The Boys from Old Florida

Inside Gator Nation

Buddy Martin

SP
SPORTS PUBLISHING L.L.C.

SportsPublishingLLC.com

ISBN 10: 1-58261-173-4
ISBN 13: 978-1-58261-173-0

Publishers: Peter L. Bannon and Joseph B. Bannon Sr.
Senior managing editor: Susan M. Moyer
Acquisitions editor: John Humenik
Developmental editor: Travis W. Moran
Art director: K. Jeffrey Higgerson
Dust jacket design: Kenneth J. O'Brien
Interior design: Kathryn R. Holleman
Photo editor: Erin Linden-Levy

Sports Publishing L.L.C.
804 North Neil Street
Champaign, IL 61820
Phone: 1-877-424-2665
Fax: 217-363-2073
SportsPublishingLLC.com

Printed in the United States of America

Library of Congress Cataloging-in-Publication Data

Martin, Buddy.
    The boys from old Florida : inside Gator nation / Buddy Martin.
      p. cm.
    ISBN-13: 978-1-58261-173-0 (hard cover : alk. paper)
    ISBN-10: 1-58261-173-4 (hard cover : alk. paper)
    1. University of Florida--Football--History. 2. Florida Gators (Football team)--History. I. Title.
    GV958.U523M36 2006
    796.332'630975979--dc22
                                        2006023877

For Joni, my inspiration for everything.

Contents

Foreword

by Woody Paige

This is not really a foreword.

It is a backward—or, actually, a *backword*.

Therefore, feel quite free to skip this section and get right to the meat of the book, which is about Florida football, and which is why you bought this book, which is the greatest and most complete work about all things Gators and Swamp and Steve Spurrier and what have you. Nobody bought the book for the foreword (or backword). And when you figure out who is writing the foreword, then you will certainly wonder and will definitely go right to Chapter One and begin reading the approximate four million words Buddy Martin has written. I don't believe the description of rise and the fall of the Roman Empire took four million words, but that was just a bunch of guys in robes over there in Europe, and this, after all, is about Gator Nation, considerably more important in world history than Roman Nation.

Et tu, Brute.

Now, then, there is a famous painting of Ulysses S. Grant and Robert E. Lee sitting at a small table in Appomattox, Virginia, supposedly showing Lee surrendering to Grant. General Grant was the commander of the Northern Troops, and Lee was the commander of the Rebel Boys in what many Southerners still refer to as "The War of Yankee Aggression." The South didn't lose the war. As they say in football, "Them good ol' boys just ran out of time."

… And bullets.

Anyway, there is one problem with that famous painting. Grant, who was a drunk and would go on to become President (figures), refused to sit at a table with Lee because he knew Lee was the better man. When Grant wrote his best-selling biography, he did not ask Lee to write the foreword, which is kind of what this foreword is like.

Martin, a man of many words and achievements—and a Gator through-and-through—has asked a Tennessee man to write the foreword to his soon-to-be best-selling epic about Florida Football. In fact, this book could be bigger than *Gone With The Wind* or "Gone With The Zook."

I have no business writing a foreword for a book about the history of Gators Football. Now, I could write one about the history of Vols Football. You remember the Vols. They kick the Gators' butts just about every year.

Peyton Manning. (Okay, so maybe he didn't.)

Well, that's our story, and we're sticking to it.

Here's all I know about Florida football:

I went to a national championship game featuring Florida and Nebraska, and Florida got its alligator purse handed to it. One of the worst two days in my life is when Tennessee lost to Florida in the Gator Bowl (where's the Volunteer Bowl?), and the next day, the Tennessee coach, Doug Dickey, took the Florida coaching job.

Can you imagine Lee quitting the South and taking the North job (except at the Senior Bowl)? In fact, Lee was asked before the (un)-Civil War by Abe Lincoln to head the northern troops. He liked the South better, which is true of everyone from Tennessee and Florida.

Which brings us, of course, to Steve Spurrier, who is the son of a Tennessee preacher man, and I met him when he and I were in high school. Later, we met when he was trying to hang onto his pro football career and signed with the Broncos in Denver, where I had somehow landed (and also met Buddy Martin there). Spurrier and I reattached and played backgammon a lot and talked South and football and his chances of being the starting quarterback for the Broncos.

After he started an exhibition in Atlanta—and while he was icing his knees on the plane later—he said: "Don't you think I earned the starting job tonight?"

"What I think," I said, "is you won't even make the team."

Spurrier looked at me incredulously and in utter shock. He didn't know what I knew. The next day he went to the head coach, who told him he was finished.

Soon Spurrier was a head coach himself—and the rest is Roman-like history.

I met Buddy Martin in Denver when we both joined *The Denver Post* as sports columnists; and Martin as editor and, in theory but not fact, my boss. Nobody from Florida ever bosses anybody from Tennessee. Buddy and I spent hundreds of nights together on the road covering events, he doing boss-type stuff and me watching professional wrestling and Jim and Tammy Bakker on television.

One day I said to Buddy: "I had a dream last night. The editor called me in and said I had been fired, and I replied, 'But what about Buddy?'"

Buddy is one of my three closest friends, I can't remember the other two, and I will love him like a brother forever—even though I don't understand this Florida thing. I studied at the University of Tennessee at Knoxville, then I moved on. Buddy studied at the University of Florida, wherever it is, but never moved on. In fact, he has returned to Florida about 15 times as an editor, a columnist, a talk-show host, an entrepreneur, a widely read author of about four million books on the Gators, and Ocala's Favorite Son.

Me, I have bought a home in Naples and a condo in Venice (I have an Italian theme going)—have bought them high and sold them low. And I have stayed in Marathon, Florida, and visited Cypress Gardens, and watched football games all over the state. Plus, I am employed by Disney. I will say only good things about Mickey Mouse, and I will not allow anything bad to be said about Annette Funicello, my first girlfriend on television—and who would have thought someday I would on the same payroll as she once was? And that I am a latter-day "Spin" of "Spin & Marty." Ask someone old what that means.

Buddy would know.

So I know Buddy Martin and Steve Spurrier, and I have bought places to live in Florida (and paid taxes, whoops, no state income taxes, bless you, Florida), and vacationed in Miami Beach and Daytona Beach, and eaten Joe's Stone Crabs, and seen football games in "The Swamp", and rode a swamp buggy in the real Swamp.

… Which leaves Urban Meyer.

I met him when he was coaching in Utah, and I thought he was the most imaginative coach in the country, and he had the best post-game barbecue spread in his locker room. And he ran for two to win the game by snapping the ball to his fullback, who faked a run and threw the first pass of his life for the victory.

Urban Meyer sounds like a government housing project on the edge of downtown. I lived in one in Memphis. It was not called Urban Meyer. It was called Lauderdale Courts, and my neighbor was a kid named Elvis.

Yes, that Elvis.

Finally, Buddy Martin was telling me Urban Meyer would be hired as the Florida coach. I went on national television and proclaimed my source (Buddy) said it would happen. Everyone at ESPN—the network that reluctantly employs me on several different shows because my demographic is 8-11 year-olds—laughed for weeks. Then Urban Meyer was hired. Oddly enough, Buddy was in New York on the set of *Cold Pizza*, at that exact time. He and I laughed and laughed and laughed. It was the first thing he and I had ever gotten right.

Then we sat down, like Lee and Grant didn't do, and had a painting of us made; and I said, "Why don't you write the *War And Peace* of Gator football, and why don't I write the backward."

And we did.

Enjoy this book. Buddy put his heart and his soul and every word he knows into it.

I can't wait to see the movie.

-WP

Preface

Saturdays with the Gators

We are the boys from old Florida
F - L - O - R - I - D - A
Where the girls are the fairest,
the boys are the squarest
of any old state down our way. (Hey!)
We are all strong for old Florida,
down where the old Gators play. (Go Gators!)
In all kinds of weather,
we'll all stick together. For
F - L - O - R - I - D - A!

The people who have lived Florida football and their back stories sparked the passion to write this book. In 2004, two years before the centennial year of Gator football, I began revisiting many central characters from the last 55 years in hopes of lacing together a tapestry through their recollection and hindsight. And while the task was mostly gratifying, the challenge of separating fact from folklore, fiction, misinformation, or even misguided notion, was often daunting. We allowed for occasional embellishment, sometimes making slight windage adjustments.

In researching *The Boys From Old Florida*, I relied mostly on interviews, including talks with every living Gator head football coach—nine of them, counting interims. I also drew from the notes of a previous interview with the late Charley Pell in the 1990s, as well as several recent conversations with his widow, Ward Pell. As for the late Bob Woodruff of the 1950s, I did speak with him several times when I was a young sports writer for the student paper, *The Florida Alligator*, but only in large groups while he was coaching at Florida. Woodruff's era as coach was mostly reconstructed through his players' remembrances.

Several things were learned from the living coaches prior to the current one:

Each still considers himself a Gator at heart.

Each has a healthy respect for the university, the athletic program, and the remarkable players who have built the legacy.

Each still cherishes the experience, even if it didn't have a happy ending for some.

And each man seems to have been the appropriate hire at the time. Some had larger roles in building Florida's program but clearly contributed important bricks to the foundation.

We could not speak with everyone, of course, so for those people whose perspectives were not included, we apologize. There are only modest references here to stars in the early days, pre-1950, and only a brief mention about the excellent 1928 team, because of limited access to information and only scant, second-hand knowledge of the first 44 years.

I meant no disrespect to those great players of the 1906-1950 era, like Dale VanSickel, and Forrest "Fergie" Ferguson, and others. Certainly there could never have been a Gator football program without these stellar All-Americans. In fact, three deceased members of the so-called "Golden Era" teams of the late 1940s were early heroes and later personal friends of mine—punter Fred Montsdeoca, center Jimmy Kynes, and lineman William "Red" Mitchum—and they played on the squad with another acquaintance, Doug Oswald. But we have begun the book with the period historians have deemed "the dawning of modern football" at Florida, so hopefully that does not in any way diminish the importance of those Gator football pioneers.

I started chronicling the ups and downs of Gator football professionally in the early 1960s as a 20-something sports editor at the *Ocala Star-Banner*. My journalistic journey took me to eight other papers, including six in Florida—the *Gainesville Sun*, the *Jacksonville Journal*, *Florida Today*, *The St. Petersburg Times*, the *Florida Times-Union*, and the *Charlotte Sun*. I left Florida briefly to become a sports writer for the *Nashville Tennessean*. Upon returning to Florida, I then went on to become columnist for Gannett News Service in New York and later sports editor of the *New York Daily News*. After serving as assistant managing editor/sports and columnist of the *Denver Post*, I spent three years as editorial consultant for *The NFL Today* at CBS. But I always kept my eye on things in Gainesville and often attended games there.

Saturdays in the press box at Florida Field, or on the road somewhere in the Southeastern Conference, were always among my favorite stops along the sports writing trail. Of course, to my out-of-state media colleagues, those Gator games were not equal in national sporting stature to some of the other events we covered—the Super Bowl, Olympics, World Series, Masters, U.S. Open, and Triple Crown horseracing series among them. But Saturdays with the Gators were always meaningful intersections that connected the dots of my youth, and therefore always resonated in the memory bank of life.

Generally, the following seasons are thought to have included the best Gator teams: 1928, 1960, 1966, 1969, 1984, 1990, 1991, 1993, 1994, 1995, and 1996. Aside from not being around in 1928, I was blessed to have covered at least a portion of all but one of those years—1984 being the exception. Heading into the 100th year of Florida football, I estimate having covered 275 Gator games. Counting this book and other columns written in 2006, I will have penned three books on the subject and over one million words.

With the researching and interviewing for this book, I was reminded how much there is yet to be learned. As one would empty the contents of a jigsaw puzzle on a table, we laid out all our questions, trusting the vagaries of the oldest form of communication—storytelling. Not all of the pieces fit.

For instance: Why did Ray Graves, after a successful 9-1-1 season in 1969, step down as head coach of Florida to make way for Doug Dickey? And why did the move backfire? Neither man claims knowledge of exactly how or why it became unraveled and ended with Dickey's firing.

How was Charley Pell able to generate millions of dollars to restructure the football program and to grow the grassroots of "The Gator Nation" through the seeding of Gator Clubs, yet free fall into the deep black hole of compliance deficit that resulted in 117 formal charges by the NCAA, leading to his dismissal? Without Pell's remarkable fund-raising acumen, "The Gator Nation" might still have only statehood status. And in the end, wasn't he more of a hero than a villain?

What was the real reason that Steve Spurrier didn't return to coach the Gators in 2005? There was a small window during which he wanted the job, but something changed his mind. What? Did Florida really have a genuine interest? And why did he never get to the negotiating table with Jeremy Foley? Both parties say they tried.

And when Spurrier left after the 2001 season, what about the note allegedly left on his desk by Foley suggesting that several assistant coaches be re-evaluated and possibly fired? Foley and Spurrier often communicated by note, but was there something different about that one?

Why won't Galen Hall talk about what most people consider the callous way he was treated and the unceremonious manner in which he was discarded in 1989? Hall was only willing to say, "Some people had their own objectives." On Hall's watch, Florida fell right back into the black hole with NCAA compliance issues.

Why was Ron Zook hired so quickly? And then fired so quickly? Was he ever really given a chance to succeed, or was his fate sealed early? What prompted the late-season dismissal of Zook in 2004; and why was "The Gator Nation" so upset and so divided about the coaching change? "We did not fail," Zook says he told his players and assistant coaches—a contention that he maintained in a rare interview about his days as Gator head coach for this book.

How soon did President Bernie Machen begin the recruiting of Meyer, and how much did the fact that he'd been Meyer's boss at Utah factor into the decision to dismiss Zook before the 2004 season ended? Was there actual contact with Meyer before the season was over through another source besides the UF? Foley had a need to be proactive in the solicitation of Urban Meyer, but he insists Florida did nothing improper. Of course, all schools use the standard line—"we have had no contact ..." Foley stands firm on that issue, but there were mitigating circumstances that caused him to accelerate his pursuit of Meyer.

I have attempted to unravel some of these mysteries and provide some of these answers. Of course, no need to demystify and oversanitize these tales. They are to be enjoyed as part of oral history. So we also embrace some of the lore—for what is Gator football without lore and mythology?

Much like Grimm would be without fairy tales.

Acknowledgments

Thanks

It took almost a village to write this book. The people who supported me and endorsed this project were vital to its concept and completion. They suggested topics, read copy, edited, helped line up interviews, and encouraged me to keep going.

John Humenik started the idea rolling and brought it to fruition through Sports Publishing LLC.

Former SP editor Elisa Block Laird, who was instrumental pushing for format change, provided the editing jumpstart, had her first baby, and handed off the script to Travis Moran. Any writer who appreciates thoughtful editing and enthusiastic support would consider working with Travis a privilege—as did I. To the exclusion of other work, Travis devoted himself to the editing of this book.

Former *Jacksonville Journal* and *Gainesville Sun* sports editor Jack Hairston had helpful input and provided many excellent proofing touches, as did John Fineran of the *Charlotte Sun*, Jacksonville ESPN 1460 talk-show host Frank Frangie, University of Florida's Norm Carlson, and *Fightin' Gators* Magazine editor Mike Hodge.

At the outset, the wise counsel of friends like Frangie helped a great deal. It was his suggestion that every living Gator coach be interviewed—and he was right. He and other friends and colleagues served as go-betweens for key subjects and supplied valuable resources on content suggestions and background detail. Among them were Franz Beard, Augie Greiner, Bob Whitfield, and Brady Ackerman.

The University of Florida Sports Information Department was most helpful, including Assistant Athletics Director Steve McClain and his staff—especially Assistant Director Zack Higbee.

My wife Joni's name should be on this book as the co-author, given that she read many chapters aloud, offered many constructive ideas, and tolerated the late-night and early-morning work sessions that often interrupted her sleep.

Sadly, over the two-year period of working on this book, we lost some special people who had strong ties with Florida football. One of them was my sister, Shirley Lovell Ritch, who grew up in our house as perhaps the most ardent Gator fan in our family and often made road trips with me on assignment. And at presstime, we grieved the loss of Bob Whitfield.

In addition, I am saddened by the death of my friends Ed Kensler, the former Gator offensive coordinator; and ex-players Fred Montsdeoca, William "Red" Mitchum, and Charlie LaPradd.

Lastly, I am most grateful for the time afforded me by The Boys From Old Florida—and to the one girl, Ward Pell. For the stories of those players and coaches make up the heart and soul of this book.

Introduction

An Introduction to the First Church of Gator Football

"The Gator Nation" resides without boundaries in a semi-mythical land, "down where the old Gators play." But it consists of very real people who live passionately on a pilgrimage that they consider almost spiritual. During the football season, they migrate to a place now called "The Swamp," more than 90,000 strong, and bond through a ritualistic swaying after the third quarter, bellowing the song, "We Are The Boys From Old Florida."

Which school actually first sang this famed "We Are The Boys" anthem is still under dispute. It may or may not have been ripped off by the University of Toledo or University or Nebraska—or maybe even by the Gators, heaven forbid. But the University of Florida claims ownership, because the song has become the Gators' trademark. If there ever were a platinum recording of it, the royalties would surely go to Florida. Today, the singing of "We Are The Boys" is probably the favorite football tradition of "The Gator Nation," that melting pot of football fanatics spread over the globe. They are legion, and they are diversified—there is no real typical Gator fan anymore. So come one, come all, brothers and sisters, and let us hear you belt it out:

"... *in all kinds of weathurrr, we'll all stick togethurrr!*"

Toledo or Nebraska notwithstanding, Florida's version of "We Are The Boys" is the invitational hymn for the First Church of Gator Football, where the pews are always packed and the disciples love to sing and shout on the Sabbath Saturday.

Though the sport began in 1906 at the University of Florida most historians mark 1950 as the dawning of so-called Florida Gator "Modern Football." Well before that, the manly menfolk in the state began to debate the pros and cons of it the way most people argued politics around the pot-bellied stove. They also swapped opinions on the worthiness of coaches, the promise of new players and the potential of the program. After all, there weren't many Gator bragging rights to be harvested until the 1960s.

A healthy skepticism has always existed among Gator fans. Cynics wondered and worried about their team ever getting to the level of their most powerful adversaries. At the same time, unwarranted optimism often abounded, and false hope became synonymous with every spring. This love-hate relationship and its political yin and yang were embedded in the culture.

Television was just beginning to beam pro football to the hinterlands of the South in the fifties—and then, only the Washington Redskins and their opponents. Once Gator fans could see the difference in the pros, they may have become discontent with Florida's stodgy offense.

For the better part of two more decades, there would be no major-league professional sports teams of any kind in the Sunshine State, except for baseball spring training. Hot-rodders were just starting to race stock cars on Daytona Beach. Dog and horse racing were flourishing in South Florida. And although a couple of professional golf tournaments, such as the St. Petersburg Open Invitational, won almost unnoticeably by a young Pennsylvanian named Arnold Palmer in 1958, the PGA Tour as we know it today didn't yet exist.

The eye of sports often focused on Gainesville. For a sports writer, the Florida Field press box was the place to be on Saturday. Usually, most sports editors or lead columnists of major dailies in the state could be found hovering over their typewriters after big games, especially if it featured a matchup of Florida-Georgia or Florida-Auburn—or later, the Gators against the upstart Seminoles of Florida State.

In addition to the emergence of the Seminoles and Miami Hurricanes, the state was eventually invaded by National Football League franchises in Miami, then Tampa Bay, then Jacksonville. National Basketball Association franchises were established in South and Central Florida. Major League Baseball and the National Hockey League were added in Miami and Tampa. Pro tennis and the PGA Tour soon had several more stops in the state as well.

Instead of shrinking, the Florida Gator football program kept growing, driven by rich alumni and escalating state and regional pride. Meanwhile, the white heat of the rivalries powered the generation-to-generation quest for retribution. Great grandsons are still trying to get even for what Georgia did to their relatives. So in the face of competition for media attention, the Gator programs held their ground, and the rivalries intensified, proving that the emotion of college football tethers alumni to their alma mater or favorite team like mothers' milk.

University of Florida football has evolved from a small colony of club athletes in the early 1900s to a gigantic, multimillion-dollar corporation nurtured by that tribal loyalty. In 2006, the projected budget for the Florida athletic department was expected to exceed $66 million. So the bedrock support of these hard-core constituents fuels a necessary political, social, and economic dynamo. "The Gator Nation"—universal in scope, yet singular in purpose—is a powerful force with which to be reckoned, politically and economically. The term "Gator Nation" has become another virtual trademark, although there is nothing on record to indicate when and how the brand originated. For so long, the school shunned the moniker, then decided to use "The Gator Nation" in a television commercial promoting academics and the pursuit of excellence. Seems the rising tide of Gator athletics has even lifted the cause of quality education.

There have been many memorable days in Gator football, but some very special ones at Florida Field. The scrapbook of defining moments colorizes each era for us all. When Florida State University and the Universtiy of Florida first met on the gridiron in 1958—and the Seminoles' Bobby Renn nearly returned the opening kickoff for a touchdown—who knew that this would seed a great college football rivalry that would blossom into a competition for the same national championship some 38 years later in the Sugar Bowl?

No moment was more unforgettable than September 24, 1960, when Ray Graves held up two fingers after Lindy Infante's touchdown run, calling for the two-point conversion, consummated by Larry Libertore's pass to Jon MacBeth that upset Georgia Tech, 18-17. That one play liberated Gator fans from Bob Woodruff's turgid four-corners offense, no-risk mentality, and the purgatory of third-down punts. Also one to cherish was the Steve Spurrier field-goal kick on October 29, 1966, that would beat Auburn and clinch the Heisman Trophy for him. Especially since he could count on one hand—or toe—the field goals he had kicked as a player at Florida. Another classic was John Reaves' pass to Carlos Alvarez, whose spectacular catch for a 70-yard touchdown on September 20, 1969, against Houston began the reign of the "Super Sophs" and set the tone for a season of unanticipated brilliance. How about gimp-legged quarterback Kerwin Bell limping across the goal line to beat Auburn, 18-17, on November 1, 1986, which would rank as a top Florida Field highlight? Who can forget the opening game for Spurrier as coach on September 8, 1990? Shane Matthews took the Gators on a hurry-up journey for a touchdown against Oklahoma State as the Ol' Ball Coach made his debut in style, 50-7. It only took one game for him to deliver the goods.

Florida fans can only hope that Urban Meyer's Gator debut—a 32-14 win over Wyoming on September 3, 2005—will turn out to have been as ominous a start for opponents.

And these are just some remembrances from home games—not even counting the spectacular plays in the Florida-Georgia series in Jacksonville, road victories like beating Bear Bryant's Alabama team in Tuscaloosa, 10-6, plus the many stellar moments in the six SEC Championship seasons and, most of all, the national championship win over Florida State in the 1997 Sugar Bowl, 52-20.

Today, there is still a strong emphasis on Gator football among the state newspapers, though diluted somewhat by the success of other college teams and the changing populace. While Gator football will never again occupy such a dominant spot as it did 60 years ago among papers in such a complex state, it's still a huge story—attracting one of college football's largest media troupes on the road. Nine of the state's 10 largest papers cover Gator sports on a regular basis. Almost every game is on television and replayed on cable. Major TV networks are regular visitors to the campus. National magazines and newspapers often feature stories on Florida basketball or football players. Internet chatter is ceaseless, and every week there seems to be another Web site devoted to the Gators. Being on national TV is regular fare. The largest crowds in the state to see any football game have all been at Ben Hill Griffin Stadium—more than 90,000—and that includes Super Bowls in three Florida cities. Gator football attendance consistently ranks among the nation's top seven.

In many ways, nothing in sports is bigger than the Gators to a large segment of state residents, and they appear to get more popular with each championship era. Florida is still THE state university with an army of patriarchs and a few matriarchs, some of whom number among the VIP-ness of a group called "Bull Gators."

Though you can buy your way into elite status, you don't have to be rich or famous—or even a Florida alumnus—to be a member of "The Gator Nation." No matter your economic clout, you'll never really outrank those fourth- and fifth-generation Gator mommas and daddies who have seniority. Longevity counts. They claim certain birthrights, including extra credit for their long suffering. But money does buy influence, including a skybox seat and having something on campus named after you.

Every so often, the pot is stirred among "The Gator Nation." As in all families, a certain amount of bickering is to be expected. The commitment and support seem to ebb and flow with eras and the changing of the coaching guard. Therein lies much of the reason: with change often come consternation, conflict, and controversy. In the end, however, "The Gator Nation" has stuck to its charter for right at 100 years. But it has also been battle-tested.

The "Year of the Gator" came and went several times—and may yet return someday. In football, the pattern is the same: always with the next coach, the next season, the next game, fresh hope abides. Expectations soar, and reality takes leave. Yet, perhaps part of being a card-carrying member of "The Gator Nation" is living in a dream world and waiting for some piece of it to become real. In between, the unhappy constituents don't always suffer silently.

Much like tormented fans of the Boston Red Sox and Tampa Bay Bucs, Gator fans endured an extended dry spell before finally tasting the champagne of championships—the first true Southeastern Conference title to be kept in 1991 and then the national championship in 1996.

Before that and in between the good times were bitter memories—the 51-0 shellacking by Georgia in 1968; an NCAA investigation in 1970 over a coaching change didn't bring any penalties, but two other probes later in the 1980s for cheating that nearly resulted in the so-called "death penalty"; a winless 0-10-1 transitional season in 1979; the stripping away of Florida's first SEC title in 1984; and then the departure of The Prodigal Son.

The casting aside of coaches has become a blood sport. The comings and goings have always been cataclysmic. It took many years to close the ranks after the debacle of Doug Dickey's hiring and Ray Graves' boot upstairs in 1970—and some don't think it was ever resolved.

The dark days of NCAA probation resulting from Pell's improprieties in the mid-1980s—and the reign of terror that followed in the late 1980s under Athletics Director Bill Arnsparger's dictatorship—were two of the school's bleakest periods. The firing of Galen Hall seemed contrived and unwarranted. Only the arrival of The Prodigal, Spurrier, and his roaring success made it possible to move beyond that ugliness.

Spurrier's exit in January 2002 began a bewildering and confusing time for "The Gator Nation" that became more muddled in 2004, when Spurrier's old school seemed to be kissing him off and then hiring Urban Meyer. In many ways, Spurrier is to blame for some of the turmoil—the way he coached so brilliantly, the way he upped the expectations, and the way he left so abruptly. Then, finally, the way he suddenly popped up without a job. Replacing a legend is impossible. Following a legend is guaranteed futility, if not a ticket to failure. Ask Ron Zook.

"The Gator Nation" has teetered a bit since Spurrier left. In the most recent litmus test, from 2002 to 2004, attendance actually slipped a hair—1,768 below average for the 2004 season. A few defectors turned in their season tickets, and disharmony surfaced over Zook's failure to meet expectations despite strong recruiting classes. Then one day, the Gator brain trusts found the coach who could maybe help compensate for the loss of a legend—or so they hoped and prayed.

In the spring of 2005, when a crowd of almost 60,000 welcomed Meyer for the Orange and Blue game, hope for the future bloomed again, too.

Meyer's first season was something short of Spurrier-esque, with SEC losses to Alabama and LSU and—worst of all—Spurrier's South Carolina Gamecocks. But after a win over Florida State and an Outback Bowl victory over Iowa, things appeared back on track as the 2006 season approached.

As the school song says, they stuck together "through all kinds of weather"—turmoil, disdain, dejection, disbelief, upheaval, political skullduggery, shame, glory, unmitigated joy, and pure ecstasy. The annual pilgrimages to Gainesville and other outposts of the Southeastern Conference cannot be stemmed or deterred by any of those forces. There were certainly some threatening tremors, but the vast majority never stopped supporting the Gators. Even in the fruitless, winless season of 1979, they still filled the stadium.

Thus the metaphor of surviving the weather. Yet nobody ever dreamed just how bad the weather could actually turn. Little did those authors of that famous school song, allegedly written in 1919 by Robert Swanson and John Icenhour, realize this would include having to survive four hurricanes in seven weeks during the stormy 2004 season, when the coach would be fired before either the hurricane or football season was over.

And now Urban Meyer had been charged with calming the storms.

The Bermuda Triangle of Coaches

If ever there was going to be a Bermuda Triangle of Gator coaches, it would come in the final days of autumn in the weirdness that was 2004. The state was still reeling after direct hits from four hurricanes in seven weeks. Having endured its own storm during the final weeks of the season, Gator football was suddenly saddled with a lame-duck coach and a family feud over his successor.

If the hiring of Ron Zook to replace Steve Spurrier in 2002 was a flash point for Florida fans, then Zook's firing three years later and the university's subsequent missed opportunity in 2004 to reclaim a legendary coaching figure was stultifying. In fact, except for those precious few informed about the process, it downright confounded most everybody, and seemed outright treasonous to a few. Some of those people caught up in the vortex were stunned—and a firestorm of controversy ensued.

Florida was coach-less again for the second time in four years, and even though Spurrier was unemployed at the moment, owned a house in Gainesville, and professed an interest in the job, Florida's brass showed no genuine interest in him. Were they crazy, or what? Thus began an especially tumultuous period for Gator diehards—tantamount to breaking off a birthright, bypassing the royalty of a crown prince in his rightful return to the throne.

As rumors swirled and facts were sorted out in early December, three different coaches encountered the swinging door in Gainesville. Ron Zook was paid off and ushered out the door prior to the bowl game; Urban Meyer flirted with Notre Dame while holding one foot in the Florida door despite his upcoming bowl game at Utah; and Spurrier was out of work and contemplating an invitation through a door that never materialized.

Few facts were known outside the inner circle. Due to Zook's clandestine dismissal and the several candidates to replace him, "The Gator Nation" was stirring. This informational blackout after such an abrupt firing precipitated a cyclone-like speculation about who might become Florida's 22nd head coach.

The lid was so tight that the media couldn't even find a good "Deep Throat." Meanwhile, the fan base was being torn apart by its own split loyalties. Dark clouds, building since week three of the 2004 season, began forming a thunderhead over Gainesville after the 35-31 loss to Mississippi State.

Then the axe fell on Zook.

During the days that followed, I had a series of private conversations with Spurrier, including one a few hours after Zook's dismissal. Spurrier confessed he was a little startled about Zook's mid-season firing.

"Aren't you surprised that they would fire him in the middle of the season?" Spurrier asked me.

"No, because the man they want for the job is available now and may not be in a few weeks," I replied, not knowing, for certain, if that man was going to be Spurrier or Meyer.

Having left the Washington Redskins the year before, Spurrier still hadn't announced his intent to return to college football or to head another NFL team. Rumors circulated about him being recruited by the Miami Dolphins. The lack of hard information started the rumor mill full tilt. Clearly, the hiring of this next coach would be a critical juncture for Florida. The scramble was on, and it was enough to give Director of Athletics Jeremy Foley some sleepless nights. One November night in 2004, right after Florida upset Florida State in Doak Campbell Stadium, as the media packed up for a midnight exit from the press box, Mick Hubert, voice of the Gator Radio Network, was encountered.

After being fired, Zook had won three of his last four games—including this one over FSU on the newly anointed Bobby Bowden field, an amazing achievement by a lame-duck coach.

Looking back on the conclusion of an upside-down, wacky year, conjecture about the next Gator football coach was an obvious conversation piece.

"If you were a betting man, would you bet on it being Urban Meyer?" Hubert was asked.

"I don't know," Hubert said. "I'd probably take the field and give you Urban Meyer. This has been such a weird football season. I think it all started with the hurricanes. They completely changed the atmospheric conditions."

Even insiders were in the dark during this period. Given the lack of hard information, Hubert's hurricane analogy made as much sense as anybody's theory.

If the first 60 years of Florida football were mediocre, the next 40 brought gradual improvement before ultimate prosperity. Florida didn't even field a team in 1945 because of World War II, and once the program was jump-started, it took another 15 years to become competitive for championships. In the 75-year history of the facility once known as Florida field and now called "The Swamp," (aka Ben Hill Griffin Stadium) from 1930 through 2005, the Gators won 268 times, lost 99, and tied 13 for a sparkling .740 winning percentage. From 1990 through 2005, Florida lost just 11 of 98 games. Against the SEC, the Gators were 50-7 at home. Stripped of that 1984 SEC title and denied a second one six years later, Gator fans ultimately saw their first dream of an official conference championship realized in 1991. The national championship came five years later.

The most forgotten thing about the 12-year Spurrier era is that he not only won championships, but he cleaned up a program that had been flirting with the NCAA death penalty for violations. He wasn't only the new coach in 1989, but he was the new sheriff, too. He was fanatical about playing by the rules and quickly let other coaches know that he wasn't afraid to blow the whistle on them if they cheated. Discipline was swift; excuses were not tolerated, and nobody was exempt from team rules.

Spurrier's impact on Florida football went beyond attainment of trophies. He left behind fingerprints of integrity, style, panache, imagination, and daring that should be stored somewhere in a time capsule.

Whether he was re-hired at Florida or not, unquestionably, Spurrier was the Coach for All Seasons because he established so many traditions—including winning championships. He was the gold standard, and he brought home the gold.

It was Spurrier who nicknamed Ben Hill Griffin Stadium "The Swamp," which became a pit of despair for rivals: he lost at home just five times in a dozen seasons.

During 1990-2001, the Spurrier years, Florida played in nine bowls and produced 21 All-Americans. Spurrier's Gators won 122 games, lost just 27, and tied one for a winning percentage of .817. Under him, Florida won four SEC titles in a row. His team was ranked among the nation's Top 10 nine times and was ranked in the national polls 202 out of a possible 203 weeks, appearing in the national championship game twice.

Ordinarily, alma maters would be sending limousines for guys with those kinds of credentials.

Who could ever have thought that the University of Florida would have a shot at a re-run of Camelot—and then would blow it? That is, if you accept the premise that Spurrier might have considered returning to Gainesville if given the opportunity, or that the Gators even wanted him.

In the early days of November 2004—during the alleged Florida coaching search for Zook's replacement and after a season of life without football—Spurrier made it known he still wanted to coach.

"I'm not retired yet," he said.

Yes, he wanted to coach, but would it be college or pro?

He first made those thoughts public as he boarded a plane in Atlanta on his way to see his new granddaughter, Lauren, born to his daughter, Amy, and her husband, Jay Moody, in Panama City. He told a friend via cell phone that he preferred to work. He also was drawn to the passion of football in the South because "… the fans seem to care more."

Certainly the Gator fans cared, as President Bernie Machen and Foley began to learn in the next few weeks. In the crazy world of Internet blogging and sports talk-show missives, as well as the blunt instrument of words fired off by newspaper columnists, Machen and Foley took a battering. In the initial blush, Spurrier was a bit enamored about returning and may have taken the job in the next 48 hours, if offered, except for two things:

1. Spurrier is not a man to make snap decisions without introspection, the Washington move notwithstanding; and—

2. Job negotiations may have already been afoot in South Carolina.

Unconfirmed rumors arose about the purchase of a lot on a lake in South Carolina—he eventually did buy a house on a lake, but a different one—but he had pooh-poohed the idea that he had accepted any deal.

When the Florida job opened up and Spurrier spoke with Foley, they agreed they'd talk more about it. But Machen and Foley didn't exactly roll out a red carpet for him. They told him the school would be doing lots of interviewing and going through the "proper procedure" in the search for Zook's replacement. Apparently, there was a misunderstanding about "proper procedure," but all that began to change as the pressure built for Florida to close the deal with the right coach.

It's true that they talked about talking, but perhaps Machen and Foley didn't put enough of a priority on the pursuit of Spurrier, presenting the perception that they may have had some kind of informal agreement with Meyer. Foley says, "Absolutely not."

The folks in South Carolina pulled the trigger immediately. When South Carolina Athletics Director Mike McGee did make contact, Spurrier was told he was the first and only candidate, and nobody said anything about having to go through a long process. Foley, recognizing the political correctness, knew he needed to get to the table with Spurrier and at least agree to show him the respect he deserved with an interview. Indeed, Spurrier even hinted at that when I contacted him on four occasions during that stretch and later in a long mid-summer interview in Columbia. Looking at the timeline from the outside, the six-day period from October 25 when Zook was fired to October 31 when McGee said he contacted Spurrier is unaccounted for on Florida's part if the intentions were to interview him. That's apparently when Foley and Spurrier were exchanging voices messages and talking briefly.

If the brain trusts at Florida weren't really going to do an extended search as previously indicated, why couldn't they hook up with Spurrier? He was already in the state, and everything had pointed to a get-together. The day of Zook's firing, Spurrier was contacted by the media on the golf course and told the *Orlando Sentinel* "apparently there are going to be some talks" with Florida.

What happened from that point is unclear. However, I received a surprise phone call from Spurrier on Friday, October 29, 2004, as I was driving to Jacksonville for the Florida-Georgia game. At that time, he appeared to be the leading candidate at UF and seemed very enthused about the notion. Among what he told me:

—He was surprised that Zook had been fired in the middle of the season and felt Ron was treated unfairly.

—He was worried about the Gators not being able to play well against Georgia.

—He thought it was to be "a long process" of hiring a coach at Florida, "… because that's what they do nowadays."

On Thursday, November 4—11 days after Zook's firing—Spurrier pulled out. Two days later, on the morning of November 6, he returned a call I had placed earlier in the week and sounded relieved. His pride was damaged, but if he had been miffed about the way he was treated, he didn't show it. There was also some concern about how University of Florida officials had glossed over his decision to pull out. Part of the reason for Spurrier's decision to retract was that the waiting period gave him 10 days to seriously ponder it before deciding the process just wasn't working in his favor. If he wanted to coach again, he was probably going to have to do it somewhere else. That somewhere else suddenly surfaced. Spurrier had done a little research of his own and wisely chose, after reviewing history of those who tried to go home again and failed, decided not to try and outdo his own records that he established in his 12 years at Florida. (Of course, he had already begun talking with McGee, but we didn't know that. Even though there were rumors to that effect, Spurrier, too, kept it close to his vest. And he wasn't talking to many people in the media except a few friends.)

A few hours later, after his plane landed in Florida and he'd rethought his previous comments, Spurrier called back and informed me that in the use of his quotes he preferred that it wouldn't appear that he was bashing the Gators. There was one clarification about how he said it was "apparent" he was going to have to go somewhere else besides Florida, but he didn't want it to sound contentious.

"This is best for all concerned," Spurrier said once again of his pulling out, but it sounded as if he were trying to convince himself as much as anybody. And he apparently also felt it would stir up too many members of "The Gator Nation," who, coach-less still, were starting to demand answers.

"I feel good about my decision [to withdraw]," Spurrier said. "You think and think and think about something, and then you make your choice and move on. This was best for everybody."

So the guessing game began. South Carolina? North Carolina?

He noted that the college game had changed a lot, even since he left in 2001. "The athletes are bigger, stronger, faster. There's the pro influence. The defenses are more sophisticated," he said.

As for Florida, "I closed the book on it after 12 years, and I never guessed this would all come up three years later. But it's time for me to close it this final time."

Spurrier simply wasn't going to campaign for the job or intrude in the process by FedExing in his résumé.

Machen's and Foley's worst fears were that he would choose to coach in the SEC again. Not many days later, they were realized when Spurrier became South Carolina's new coach. You could feel the ice coming through the television. "Again," Spurrier said on screen, re-emphasizing why he wasn't coming back to Florida, "I was never asked to come back. So it's not like I turned down my old school."

But South Carolina?

"The job opened up while I was available and looking to coach," Spurrier told ESPN's Steve Cyphers. Then he went on to laud the facilities, the fans, the state, and the potential of the Gamecock program.

"This seemed to be the perfect place to me," Spurrier said.

The "perfect place"?

That was a bizarre description, if not outright heresy, to many members of "The Gator Nation," some of whom had been campaigning to bring him back home. A group of well-connected Spurrier loyalists had signed a petition asking the school to hire him back. There was only one "perfect place" for the Head Ball Coach as far as they were concerned: in "The Swamp."

Ben Hill Griffin Stadium was to Spurrier what Yankee Stadium was to Babe Ruth—the house that he built. When Spurrier set foot on Florida Field as a player in 1964, Gator football was still struggling for an identity—an identity that began to materialize only when Ray Graves infused offensive excitement into the program. Spurrier helped generate even more excitement four years into Graves' era.

When Spurrier came home as coach 24 years later and won six conference titles and a national championship, his revered stature in Gator annals was guaranteed. All that has won him the kind of iconic admiration that many Gator fans feel should be recognized by a statue of him being erected at "The Swamp," an honor that Seminole supporters have already afforded Bobby Bowden while still coaching at FSU. Yet it was always Spurrier who asked that no tribute to him of any kind be erected while he was there—an argument that he finally lost to Foley when his name was painted on the stadium face as one of two Heisman winners.

So given all this, how could Steve Spurrier not deserve a mulligan from Machen and Foley at Florida? The inference that he should take a number and send in his résumé—real or imagined—was a humiliation and pure political poppycock to his friends and followers.

What happened?

Foley was forthcoming about his role. He remembers exchanging a series of telephone messages with Spurrier; and while attempting to call back another time and leave word, he actually reached him live.

"We talked about getting together in about two weeks, as I recall," said Foley, "and he seemed fine with that."

Spurrier acknowledged six months after he had taken the South Carolina job that "… the new president didn't know me very well." But he also found no fault with Foley. "It had nothing to do with Jeremy. He let me know when they fired Zook, 'Hey, the president wants to get with you … wants to see where the interest level is.'"

So they were attempting to set up a get-to-know-the-president meeting when Mike McGee called and said Lou Holtz had retired. McGee said he wanted to come to Virginia and talk the next day. The South Carolina athletics director then got on a private plane and brought Spurrier a fistful of media guides, informing him: "When I come up next time, I want to talk seriously."

To which Spurrier responded: "Okay, come on!"

On the next trip up to Virginia, McGee brought a contract. Steve looked it over and told his wife Jeri, "We need to go do this. Let's go."

There were other little public relations gaffes by Florida that might have made things indelicate. Machen downplayed the idea that he'd ever really met Spurrier, despite the fact that they'd actually spoken at a Southeastern Conference basketball tournament, according to witnesses. Maybe Machen did forget, but critics would say that would indict him for not grasping Spurrier's contributions to Gator football.

This is where things get fuzzy: unconfirmed reports that Machen had contacted Meyer much earlier in the season did arise, but cautiously and circuitously left behind a cold trail. Shelley Meyer had befriended Machen's wife, Carol, while at Utah, and it has been suggested that the two of them had serious conversations that were relayed to their husbands even before Foley's official visit in late November. Without clear entries on the timeline, however, that remains conjecture. Foley was vague on this, but insists the coaching hire was his call and that he had told Machen that Meyer was his No. 1 choice.

Meanwhile, the Meyer deal still had to be struck, and Florida was without a coach. For sure, Machen and Foley had Meyer on "the list," official or otherwise, before Spurrier came into the picture. This experience began to conjure up flashbacks of Spurrier's abrupt departure to the Redskins. Foley had no intention of allowing that "empty basket" to re-occur.

Following Spurrier's departure in 2002, Bob Stoops of Oklahoma and Mike Shanahan of the Denver Broncos turned Foley down, leaving him to his third choice, Zook. Some Gator insiders wondered why Foley stopped there and didn't consider top-flight candidates like Jon Gruden, then coaching the Oakland Raiders. Little messages had been sent out to Foley about Gruden—Jon's father, Jim, even told the press his son was interested— but Foley seemed in a hurry to get the Zook deal done for what he considered good reason: recruiting season. Foley denies that he was premature in the Zook hire, but acknowledges the lack of leverage.

This time, however, Foley would be more cautious. But there was a sense of urgency because his candidates were in danger of being picked off. At least two of them were tied up in late-season games that had been cancelled by (here we go again) hurricanes as well. Once again, Stoops' name was floated for the Florida job, but Oklahoma quickly signed him to an extension. Louisville's Bobby Petrino seemed to be the dark-horse favorite.

Even if Machen and Foley could never address it officially, clearly Meyer had moved into the top-choice slot, which became even more apparent when other schools began to show interest in the Utah coach. With Spurrier going to South Carolina and Meyer being romanced by other schools, the pressure intensified on Machen and Foley.

Claiming he was committed to the principle of not contacting any coach during the regular season, Foley had hired a consultant to feel Meyer out on the proposal—"… but only after Utah's last game." That way he could say, unequivocally, that neither he nor Machen had tampered. "I will tell you this," Foley conceded 16 months later. "As part of the process, we usually hired a consultant to find out if [a candidate] is interested in our job; and who is moveable and who is not."

In this case, that consultant was very credible: Chuck Neinas, president of Neinas Sports Services, former executive director of the College Football Association. Neinas got the answers quickly. "He [Neinas] found that Urban was maybe interested in talking to us after the season was over—so that was the only communication with Urban," said Foley.

So by being allowed to claim that, without actually any University of Florida staff members contacting Meyer, Foley would know whether he was interested. Meanwhile, Foley and Florida would go through all the "proper procedures" in interviewing others—or, least, they had hoped—and start doing all the research on the Internet, talking to college and pro coaches, players, media, etc., about their candidate.

Foley, fearing the "empty basket," suddenly had to escalate his moves. Therefore, once Meyer sent back word he was interested, they all agreed they would talk after Utah's final game against Brigham Young, which the Utes won, 52-21, on November 20, 2004, to complete an undefeated season.

"After he beat BYU, I gave him a day," said Foley, "and obviously I'm telling Bernie Machen about this and all the other names on the list."

Two of the names still on the list were Petrino and Jeff Tedford of California, but both still had games to play due to—here we go again—the hurricanes that had elongated their seasons.

That Sunday night, November 21, Foley called Meyer.

"I told him a little bit about Florida. We had put some information together about University of Florida that we FedExed out."

Meanwhile, Foley figured he'd spend Thanksgiving at his home in Vermont. Also, that would provide cover for his side trip to Utah. "Again, cognizant of the decision three years earlier, I made the decision to go to Salt Lake City from Vermont because nobody up there would know who I was—and they don't."

The day after Thanksgiving, on November 26, Foley traveled to Salt Lake City, with reservations under the name of a Utah staff member. He was going stealth this time to avoid anybody tailing him as they did when he had flown out to Norman, Oklahoma, Denver, and New Orleans on his coaching search expedition three years prior.

Foley came away impressed with Meyer. "He was organized, straightforward, and he asked a lot of good questions. He showed me his academic plans, his discipline plans, his plan to win. He asked questions about Florida. We talked about staff, weight room, academics, training room—he was prepared."

The two men hit it off. Foley had a sense that he was *the* guy, much like when he had interviewed basketball coach Billy Donovan. Still, memories of his decision to hire the first football coach under his regime may have been nagging at him—and so Foley didn't want to make a mistake twice.

One of his biggest challenges was to get Meyer and his wife Shelley out of the state of Utah, which they loved.

"So it was no slam dunk," said Foley, even though the money at Florida was twice as much.

When Foley returned to Gainesville, he suggested immediately that Meyer to talk with Donovan and for his wife, Shelley, to talk to Christine Donovan about coaching there, about living in Gainesville, the schools, etc. It would prove to be a good connection, because very few people can recruit like Donovan—or, in this case, the Donovans.

As the "process" began to take place, there was still no offer extended. But that process quickly came to an abrupt halt when Notre Dame fired Ty Willingham and made it known they were going after Meyer, a former Irish assistant coach.

Consider the migraine headache that was suddenly starting to envelope Foley. Haste is what rushed him into a decision to hire the man he had just fired. And while he stops short of calling Zook's hiring a "mistake," Foley does admit he was under pressure back in 2002 to move quickly to accommodate recruiting and to keep star players like quarterback Rex Grossman and wide receiver Taylor Jacobs from defecting to the pros.

Now this unexpected curve: he had to win the recruiting war of coaches against perhaps the most storied college football program in America. If there had been a Las Vegas line on the favorite in South Bend, it would have been 2-1 in favor of former Notre Dame assistant Meyer taking over the Irish program, and not Charlie Weis—a Notre Dame alumnus working as the offensive coordinator for the Super Bowl champion New England Patriots.

And so all the so-called "process" had to be scrapped after Willingham's firing.

"That turned up the heat immeasurably," said Foley. "So I called Urban and said, 'I'm coming back out there.'"

This time Foley brought the contract and made the offer, but Meyer said, out of respect for Notre Dame, he would have to go to South Bend for the interview. There was some anxiety ahead. That Thursday was a tough, restless night because Foley was targeting Meyer, and Spurrier was now out of the mix.

"Out of this whole process, the thing that kept me up at night was not failure—failure is not fatal, of course—but the fear that the basket would be empty again," Foley recalled. "This coach says, 'I'm going to stay here' or go there, or this guy decides at the 11th hour 'I don't want to talk to you.' [Then] the guy you think you're going to get decides to go to the NFL. … All of a sudden, you're looking in your basket, and there's nobody there again. There's not that name, not that guy.

"And then you hire someone who comes in here; and maybe the house is divided again and the uphill battle again. And that's how programs get on a downhill slide for a number of years. And *that's* what kept me up at night."

The moment a coach is fired and the rumor mill starts churning, members of the Gator media go on alert. They are consumed, almost afraid not to chase after every wild rumor, no matter how vague or silly they may seem. So a feeding frenzy was about to unfold. The coaching dominoes had started to fall, and when Notre Dame fired Willingham. The landscape changed dramatically.

I got off a plane in New York early in December, 2004, and after checking my messages, learned I had received a call from a Gainesville businessman who asked: "Do you know anything about a 10-year, $40-million contract Florida offered Bob Stoops?"

Right around the same time, ESPN was reporting Stoops had received a Florida offer that had been matched by Oklahoma.

By the time I reached my hotel later that night, back from dinner, I had a message from veteran Atlanta sports writer and CBS correspondent Tony Barnhart, asking: "I'm hearing crazy stuff, like Jeremy [Foley] is on a plane to Salt Lake City, and that Bob Stoops is a done deal at Florida."

Before bedtime Thursday, my phone rang, and it was ESPN's college football analyst and my curmudgeon friend Beano Cook, who admonished me: "See, I told you Urban Meyer was going to Notre Dame. You were wrong! You said he was going to Florida."

Indeed, it appeared Meyer was headed to South Bend. (And to his credit, Beano later apologized on ESPN radio and said he was wrong.)

The next morning, while walking in downtown Manhattan on a crisp, cold Friday, my WMOP-WGGG radio-show partner, Brady Ackerman, called to tell me the *Florida Times-Union* was reporting Meyer was turning down the Irish in favor of the Gators—stunning news if true.

In New York while I was on the set of ESPN's *Cold Pizza Friday*, Woody Paige, the show's co-host, was still taking a beating for having previously said many times, "My Florida sources—hint, hint—say Urban Meyer is the new Florida coach," more than two weeks before. And Paige was still out there on a limb.

His counterpart, Skip Bayless, chided Paige: "The next thing you know, Woody will have Bill Belichick fired and the New England Patriots hiring Urban Meyer." Speculation was rampant and, as Bayless was pointing out with his caustic comments, everybody seemed to have a different opinion.

Foley had hit a preemptive strike Thursday morning, telling Meyer he was his No. 1 choice and laying out an attractive financial plan. A huge Boston Red Sox fan, Foley had hit the equivalent of a walk-off home run in the bottom of the ninth against the Yankees.

And in the end, the friendship between of Machen's wife, Carol, and Shelley Meyer may have played a huge role as well. Or maybe it was, as Mick Hubert said, just those damn hurricanes.

A small amount of irony accompanied Meyer's arrival for duty on December 7, the anniversary of Pearl Harbor. Machen and Foley had been under siege by critics for slow dancing with coaching candidates. Conditions were hardly ideal, then, when the dapper 40-year-old Ohioan stepped to the front and placed his hands comfortably on both sides of the lectern, like a captain taking firm grip of the wheel to right the course. He had just come back from talking to the Gator players for the first time, which he noted was probably more uncomfortable for the players but also a little tense for him, and here he was facing over 200 members of the media, about 195 of which he'd never seen before.

Meyer was impressive. He stood firm, fielding all questions without a flinching body language, fixing his eyes on the questioner and responding in a staunch-but-unhostile manner. The way in which he embraced the past tradition, lauding the style and success of Spurrier, scored big. He said he wouldn't be wearing a visor a la Spurrier, because wasn't a visor man—"… but I wouldn't wear one around here even if I was." However, Meyer was a huge fan of the Fun 'N' Gun offense and everything Spurrier.

"I fell in love with the way they played, the way they talked, the way walked, the way they took the field, the way they came off the field, the way they scored points," Meyer said of Spurrier's teams. "A coach would be lying to you if they said they sat there and watched the University of Florida play under Coach Spurrier and didn't get excited.

"When I saw them come across TV, I sat down and watched the University of Florida play because of their swagger."

Meanwhile, Urban's wife and their three kids were sitting in the press conference. As a committed football coach's wife, she always said she considered herself a single parent nine months a year. And she'd not seen much of Urban lately, who had been somewhat sequestered from them in recent days. He had a Utah football team back in Salt Lake that had lost its coach. And he was trying to take care of the unfinished business—an unbeaten record and the school's first BCS bowl game.

Could it have been tougher? Well, yes, he could have been on the wrong end of that 11-0 record at Utah, or looking for a job like some members of Ron Zook's departing staff. So while it may have been tough duty, Urban Meyer was equal to the task and seemed to relish the pressure of this day.

This wasn't his first visit to "The Swamp." That had come in 2000 at the end of a recruiting trip when Meyer happened to be driving through Gainesville on the way back to his assistant coach's job in South Bend. He decided to see for himself what his ESPN pal Kirk Herbstreit was talking about when he told Urban "The Swamp" was the best venue in college football. Meyer parked his car illegally (for which he received a parking ticket), walked down on the field to the 50-yard line, where he was wowed immediately. He knew, at that moment, what Herbstreit meant. He called Shelley and told her he now understood why he could never get any of the Florida high school players to forgo the Gators for Touchdown Jesus and the Golden Dome.

Perhaps it was at that very moment he began to choose the University of Florida, or that Florida was choosing him as its 20th head coach—22nd counting the interims.

Some 28 minutes into the Urban Meyer press conference, I asked a question that never showed up on any of the official University of Florida transcripts:

Q: *"Did you have an epiphany on this decision, and can you talk about the moment you made up your mind? And also, did you have your mind made up before you talked to Notre Dame?"*

Meyer's eye twinkled a bit, and then he reflected during an eight-second pause before responding. He never really answered the question directly, but that may be the questioner's fault for not framing his inquiry properly.

"Tough question," Meyer began. "The University of Florida ... During the season it would be absolutely unfair to everybody at Utah to consider, think, discuss, look at any other university. We had high expectations from day one at the University of Utah to finish undefeated. Expectations were there. I noticed Kirk [Herbstreit of ESPN] is here ... From August, you cannot stub your toe. All of a sudden, the goal shifted from the Mountain West Conference championship to the BCS. That's a heck of a thing to have a coach and a bunch of seniors go through every week in and week out.

"There was no discussion, no looking, no evaluation of any job possibilities until following our last game of the season. When that occurred, we spent two weeks studying it closely. When that other situation [Notre Dame] arrived, I'd say it was the 11th hour. A group of kids and a wife and a coach were pretty close to a decision. However, having such great respect for the other university, there was a little discussion. But it was not this versus them. I tried to make that clear about a week ago. But that wasn't the case at all."

It sounded scripted, even if true. There was no mention of talking to a consultant. Understandably, he couldn't say much. Perhaps we'll never know exactly when Machen and Foley began recruiting Urban Meyer.

Eventually, "The Gator Nation" did all stick together, despite the hurricanes. But as much as he thought he knew about being the coach of Florida, Urban Meyer had many surprises in store.

Some angry, pro-Spurrier Gators at first may have perceived Meyer as a bit of an interloper who deprived "The Gator Nation" of a happy ending to their football fairy tale. You don't think longtime Gator fans believe in fairy tales? You never suffered through the mediocre years of their forefathers. Meyer allayed those fears with his fiery personality, openness to the insight of others, and his dedication to building a program of high-character athletes with academic ambitions, and his strong desire to integrate them with the student body culture. But the immediate buzz was met with a backlash.

Right or wrong, Machen perhaps will always be called into question about Spurrier. However, he could have resolved some of the harsh reaction with a simple courtesy call to Spurrier and an interview over lunch, even if Spurrier would wind up taking the Carolina job, which he likely would have. Because he didn't, it will be forever perceived by most that Machen had an agenda—that Meyer was the choice all along, and Machen was the man who thumbed his nose at the all-time Gator legend to bring in his guy from Utah. Otherwise, what was the hurry in firing Zook? These issues jeopardized good will. Perhaps some of it was fostered by poor communication created by the cloak-and-dagger business of hiring coaches with the intent of not creating a circus and a public spectacle.

The specter of Steve Spurrier will always be hanging over Urban Meyer's head. When one of the greatest players in school history and its most successful coach has preceded you by only four seasons, your charge of greatness is clearly defined for you. You only need to look in the Gator trophy case for proof.

When the subject of greatness comes up for discussion, no chapter can ever be written without the acknowledgment of Florida football's gold standard, as players and coaches. If they ever carve the faces of Gator football heroes on a mountainside, you can bet Steve Spurrier's face will be on it.

2

The Mount Rushmore of Gators

Football greatness is a subjective superlative that is bound to provoke argument and prompt diverse opinion. Perhaps impossible is accurately quantifying greatness until after the passage of time. One cannot mistakenly wait to equate the success or failure of a player in the pros with his career in college, because the two are distinctly different. So when you talk about greatness it must be measured in context of time and competition. To compare eras, however, is unfair and futile.

Trouble is, greatness is mostly in the mind of the beholder and tends to either diminish or over-inflate in the rearview mirror. With each passing season, our memories dim and our parameters get fuzzy. When too many seasons have faded and gobbled up the impact of achievement, we often lose track of many extraordinary deeds. We tend to think the players and coaches of our own era are better than the ones since or in the past—especially our own favorites. If you don't believe it, the next time you're in a room of Gator football fans, ask each of them to draw up their "Mt. Rushmore of Gator football greats." Then tell them they can't carve the faces of any coaches or Heisman Trophy winners on their mountain. See if there isn't a disparity of choices between the ages of your respondents.

Very little argument is made about the Greatest Gator Team of all-time because of the 1996 national championship won by Steve Spurrier's players. After that, you could make a case for the teams of 1928, 1960, 1966, 1969, 1984, 1990, 1991, or 1995. In most quarters, second place would likely go to the 1984 team of Charley Pell and Galen Hall. That Gator team lost the opening game 32-20 to Miami's defending national champions, with Bernie Kosar at quarterback. The next week, the Gators tied LSU, 21-21. In Charley Pell's final game, they beat Tulane 63-21, and then interim Galen Hall took them to eight straight wins for a 9-1-1 record. But because of

NCAA probation, they weren't allowed to keep the SEC title or go to a bowl game.

Based on a regular season, however, the 1995 team of Spurrier was the best ever, posting 12-0 record. The blemish of a lopsided 62-24 loss to Nebraska in the Fiesta Bowl marred an otherwise-perfect season.

When it comes to judging players, perhaps we are best served in taking the best from each era, putting them in a sack, shaking them up, and pulling out the ones whose faces belong on the mountain. Even though it's a purely subjective measure, it's likely as accurate as any other method—but making up your list for a lively dinner conversation can be fun.

One important factor that skews the data is how well players perform after leaving Florida. Neither of Florida's Heisman Trophy winners— Spurrier in 1966 and his quarterback, Danny Wuerffel, 30 years later—came close to achieving in the NFL what they did in college, but we must remember that the Heisman is a college award. At the same time, players such as Jack Youngblood played even better in the NFL and, therefore, probably cast a bigger aura. Yet, few would argue Youngblood's rightful place among Gator greats.

Except for the overwhelming statistical comparisons, which wouldn't be apples to apples, one cannot make an honest case that Clyde "Cannonball" Crabtree was any less vital or great a player in 1928 as Heisman Trophy winner Danny Wuerffel was in 1996.

Or that VanSickle of Charles Bachman's '28 team wasn't every bit as good or critical to the success of his team as Wuerffel's three first-team All-America wide receivers on the national championship team—Ike Hilliard, Reidel Anthony, and Jacquez Green.

So which, other than our personal choices, would be the best criteria for judging greatness? Certainly not mere statistics; or an offensive lineman would never be on any All-America team. Systems often dictate the offensive stats. For quarterbacks, wide receivers, running backs, defensive players, and even kickers and punters, the numbers may speak volumes, but don't tell everything.

Individual honors—like the Heisman Trophy winners and All-America and All-SEC designations—serve as a barometer. But even those honors are completely subjective, imbued with our own regional bias, and could be called somewhat of a popularity contest. And most of them are usually tied to the performance of championship teams since football is a team sport, and individual numbers cannot suffice as a standard.

Sometimes the talent comes in clusters at a position, as it did with the three All-America receivers who caught balls for Danny Wuerffel. How many teams can claim three All-America wide receivers as in the aforementioned

Hilliard and Anthony in 1996, then Green in 1997? All three were acrobatic and ran fast-break patterns underneath the passes of Wuerffel, out-galloping and out-leaping the defensive backs.

No wonder Wuerffel was able to become the most accurate passer in the history of college football. The fact that he also won the Heisman and led his team to the school's only national championship locks Wuerffel in as one of the forever faces of Florida football. In fact, you be would hard pressed to name any Gator who was greater.

Another unit that will be long remembered was "The Great Wall of Florida" in 1983-84, generally considered the school's best offensive line: left tackle Lomas Brown, left guard Jeff Zimmerman, center Phil Bromley, right guard Billy Hinson, and right tackle Crawford Ker.

The most All-Americans came in the Spurrier coaching era, during which 10 were named first-team AP. Lest it be forgotten, Spurrier produced two All-America quarterbacks—Wuerffel in 1995-96 and Rex Grossman in 2001. As a sophomore, Grossman was runner-up to Heisman winner Eric Crouch of Nebraska that year, but wasn't invited back to the Downtown Athletic Club the next year under Ron Zook's regime.

Even Spurrier's first quarterback at Florida, Shane Matthews, was ninth in the Heisman voting. Despite his remarkable stats and twice being named SEC player of the year, Matthews never made All-America. Though Spurrier was known for his offense, his staff produced nine defensive All-Americans: linemen Huey Richardson, Brad Culpepper, Kevin Carter, Alex Brown, and Jevon Kearse; linebacker Mike Peterson; and defensive backs Wil White, Fred Weary, and Lito Sheppard.

From 2001 through 2005, Florida produced only three All-Americans—and just one consensus. Cornerback Keiwan Ratliff was Zook's first consensus pick, listed on four teams, including The Associated Press. Offensive guard Shannon Snell made it on *The Sporting News* squad. That means after 33 All-Americans over the 21-year period from 1980 through 2001, only two Gators gained that honor in the next four seasons.

In the first 50 years of Florida football, few opportunities arose to be selected for All-America teams because only a few were picked. If not for Walter Camp and Grantland Rice, there would have been even fewer. Media coverage of the Florida Gators was certainly not intense, as they drew little or no national acclaim. The Gators were barely on the college football map until the Ray Graves era began in 1960. Prior to Graves' arrival, only five All-Americans were named in the first 52 seasons of Gator football.

Therefore, since we are dealing only with the so-called "Modern Era," we won't get a representative head count of the greatest Gator players over the

99-year span, focusing just on those after 1950. Only two were chosen prior to then—Dale VanSickel and Forrest "Fergie" Ferguson, both ends.

There have been 55 other first-team All-Americans at Florida since 1950, eight of them named twice. Twenty-one Florida players have been named All-America first team by The Associated Press (including VanSickel), generally considered the most prestigious. Just six have been consensus choices, starting with offensive guard John Barrow.

In the 10 years Bob Woodruff coached at Florida, when defense was the mantra, just three players were named All-America—all linemen. The first, Charlie LaPradd in 1952, was a defensive star on Florida's first bowl team and is still considered one of the elite players. Then came Barrow in 1956 and defensive tackle Vel Heckman in 1958.

Several players of that era were never All-America but would rank among the best in Gator annals, except they never completed their careers: quarterback Haywood Sullivan and fullback Rick Casares of the early 1950s among them. Sullivan signed a contract with the Boston Red Sox, and Casares volunteered for the U.S. Army, later enjoying a long career with the Chicago Bears.

From 1960-69, Graves' teams produced 11 All-America players, one of them a Heisman winner. Graves can easily identify his best player: Spurrier. He was a master at pulling out games in their waning moments and called plays brilliantly—sometimes even improvising with his own version of the play.

Yet when you ask somebody like early-1960s quarterback Tommy Shannon to name his favorite Gator teammate, he says unequivocally, "It was Larry Dupree," the All-America running back from Macclenny.

Shannon meant no disrespect to his good friend Spurrier; it's just that they only played together for one season and never shared the field. "And I had a great vantage point for watching Dupree cut back after handing him the ball," said Shannon.

Certainly a case could be made for All-America wide receiver Carlos Alvarez, who was one of the rare consensus choices as a sophomore before becoming injured and being forced to play two more years on bad knees. When Alvarez was healthy, he drove defensive backs crazy with his changes in speeds and his ability to snag the long ball at full stride.

His teammate, John Reaves, an All-America quarterback, broke the NCAA record for total passing yards and definitely deserves mention. Reaves had the gift of a powerful arm and a feathery touch that produced an easy-to-catch pass.

There were six All-Americans in the Doug Dickey regime, one a holdover from Graves' era—Youngblood. The All-American from Monticello is considered the best defensive end in Gator history and was named to the All-SEC team of the 1970s decade. He went on to become a five-time All-Pro—playing in seven straight Pro Bowls—and was elected to the Pro Football Hall of Fame and College Football Hall of Fame.

During that era, six years later, Wes Chandler emerged as the school's first two-time AP All-American (1976-77). Amazingly, Chandler did it by becoming a world-class receiver in a wishbone offense. Chandler's favorite player? "Carlos Alvarez,'" he said, although he played a half-dozen seasons after him.

"I remember the first thing I saw when I came to Florida was a picture of Carlos Alvarez making a great catch and said, 'Man, that guy is awesome!'" recalled Chandler.

Dickey proclaims Chandler as good a football player as he coached at Florida, but he also was proud to coach linebackers Ralph Ortega, Glenn Cameron, and Sammy Green (a first-team AP All-America choice) calling them, "… as good a group as I've ever had."

During the Charley Pell-Galen Hall decade, from 1980 to 1989, 12 All-Americans paraded through Gainesville, six of them first-team AP, two consensus choices. None more revered than linebacker Wilber Marshall, or more highly regarded than running back Emmitt Smith, a consensus and AP All-American during his junior year of 1989. Marshall, later to become an All-Pro as a member of the 1985 Chicago Bears Super Bowl Champions and the 1991 Champion Washington Redskins, was a first-team selection on *The Gainesville Sun's* "Team of the Century" and was also named "Defensive Player of the Century."

Emmitt would go on to become an NFL superstar, establishing a record for rushing yardage and becoming both MVP of the league and MVP of the Super Bowl.

Smith came to Florida with a big rep. When he first arrived as a Gator assistant coach, Galen Hall started watching film on Emmitt. Smith was then a high school freshman in Pensacola. As a prep All-American, Emmitt rolled for 8,804 yards and 106 touchdowns.

"We looked at him in high school—I think when I got there in 1984, he was a sophomore—and they said, 'There's a kid up there in Pensacola that everybody's going to be chasing in a couple of years,'" Galen Hall recalled.

Very few ever caught him.

The game of chance figures heavily in the search for football talent. Even with all the sophisticated scouting systems, computer data, and millions of dollars spent on recruiting, mistakes in judgment and oversight of talent occur in every program, including Florida's. And quite often, some of the most talented ones in the state choose other schools, although Florida's recruiting program has become extremely strong.

• • •

Were it not for some of these "walk-ons, long shots, and near-misses," however, Gator football would have been much the poorer.

On occasion, Gator football stars literally grew up right in Gainesville. Some of Florida's best have also come from outside Florida—Tennessee, Georgia, Alabama, Louisiana, Texas, and Pennsylvania. Still others are just barely noticed enough to land scholarships; others are invited to try out; and some just show up.

They found Dickey working on the school's grounds crew and asked him to come out for football, being familiar with his background as an athlete at Gainesville's P. K. Yonge High School. And although he wasn't All-America or even All-SEC in college, Dickey wound up playing safety and quarterback, the latter in what many considered the best backfield ever at that time. He was in that 1952 group with Rick Casares, J. "Papa" Hall, and Buford Long. And, of course, Doug went on to become head coach.

P. K. Yonge also produced All-Pro Cleveland Browns defensive back Bernie Parrish, All-SEC; record-setting pass receiver Chris Doering, a walk-on; and all-round player/running back Terry Jackson, a key contributor to the national championship team. Parrish was also an All-SEC baseball player and signed a contract with the Cincinnati Reds before giving it up to play in the NFL—and he had to beg for a scholarship at Florida.

Walk-on Lee McGriff, now the game analyst for Gator Radio Network, was All-SEC and led the conference in receiving, later playing for the Tampa Bay Bucs as one of Steve Spurrier's receivers.

Defensive end Preston Kendrick, whose brother Vince Kendrick was a Gator running back on scholarship, came to the UF without one and made All-SEC in 1974. David Posey, another walk-on, was an All-SEC place kicker in 1975. And fellow kicker Bobby Raymond broke four records at Florida in 1983-84 after trying out for the team. John James (1970-71), executive director of the Gators Boosters, punted without a grand-in-aid initially and later became an All-Pro punter with the Atlanta Falcons.

What if Kerwin Bell of tiny Mayo hadn't walked on to become All-SEC and one of the best quarterbacks in school history—starting out as eighth string in 1983, to help hold the program together during probation? Bell's teammate, defensive back Louis Oliver then walked on a year later, was named All-America twice, and later became a first-round draft choice of the Miami Dolphins.

All-America placekicker Judd Davis, winner of the Lou Groza Award in 1993, and placekicker Jeff Chandler (1998-2001), the all-time leading scorer, came to play without scholarships.

Gary Rolle (1982-84) was an outstanding walk-on wide receiver who graduated and became an orthopedic surgeon in Tallahassee.

Allen Trammell, now a successful Orlando businessman, came from Alabama without a scholarship and was a three-year starter in football and an All-America baseball player who led the SEC in hitting in the mid-1960s.

• • •

Other scholarship players became stars but easily might have been overlooked.

Dr. Daniel Grossman of Bloomington, Indiana, the father of quarterback Rex Grossman, made an appointment with Steve Spurrier to show tapes of his son's high school exploits. Otherwise, it's not likely Rex would have been plucked from Indiana to become one of the school's few All-Americans as a sophomore, runner-up for the Heisman, and the SEC Player of the Year in 2001. Rex was brilliant in his sophomore season under Spurrier, making first-team All-America and finishing runner-up to Heisman winner Eric Crouch of Nebraska.

Little Jimmy Dunn, all 142 pounds of him, was invited to play for the Gators after the 1955 high school all-star game by assistant coach Dick Jones; and when he came out for freshman ball, there were over 100 players uniformed. He was mired in 13th place on the quarterback depth chart but fought his way up through the "B" squad, and wound up a two-year starter on offense and defense. Later, Dunn returned as an assistant coach.

Lanky All-America lineman Jack Youngblood, from Monticello, almost went unnoticed out of high school. Were it not for Dave Fuller, who signed him on the spot, Youngblood might have gone to junior college.

One famous-to-be NFL coach predicted Jack "… would never play college football." Only after working under the tutelage of defensive line coach Jack Thompson did Youngblood find his stride, becoming the No. 1 pick (20th overall) of the Los Angeles Rams.

Larry Dupree wasn't even recruited by Florida until late in his senior year and then only because Georgia had paid a visit to Macclenny. He went on to become an All-America running back at Florida whose talent and determination awed his own teammates.

Two-time Southeastern Conference Player of the Year Shane Matthews may have been lost in the maze of the depth chart had Spurrier not come along and picked him out as the No. 5 quarterback in the spring of 1990. He had almost quit and transferred to Ole Miss just before Spurrier arrived.

All-America receiver Wes Chandler says the coach at Bethune-Cookman originally turned him down by because he was too small at five feet, 11 inches, 155 pounds. He grew up to be 190 pounds and a two-time All-American at Florida, and later a four-time Pro Bowl receiver for the San Diego Chargers.

As far as small goes, old-time Gator fans will tell you about little guys like Larry Libertore, who didn't weigh much more than 138 pounds but starred in that famous two-point pass play that beat Georgia Tech. And that's without going all the way back to 1928 and the five-foot-eight, 148-pound "Cannonball" Crabtree, who reportedly was a "quadruple-threat" back who could run, pass, hand off, or punt.

You can get yourself in an argument quick when you start picking out the greatest Gator players. During a slow period for sports-talk radio in early 2006, ex-Gator player Brady Ackerman of WMOP/WGGG asked callers in Gainesville and Ocala to pick the faces on a "Florida Gator Mt. Rushmore." There was one caveat: Spurrier and Wuerffel couldn't be picked. To that twosome, Ackerman's callers added Smith, Youngblood, and Marshall. Frank Frangie of Jacksonville's ESPN 1460 didn't disagree with that, but also mentioned Rick Casares, Chandler, and Matthews. Although players such as Casares and Matthews weren't named first-team All-America, their football accomplishments were abundant. Matthews was named SEC Player of the Year twice, quarterbacked Florida to its first real SEC title, and set 50 schools records. Casares, whose career was shortened by a car accident and an induction into the U.S. Army, was one of the greatest athletes in Florida history. He was an All-SEC back and a starter on the basketball team.

"And I believe Rick came out for baseball one time," recalled former teammate and head coach Dickey, himself a catcher for Fuller. "If he'd have worked at it, he would have been an excellent baseball player, too."

Athletes like Sullivan, Casares, Spurrier, Marshall, Emmitt Smith, Reaves, Scot Brantley, and All-America running back Larry Smith were highly recruited blue-chip prospects who had success written all over them. Yet many other of those 57 Florida All-Americans came in under the radar and blossomed once they became college players. A number of them grew into successful NFL performers as well.

Florida has also been rich in high draft choices. From the Pell/Hall era from 1980-89, there were 11 first-round NFL picks over nine seasons: linebacker Wilber Marshall (Bears) 1984; running back Lorenzo Hampton, (Dolphins) and offensive tackle Lomas Brown (Lions), 1985; running backs John L. Williams (Seahawks) and Neal Anderson (Bears), 1986; wide receiver Ricky Nattiel (Broncos), 1987; linebacker Clifford Charlton

(Browns), 1988; defensive tackle Trace Armstrong (Bears), offensive tackle David Williams (Oilers); and free safety Louis Oliver (Dolphins), 1989.

Since they started keeping records of draft positions, the highest overall first-round pick of any Gator player was third, held by Steve Spurrier (49ers) in 1967 and Chandler (Saints) in 1978.

The NFL really wasn't all that big of a deal until the 1950s, but the first Gator ever to play at that level was Walter Mayberry, a sixth-round pick in 1938. Mayberry was the first of 204 Gator names that would appear on NFL rosters over the next 66 years. From 1983-2005, Florida produced 26 No. 1 picks, third most in the country.

• • •

Coaches are easier—it's all about the victories, the championships, and the legacy of values. The four barometers of greatness at Florida are national championships, Southeastern Conference titles, Heisman Trophies, and All-Americans. On that count, Spurrier is without peer. After he named "The Swamp" in 1991, Gator teams posted a remarkable record of 81-11 through 2005. Spurrier's record there was an astonishing 68-5.

You could also give coaches points for developing tradition. On that count, Spurrier was among the best. He never let his players forget who came before them. Sometimes at practice, he would give the spontaneous quizzes like, "Who was Florida's first All-American?" or "Who was Charlie LaPradd?"

Spurrier also mandated the singing of the alma mater in postgame ceremonies and put the Gator head in the locker room narthex for players to touch before going into the tunnel. In addition to having won six SECs and one national championship, Spurrier brought a swagger to the program. He was, after all, a Heisman winner and a two-time All-American. We're not talking solely of his offense: nine of his 21 All-Americans were defensive stars, and one was a kicker. Maybe that's why Spurrier was the only Florida coach of the last five who didn't get fired.

Each coach had his own specialty. Ron Zook replenished the supply of talent with an aggressive recruiting effort and stockpiled players for Urban Meyer. Before Spurrier, Galen Hall brought Florida its first SEC title—even if it was taken away—and held the program together in tough times. What Charley Pell did must not be forgotten, his improprieties not withstanding. Pell broadened the circle and brought in supporters who weren't necessarily Florida alumni. The success of the Gator Clubs today is due directly to Pell's tireless state campaigns. He also taught Florida fans to dress right: he encouraged them to wear their colors to the game, which they do today en masse. Several gifted African-American players were brought in thanks to

Doug Dickey. And Graves brought national attention to the program with a wide-open offensive philosophy and began packing Florida Field.

And Bob Woodruff laid the foundation with a solid business operation as athletic director and moved into the big-time era.

Preface II

Over the Decades with 'The Boys'

In 1906, the same year as the San Francisco Earthquake, one year after Thomas Edison produced the first talking movie, and four years prior to Albert Einstein's announcement of his Theory of Relativity, Florida football was officially born. That first Florida team had a bit of a do-over. Even though there were games played prior to 1906—before the school moved to Gainesville and came under the University of Florida auspices—they are not counted on the official ledger.

As early as 1900, Dr. James M. Farr coached what newspapers dubbed "The Blue and White of Florida Agricultural College" at the Lake City Fairgrounds against the "Green and White of Stetson." They weren't even called the Gators back when they lost 6-0 that day. And they wouldn't adopt the name until 1908. But, it seems, the blue caught on as a team color, with orange added later.

Whatever the official colors, black and blue were most prominent thanks to the beatings suffered in those early days. Few of which were recorded thankfully, outside of a handful of North Florida newspapers. In addition to losing to Stetson, the pre-1906 team took railroad trips to be hammered by Alabama (29-0), Auburn (44-0), Georgia (51-0), and Georgia Tech (77-0). There were also losses to a team from Tallahassee called Florida State College.

Some confusion remains about what happened after that, because one report on the Florida State Website appears to suggest that the roots of winning football actually came from Tallahassee and were transplanted to Gainesville. According to Florida State's historical documents: "In a 1905 reorganization of Florida's educational system by the Legislature, six state institutions of higher learning were consolidated into two when the University of Florida in Gainesville was established and designated a men's school, and the Florida State College became a women's school called the

Florida Female College. The male student body moved from Tallahassee to Gainesville, taking with it the fraternity system and the college football team, which had been state champions in 1902, 1903, and 1905."

Once the University of Florida moved from its early beginnings in Lake City and Ocala to Gainesville, the scores counted. Coach Jack Forsythe's team had beaten a group called "Gainesville AC", but was then flattened by Mercer several weeks prior in road games. It wasn't until the third game that Florida football was played before the home folks that season. Forsythe's club football team took the field on a plot just north of where Ben Hill Griffin Stadium is today and defeated Rollins College, 6-0. The victory over Rollins was one of five recorded that year against three losses. From such humble beginnings, though, rose enormous aspirations.

Twenty-two years would pass before the Gators could become competitive and then nearly six more years for them to become a factor on the national scene. Jinxed or otherwise, these Gators seemed destined for mediocrity the next 60 years, with the exception of a six-win season here and there and the eight-win seasons of 1928 and 1929. According to the school's official history, written by former Assistant Athletics Director Norm Carlson: "Gator football earned national recognition and respect in the 1920s, beginning in 1923 under new head coach Major James A. Van Fleet, who was also senior officer in charge of the school's ROTC program. Van Fleet's team tied Georgia Tech, the ruler of Southern football, 7-7, in Atlanta; and later that season, they pulled off one of the biggest upsets in college football by beating Alabama and Coach Wallace Wade in Birmingham, 16-6."

The real gem of that era was the '28 Charles Bachman team that led the nation in scoring and featured the school's first All-American, end Dale VanSickel. Bachman's undefeated team lost to Tennessee in Knoxville, 13-12, in the final game of the season. The Gators' extra point was blocked by Bobby Dodd, later a coaching legend at Georgia Tech.

During the 1920s, Florida football achieved notice under the guidance of coaches William Kline (1920-22), Van Fleet (1923-24), H.L. Sebring (1925-27), and Bachman (1928-32), posting a combined record of 64 wins, 25 losses, and nine ties for the decade. Bachman followed up the 8-1 season with an 8-2 mark in 1929. Over the next 19 campaigns, the most games won by a Gator team was six—and that mark was achieved only twice.

One of the few highlights after that was the naming of the school's second All-American, end Forrest "Fergie" Ferguson, who was chosen to the first team in 1941. That would end the bulk of Gator football prosperity, however, until the 1950s.

By 1949, Gator fans were starved, having just endured the bleakest period in the 54-year history of their college football program: "The Golden Era," a satirical reference to the ineptitude for four years leading up to 1950. Coach Raymond B. "Bear" Wolf didn't have much to work with when he replaced Thomas J. Lieb in 1946, but coming out of the box with 12 consecutive losses didn't exactly elicit a vote of confidence. After posting a pathetic 13-24-2 record in those four seasons, Wolf was dismissed. An upgrade in coaches was imminent.

As it often has, politics entered the Florida football arena in the late 1940s. In this case, the election of Fuller Warren as governor of Florida proved to be beneficial to the state's biggest university. Warren, a tough-talking Northwest Florida boy from Blountstown who actually was elected to the Florida House of Representatives while going to school at Florida, was a big proponent of the state's turnpike when he ran for governor. He was equally enthusiastic about Florida football. As he noted along the campaign trail: "Next to my pledge to get the cows outlawed from the public highways, my pledge to try and get that winning football team at Florida seemed to get the most applause."

Florida needed a new coach and better players, but hiring a good one with a high profile and increasing the scholarship fund would require money that was in short supply. One way to get it was helping coax the State Legislature to pass a bill that would tap into the cash flow of pari-mutuel gambling. The bill would eventually pass, allowing a percentage of the proceeds from the dogs, horses, or jai alai frontons to be accrued for the Florida football program one night or day each year.

The aim for a coach was high. Among those candidates in the crosshairs were UCLA's Henry R. "Red" Sanders and Maryland's Jim Tatum—two huge names. Sanders purportedly shook hands on a deal and then changed his mind. Tatum apparently felt the salary was too low. With the two leading candidates out of the picture, a new search began. Florida officials made a telephone call to Southeastern Conference Commissioner Bernie Moore, who recommended they consider the head coach of the Baylor Bears, Bob Woodruff, whose football pedigree was impressive. He had played lineman for the legendary General Bob Neyland at Tennessee from 1936-38. After graduating in engineering, he became a student assistant before joining the U.S. Army and rising to the rank of major. He served under Earl "Red" Blaik in the era of Doc Blanchard and Glenn Davis, All-America running backs known as "Mr. Inside" and "Mr. Outside."

Following the Army job, Dodd hired Woodruff at Georgia Tech. While in Miami, on the North-South Shrine Bowl staff of Hurricanes coach Andy Gustafson, Woodruff received the call about the Florida position. Woodruff immediately demonstrated his knack for business with his own negotiations. He struck a seven-year deal at $17,000 a season, considered by some a staggering sum. But with that came the mandate: "You have to beat Georgia!"

On January 8, 1950, the 34-year-old Woodruff became Florida's 13th head coach and immediately went to work hiring top-flight assistants.

3

The Bob Woodruff Era

1950 - 1959

Different Ideas

Bob Woodruff was not without brilliance in some non-coaching matters, but often had difficulty conveying his thoughts to players. To counteract that communication deficiency, Woodruff relied heavily on his assistant coaches—all of whom were first-rate teachers, strategists, and motivators. Most players considered Woodruff aloof, yet some also spoke of random acts of kindness and respect. Still others felt he was a misfit. Therefore the portrait of Woodruff is skewed; and depending upon whom you ask, he is described as either brilliant or a buffoon; kind-hearted or a mercenary; progressive or totally out of touch; generous or miserly.

"Bob always had an idea that was different than anybody else in the room," said Doug Dickey, who played for Woodruff at Florida and coached under his athletic directorship at Tennessee. Though blessed with sharp business acumen, Woodruff sometimes was regarded as an absent-minded professor as well.

Sometimes Woodruff also had a different idea than anybody on the bus— or the street. According to linebacker Arlen Jumper of the 1951-52 teams, Woodruff would often take the team for Saturday morning strolls around the city when playing a road game. "Here we might be walking down the street in Jacksonville, wearing our regular street clothes, and we'd pass a parking lot," recalled Jumper. "And suddenly coach Woodruff would stop and stay, 'Okay, first-team offense, first-team defense—line up right over here.' He'd thought of some play he wanted to run, and so we lined up right there in the parking lot, in our street clothes."

Among his many personality quirks, Woodruff notoriously bummed cigarettes, could never remember the real names of his players (but gave some nicknames), and would take long pauses in conversations during which he appeared to be off on another planet. His lengthy pauses became almost comical to many of his players. "You never knew if Coach Woodruff was 30 minutes ahead of you or 30 minutes behind," said the late Charlie LaPradd, an All-America tackle.

Woodruff often surprised his teams with what seemed like nonsensical situations—such as the day he was watching film with his players, grumbling about the lack of ventilation. They were in a dark, non-air-conditioned room, sweltering in the heat when Woodruff shouted gruffly, "Somebody open a window in here—it's stuffy!"

The movie projector continued to whirr and nobody moved.

"Somebody open a window in here!" Woodruff bellowed a little louder. Nobody moved. Angrily, Woodruff shut off the projector and turned on the lights. Peering around, he then realized there was no window in the room.

The eccentric coach also found himself preoccupied with the perfection of grass, but luckily found unpaid labor to scratch that constant itch—the freshmen. Former Green Bay Packers and Indianapolis Colts head coach Lindy Infante was a first-year player during Woodruff's last season and rarely got to see the head coach "… because we were all just cannon fodder for the varsity." But every week Infante and his fellow freshmen were brought out to Florida Field and asked to stand shoulder to shoulder, then hand to hand. "And we walked the entire length of the field, picking up every divot made by the varsity players and replacing them," Infante said. Woodruff wanted everything to be right and was often obsessive about detail.

Woodruff also communicated in a strange language. One of his favorite mantras on the field was "Oski-Wow-Wow!" which he would ask his players to yell in unison, almost like a cryptic battle cry. Some of them never knew what it meant, except that when a Gator defender intercepted a pass, he was to yell "Oski!" to his teammates as the signal for a block. "It took Woodruff five minutes to say, 'Oski-Wow-Wow,'" joked halfback J. Papa Hall of the 1952 backfield. "So we had to shorten it."

On several occasions, Woodruff's different ideas involved a bit of skullduggery—especially when his mind turned to beating archrival Georgia. Doug Dickey remembers when his coach enlisted him to break the Bulldogs' code and counter with some espionage of their own.

"We were playing Georgia my junior year [1952]," Dickey said. "Freddie Robinson [second-string quarterback] and I were rooming together, and the phone rang about 9:30 one night. It was assistant coach [Hank] Foldberg, and he said, 'Come over here to the room—Coach Woodruff wants to see you.' So we go over there, and Woodruff [said], 'Georgia is a cheatin' bunch of bastards.' I was shocked. And he said, 'They're calling the defensive signals from the sidelines.'

"Nobody was signaling in plays in those days," Dickey continued. "He said, 'We've got their signals. When you go back to the huddle, the end over there on that side of the huddle is going to look over there and get their signals, and you call out the play. And when they're in this defense, you run this play; and when they're in that defense, you run this play.' They only had two defensive formations anyway—the 6-2-2-1 and the 5-4-2. So if they ran one defense, we would give the ball to [Rick] Casares off tackle. If they ran the other, we would run Rick up the middle. Rick made about 250 yards rushing that day. And he gave me credit for 'reading Georgia's defense.'"

The Gators chomped on those Bulldogs of Wally Butts, 30-0.

Other times, Woodruff employed his own espionage. When substitutions were limited by college football rules changes and it was difficult to relay plays in the game, Woodruff and his staff members found ways to sneak in information in, according to J. Papa Hall. Back then, during time outs, only the team managers and water boys were allowed on the field—no coach-to-player communication. Using an ingenious scheme involving writing on the bottoms of water cups, unwitting couriers circumvented those restrictions. "Sometimes during a timeout," Hall said, "you would look down in the bottom of the cup and just happen to see some writing on it."

If you were looking for an Anthony Robbins-type motivator with a Kreskin memory and a Jerry Seinfeld sense of humor, Woodruff wasn't your man. His former quarterback and assistant coach, Jimmy Dunn, thinks Woodruff was a little shy.

"He was probably introverted. He didn't communicate that well, so most of his assistant coaches did that for him," said Dunn. "But he was extremely smart, and he hired some good people to coach for him. And he was extremely loyal, just seeing how he reacted around his assistant coaches. When everybody was yelling at him to get rid of them, he wouldn't do it. We had a lot of good assistant football coaches. But he probably was more distant to the players than the coaches are today."

Woodruff's regime, which was marked by solid defense, the kicking game, and low-risk offense, boasted nothing fancy. However, he did have plenty of good coaching help. Over the years, his staff proved to be an all-star cast. Frank Broyles would become head coach at Arkansas; Tonto Coleman would become SEC Commissioner; Dale Hall would become a future head coach at Army; Hank Foldberg became head coach at Wichita State, then at Texas A&M; John Sauer came from Earl Blaik's Army staff and would become a professional coach; John Rauch became head coach of the Oakland Raiders and the Buffalo Bills; Harvey Robinson was previously Tennessee's head coach; and finally, Charlie Tate, later head coach of the Miami Hurricanes.

"Coach Woodruff did an outstanding job of picking assistant coaches, and they stayed there with him the whole time," said Dickey. "They came from outstanding football programs, and it gave Florida a big boost. They kept us turning the corner and getting better, even though we weren't quite ready to play with the big boys."

• • •

After the 1949 season, the Gators had lost two-time All-SEC first-team halfback Chuck Hunsinger, the No. 1 pick of the Chicago Bears in the 1950 NFL draft. There was a dearth of good players when Woodruff arrived. The cupboard was bare with only a few exceptions: returning quarterback Angus Williams, running back Sammy Oosterhoudt, running back-defensive back Loren Broadus, lineman Carroll McDonald, and punter Fred Montsdeoca.

Woodruff started replenishing the interior linemen. All-America tackle Charlie LaPradd, would be a walk-on, fresh out of the paratroopers. Tackle William "Red" Mitchum, end Curtis King, and guard Joe D'Agostino were three of his top early recruits. With Woodruff's background at Baylor, he reached back to get a junior college transfer or two, like Arlen Jumper, a linebacker from Waco, Texas. He found a fullback, Floyd Huggins, at a Kansas junior college. He had also expanded recruiting horizons out of state in places like Alabama, Texas, Ohio, and Pennsylvania. Coupled with an offensive scheme that was considered progressive in those days, this attracted a blue-chip quarterback prospect from Dothan, Alabama: Haywood Sullivan.

Sullivan: A Man Among Boys

The Florida Gators were about to land their first big superstar of the modern era: Haywood Sullivan. Thanks in part to halfback William A. "Bubba" McGowan, already on the squad as a holdover from the 1949 "Golden Era," they had a direct connection. McGowan was a friend and former high school teammate of Sullivan at Dothan (Alabama) High School, where Haywood was setting passing records in the "T" formation.

Sullivan was recruited heavily by both Auburn and Alabama, but did the politically correct thing and opted for Florida instead. He said one reason he picked the Gators is that their offense was more wide open and featured passing. (In view of the fact that Woodruff was fired nine years later, in part, for his conservative offense, that's quite ironic.)

McGowan thinks another reason Sullivan followed him to Florida was that Haywood's family would have transportation to the home games. "My parents had been driving down to Gainesville to see me play. And Sully's parents didn't own a car," said McGowan. "So I definitely think that was a factor."

Growing up with Sullivan on the playgrounds in Dothan, McGowan had an excellent vantage point to witness the quarterback's potent arm. McGowan swears he once saw Haywood stand on the goal line and throw a baseball into the other end zone "on one bounce." McGowan also compared Sullivan to a player he later helped coach in 1969, All-America quarterback John Reaves.

"Sully could set in that pocket, he was tall enough to see you and had such a quick release," said McGowan. "He had such a soft touch, and you could catch his passes. He could lay that thing out. And he had what Reaves and Steve Spurrier had—a catchable ball. Broyles [then a Florida assistant] took him under his arm and coached him up into an All-SEC quarterback and really should have been All-America."

At 6-feet-4, 215 pounds, Sullivan was also the 1950s version of John Elway, though not as elusive a runner, and he made Dickey, who was 6-feet-3, 180 pounds, feel like a child. "I was a skinny little kid, and he was a man," Dickey recalls. "He could fire the baseball, he could hit it, and he could flat throw the football. He had a great arm. Haywood was a man among boys."

Meanwhile, Dickey was about to become Sullivan's understudy. Although Doug wasn't even on the radar yet as Sullivan's backup, attrition began to work in his favor. By the spring of 1951, Dickey had moved all the way up to second string. And about then the new quarterback from Alabama would begin to make a big impact on Woodruff's ever-improving program.

Defensively, the '51 Gators were lacking. They ran up against a strong schedule, including No. 5 Georgia Tech and No. 15 Kentucky. Losing to Tech and the Wildcats, the Gators were also knocked off by rivals Auburn and Georgia by a single point, as well as Miami, 21-6. Although the 1951 team is considered better than its 5-5 record, everything pointed toward a banner 1952 season.

Clearly, Sullivan was going to be a huge asset and a strong pro prospect. Even though Sullivan's numbers would be paltry in comparison to today's wide-open offenses, his ability and physical stature were impressive. Today, NFL scouts would have been throwing money at him, but pro football didn't pay as much as baseball in those days.

As the baseball scouts begin to sniff around, Woodruff smelled trouble emanating from a $75,000 bonus the Boston Red Sox were dangling in front of his star quarterback. A member of a working-class family, Sullivan would be unable to resist the temptation of such a large "bonus baby" sum. So Woodruff sought advice from a baseball Hall of Famer, former New York Giants first baseman Bill Terry. The quarterback and the coach drove to Terry in Jacksonville. Expecting Terry to advise Sullivan not to leave, Woodruff was shocked when Terry said:

"Do you mean to tell me you get this money even if you don't make it to the big leagues?"

Sullivan nodded in the affirmative.

"Then boy, what are you waiting for?"

Years later Terry told *Jacksonville Journal* sports editor Jack Hairston: "I didn't know he was going to ask me to try and talk him [Sullivan] out of it."

The money impressed everybody. Sullivan signed.

After his first season with the Red Sox, Haywood came back to Gainesville to scout and coach the B-team for a year, but he was done as a player there. Thus ended the dreams of an All-World Gator backfield and possibly a conference title. There were still plenty of good players on the roster, however, and Woodruff was about to enjoy his finest season.

The 'Dream Backfield' Minus One

Florida's "Dream Backfield" would be without one member, and Dickey would be missing his friend when the 1952 season began. He and Sullivan had become pals, and he was also the backup catcher to Sullivan in baseball. "We were around each other a lot, and he was like a big brother to me," Dickey recalls.

Even without Sullivan, three other talented backs remained to carry the brunt of the offense. The offense needed brain-works—coaches didn't call plays back in those days—and somebody to choose the right play and hand the ball off to the right back. That would be Dickey, but it didn't take a genius to find somebody who could make good yardage. "You couldn't make a bad choice. Whichever way the other team shifted, you gave it to the guy going the other way," Dickey said.

In a very short time, Woodruff began to see the results of his talent search, thanks to the landing of players like Sullivan, Hall, LaPradd, Rick Casares, and Buford Long. Even though he was distant to most of his players, many of them formed long-lasting relationships that they cherished.

Probably nobody was closer to Woodruff than Dickey, who played for him at Florida, went to work for him as head coach at Tennessee, left to become Florida's head coach, and ultimately succeeded him as athletics director in Knoxville.

Doug wasn't a heralded high school player. It was a total fluke that he wound up being a Gator athlete and perhaps even more remote that he'd be head coach. He only started playing football at P. K. Yonge High in his sophomore year—and even then, just the six-man variety. He had enrolled at Florida in need of a job, so he went to work in the grounds department and figured he would walk on as a baseball player.

One day, while riding on a truck at work, Dickey passed and waved to Dave Fuller, head baseball coach and freshman football assistant. That night Fuller called Dickey at home and said, "You were a pretty good football player—why don't you walk on for football?"

"I said, 'Well, I'll give it a try,'" Dickey recalls. "It's better than working in the grounds department."

Dickey started out as the seventh-string freshman quarterback. It was also his entry into the world of Woodruff, who would one day impact Doug's career in a big way. Never a very gifted athlete in one sport, but versatile enough to play several, Dickey was intelligent and quickly picked up Woodruff's simple schemes. Since he wasn't much of a passer, coaches brought in stronger-armed Fred Robinson on passing downs.

J. Papa Hall remembers that Dickey made the most of his skills. "Doug was not the greatest runner in the SEC," Hall said. "He was not the greatest passer, because he had an unusual delivery that had the nose down. And at about 15-20 yards, it started looking like Hoyt Wilhelm's knuckleball. But he was the smartest quarterback in the Southeastern Conference—hands-down, bar-none. And we knew it. In the huddle, there was never a question of 'should we do that?' He called the play, and we did it."

Dickey and Woodruff developed a simpatico relationship. "Bob was very, very kind to me," Dickey recalled. "In those days, the quarterback called the plays. Basically, my job was to pick out the guy who I wanted to give the ball to, and we let him run with it. We ran the ball about 95 percent of the time, and I think I threw it about 35 times the whole year. Robinson probably threw it as much as I did and he probably played about 30 percent of the time that I did. So Bob and I got along fine. I kinda knew what he wanted to do. I didn't have any trouble figuring out how to call the plays. And that's the way we went."

By the fall of 1952, the talent had started to meld. The "Almost" Dream Backfield had size and speed: Long, Hall, and Casares.

Casares was an all-round athlete and an outstanding inside runner. Hall was swift, with long legs and a big stride. Long was elusive and could juke tacklers.

"[Buford] Long was a little more of a jitterbug runner who had quick feet and could bounce it outside and find extra yardage," recalls Dickey. "He held the Florida scoring record that stood for a number of years. You could give him the ball on the goal line with the other two guys blocking. Buford ended up playing in the pros, as a defensive back for the Giants. He was a special athlete and he was tough. J. Papa Hall was probably the fastest—he could get out around the end and make more yardage. He was probably the best receiver of the group, too."

Looking back at what might have been, Dickey said of Sullivan: "If he'd have stayed around as quarterback his senior year, instead of me, we might have gone undefeated. He was a great player."

Hall, who served four terms as a circuit court judge and currently resides in Winter Park, where he is still a senior judge, remembers the 1951-52 backfield for boasting unusual size for that era. He reflected on the 8-3 record and the 1952 season-opening 33-6 win over Stetson and the 33-0 victory over The Citadel in the third game of the year as no-brainers.

"At that point, Haywood weighed about 220. Rick weighed 222. Buford was about 197 or 198, and I played at 207. In those days, that was a *huge* backfield," Hall said. "Buford could click [run] about a 10-flat [100-yard dash], and my best was 9.6. So we could go, we could fly. Then we moved to our senior year; and we still had three pretty big kids in the backfield, and Doug [Dickey] was tall."

When Florida opened the season, however, it was Casares at quarterback. The Gator record was 2-1 when Woodruff made the move to Dickey behind center, with Robinson as the passing specialist. Casares was so versatile that he also kicked extra points and field goals.

"The truth of the matter is, we would have won those first two games that Rick played quarterback with Forrest Gump playing quarterback and Rick as the fullback," says Hall.

About the elusiveness of Long, Hall said: "Buford had more fakes up his sleeve than Houdini. He had a real good nose for the goal line, and he could hit a crease and go through it. And Buford was a good teammate—good runner, good blocker, and good pass receiver. And he was fun to be around."

Hall, himself a gifted athlete, became NCAA high-jump champion.

Seven Gators were All-SEC that season. In addition to that outstanding backfield and a solid offense, Woodruff could also rely on defensive stalwarts like All-America and All-SEC first-teamer LaPradd, first-team All-SEC D'Agostino, second-team All-SEC linebacker Charles "Bubba" Ware, and third-team All-SEC Jumper. Players like LaPradd and D'Agostino provided toughness and leadership to the defense.

"Charlie [LaPradd] was a good leader," recalled Hall, his teammate. "He kept everybody focused. Nobody cut up around him. He not only talked about 'You play hard,' but he demonstrated it by playing hard himself—and he played very well."

D'Agostino loved to eat, as you could see by his belly and tell from his ownership in a Winter Park Italian restaurant, but he was also cat-quick in the middle of the line and a forceful run-stopper.

Old-time Gator fans will always wonder, however, what might have been had "The Dream Backfield" stayed together. Hall, Long, Sullivan, and Casares were all drafted by NFL teams. Long signed with the Giants as a defensive back and Casares with the Bears. Sullivan stayed with the Red Sox. Hall, picked by the Giants, went to law school. Dickey went off to the U.S. Army, where he would first become a coach. Once out of the Army, he moved on to coach at Arkansas on Broyles' staff; then at Tennessee for Athletics Director Woodruff; and then at Florida, his alma mater.

Sullivan wound up as the Red Sox catcher from 1960-1963 and, eventually, as one their co-owners. He also caught for the Kansas City Athletics and later managed them before going to work in the Red Sox system. Dickey's and Sullivan's friendship lasted right up until Sullivan's death. Sullivan died in February 2003, of a stroke in Southwest Florida, where he was a successful waterfront developer.

"When he was managing the Birmingham Barons, they would come to Knoxville to play against the Smokies when I was coach at Tennessee; and we would visit. He came out to the house a few times," said Dickey. "He was quite a guy."

Casares: Bad Boy, 'Great Teammate'

Of all the athletes who have passed through Florida, none was more talented or mysterious than Casares, who had moved to Florida from New Jersey and attended Jefferson High School in Tampa.

Though distant socially, Casares was described as "a great teammate" by players on both the Gator basketball and football teams. He was also termed "a great athlete" by many, as evidenced by his 12-year career in the NFL and five-time Pro Bowl selection. He was a starter on John Mauer's Gator basketball team and could have played other sports if he had chosen.

"Not only that, but parenthetically, Rick Casares had all of his individual exploits and accomplishments that are well known. But less well known is that Rick Casares was a helluva teammate and great team player. I always thought real, real highly of him," Hall said.

Dickey recalls the first time he ever saw Casares at a high school track meet in Tampa. "I thought, 'Wow, I've never seen anybody like that as a high school athlete,'" said Dickey. At Florida, Casares stuck to football, basketball, and, sometimes track, although he dabbled in other sports.

"He was a boxer, a football player ... he came out for baseball a few days during my freshman year [at Florida]—played first base and looked like he had been there all his life. He threw the javelin and won a lot of meets," Dickey said. "He was a great guy to have on your team—he could play linebacker or quarterback or punter, kick extra points and field goals. He didn't complain, just lined up, kept his mouth shut, and did whatever he needed to do to help the team. He was just absolutely a fantastic athlete who probably was not 'academically inclined.' I think he could have done it, but he wasn't inclined. His background just wouldn't let him concentrate on things like academics. He didn't need it. He was so far ahead of everybody else in college, and he was going to be a pro athlete. In today's world, he would have already been a pro—and they would have offered him $10 million."

An academic casualty, however, didn't end his college career. Unfortunately, Casares' college football days were cut short by an automobile accident that involved a woman's death. He came back to school, tried to play several games, but was too injured. In a special arrangement with prosecutors, a judge ordered Casares to enlist in the U.S. Army. After his service, he was signed by the Bears, and in his second season rushed for more than 1,000 yards.

Casares had a different group of off-campus friends. Most of the football players roomed in Murphree Hall. Jumper said he used to see "... long black cars pull up outside the dorm and people get out with black shirts and black sport coats who headed for Rick's room."

That jibed with the recollection of Casares' roommate, former Gator basketball player Augie Greiner, who recalls that older friends from Tampa would come to their dorm room before a game.

"Rick would say to me, 'Augie, you're going to have to leave for a little while now,'" said Greiner, "And I'd take off somewhere until they left. Another time, he said, 'You know, Augie; the night before a game, you really need to go and bunk out somewhere else.' So I did." Like Dickey, however, Greiner was fond of Casares and recalls that, if there was ever any kind of scuffle on the basketball court, he could count on Casares top have his back.

Dickey remembers a fight broke out during a basketball game on the road. Casares went down to the other team's locker room after the game and resolved the issue. "Rick straightened out some folks."

While McGowan was in the U.S. Army with Casares, he witnessed unleashed rage in a so-called controlled environment. "I saw him tear up a guy in the ring when they were just sparring. The guy got mad and they had a real fight," McGowan recalled.

Trouble followed the big fullback from Tampa. Despite his bad-boy image, Dickey liked Casares and found him to be pleasant company. "Rick was a great guy who loved life, was great fun off the court or the field, and had a good temperament about him." And then Dickey tempered that comment with, "Of course, I would become the one deciding who would get the ball—so everybody was nice to me."

With Sullivan signing a baseball contract, no experienced quarterbacks were left to start the 1952 season. In a mystifying move, Woodruff took his best runner, the massive Casares, and put him at quarterback, taking him out of the running attack. After three games at the position, Casares pointed out that he had a clean uniform and wasn't getting to run the ball any.

"Let Dickey do the quarterbacking," he said to Woodruff. "All he has to do is hand it off." Woodruff made the change. Dickey took over for Casares in the fourth game, and the big fullback back flourished at his natural spot, where he earned All-SEC second team.

After leaving for the service the following season, Casares' former teammates watched him playing on television for the Bears. His career ended after playing with the Miami Dolphins' 1966 expansion team. After hanging around Tampa briefly, he then faded into the West Coast.

"I'm not sure what Rick is doing these days," tackle Jackie Pappas of Tarpon Springs said of his friend in early 2006. "Every now and then, he shows up down here on the docks, but he won't tell me what he's doing out there in California."

In the summer of 2006, Casares told the *Tampa Tribune* he was torn between going to Kentucky and playing basketball for Adolph Rupp, or going to Florida and playing football. "I probably didn't have the [college] career I could have had. But I'm proud to be a Gator. I made the right choice."

Not Over the Hump Yet

Woodruff had his best year in 1952, beating Georgia, Auburn, Kentucky, and Miami. One of the three teams he lost to was No. 3 Georgia Tech, 17-14. The person who kicked the winning field goal for Tech was Pepper Rodgers, who would later be a big factor in the early success of Ray Graves' coaching staff.

After two .500 seasons, Florida played in its first postseason game against Tulsa. Even though the Golden Hurricanes knew what was coming, they had trouble stopping the big Gator running backs.

"When we played Tulsa [in the Gator Bowl] and time was running out, it was something like third-and-4, and we sitting on about our 15-yard line. Everybody in the stadium knew who was going to get it, and it was going to be Rick," Hall said. "All you could hear was *boomp, boompf, bboof,* and it was first down. We ran the clock out. Big Rick took it right up the middle against their two-time All-America linebacker, Marvin Matuszak; and we won our first bowl game."

Florida beat Tulsa, 14-13, in the January 1, 1953, Gator Bowl as Casares kicked the extra point. The Gators would end up with an 8-3 mark. Hall was the leading rusher and most valuable player. Dickey pulled a hamstring and suited up, but only played in "… about four or five plays."

Dickey unwittingly played a part in a key play "… that probably won the game for us."

"Coach Woodruff got confused on the downs," Dickey said, "and he sent Robinson in for me and had him throw a pass on fourth down that he completed and probably won the game for us." (Except Woodruff had thought it was third down.)

Things looked to be on the upswing for Gator football. Woodruff began to operate the athletic program as a business. "Prior to that," said Dickey, "Florida didn't have much support of the people. It was Bob who started the Gator Booster Club."

He also introduced a plan to grow Florida Field from its original 22,000 capacity of 1929 to over 40,000. With talent on both his coaching staff and his roster, Woodruff was able to stay at or just above the Mendoza line for football coaches: the .500 mark. However, Florida football soon proved it was not yet over the hump.

By 1953, his senior year, Dickey decided to focus on football and baseball as a catcher-outfielder.

With Long, Hall, and Casares gone, the 1953 Gators stumbled out of the gate without a win in three starts before trouncing Stetson, 45-0. They lost three of the last four and slipped to 3-5-1—the worst season since the winless 1946 campaign of "The Golden Era." They did manage to beat Georgia, 21-7, a game in which Dickey threw his only career touchdown pass.

The 1954 Florida team went 5-5, beginning a stretch of three losing seasons. Florida boasted the highest SEC finish in school history that year, third place, with a 5-2 league mark. But the Gators suffered three other non-conference losses to Rice, Clemson, and Miami.

In 1955, the Gators slipped to 4-6 as the substitution rules began to change, and according to Woodruff, Florida still lacked the depth to compete. However, a fresh new crop of talent arrived in 1956, and they brought the program back. Among them were munchkin quarterback Jimmy

Dunn, who became a steady two-way performer. And already there were two special All-SEC running backs, Jackie Simpson and Jimmy Rountree. One of the fiercest three-sport competitors ever to wear the uniform was Bernie Parrish, who would later prove that with the Cincinnati Reds and Cleveland Browns—but not until after his tumultuous encounters with Woodruff.

Parrish and Fleming: Heart and Hustle

All Bernie Parrish ever wanted to do was become a Gator football player. Growing up in Gainesville and sneaking into the games to see people like Sullivan and Casares play, he worked toward that goal as a three-sport star at P. K. Yonge in Gainesville. Parrish was a gritty competitor, a hardnosed football player, an excellent scorer in basketball, a vicious hitter and Charlie Hustle-style baseball player who could also pitch.

Parrish's formative years were spent facing some of the best competition he had ever faced, he claims—college or pro—and helped him prepare for future tasks. Parrish grew up with a group of guys that played all sports together at P. K. Yonge—guys he felt could all become scholarship football players. At one point, they helped the Blue Wave win 17 straight football games, and people began to take notice. Then one day in 1954, Parrish and his three P. K. pals got a call from Woodruff, asking them to report to his office. Excitement filled the air.

Bernie was the runt of the litter at 145 pounds. His three football teammates had size and athleticism and appeared destined for big-time football. Fullback Tommy Bronson, guard Dickie Mann, and halfback Harry Swilley were ready. The four of them had competed since grade school, along with other friends like Gene Ritch and Jerry Daniels, who would wind up going to rival Gainesville High School. This was the big day for the four Blue Wave athletes, however, and they were all very thrilled.

"Gainesville was a great place to grow up," said Parrish. "Florida football meant an awful lot. We were just *supposed* to go there and play ball. We expected to get a scholarship to Florida. So we get a call from Woodruff, to come over to his office at the stadium, to tell us he was *not* going to give us a scholarship. None of us. He said we could play if we would live at home, eat at home, and use the used books at the athletic department, but he was not going to give us a scholarship. We were flabbergasted. I've never heard of a coach calling you to tell you 'We're *not* going to give you a scholarship.' When we left, our high school coach—Hank Bishop, a wonderful guy— called several schools. He got Tommy a scholarship at Tennessee. Vanderbilt gave Dickie Mann a scholarship. Harry Swilley went into the service, and when he got out, he went to Tennessee."

Ostensibly, Woodruff had calculated that move would save him four scholarships.

Parrish stayed around to settle the score. "I was *supposed* to go to Florida on a scholarship and play football for the Gators. Stetson gave me a scholarship, and I went over there [Deland] for a couple of weeks, but I just couldn't accept that." He just felt he had been ordained to be a Gator. So Parrish enrolled at Florida without a scholarship, but got help from a friend in the Gator Boosters Club.

"They called me and said, 'There are some alumni here who don't want to see you go to school somewhere else and come back and beat our brains out. So how much do you need to go to school? You can play any sport you want, or you don't have to play anything if you don't want to.'"

Parrish says he received money for his dorm and meals and was told to come back when he needed more. He figured it was probably illegal, but didn't stop to think about it then, he said. Still nursing a shoulder injury from his last football game at P. K. Yonge, Parrish played basketball and baseball as a freshman at Florida and went out for track. But he still coveted a real athletic scholarship in order to fulfill his lifetime dream.

Dave Fuller only had one baseball scholarship to give, which would go to Dale Willis, who one day would pitch for the Kansas City. After his freshman season, Bernie was assigned to play semi-pro baseball in the Industrial League and went to South Carolina. "Each coach in the SEC was allowed to send their best players," said Bernie. "I was MVP of the league. I figured that was pretty good and that would help my chances of getting a scholarship."

Confident that he would be rewarded, Parrish returned to Gainesville only to encounter his despondent baseball coach, Fuller. "I thought Fuller was going to cry. He said, 'Bernie, he won't give it to you. The only way he's going to give it to you is if you go out for football and make it.' So, I went out for football. And I tore that damn scholarship out of his hide. I made a lot of guys pay for it in practice, and they were awfully unhappy about it."

Ever since he was 13, Parrish had carried a competitive chip on his shoulder, perhaps trying to outdo the exploits of his older brother, also an excellent athlete. Something drove him toward overachievement. "I can't tell you exactly why, but I had to be the best damn football player on that field. I wanted to have a head-on collision with the toughest guy on the other team all the time. I have no idea why I did that. Fortunately, it didn't kill me—but I'm not so sure that it helped my brain a lot."

With a redshirt year left, Parrish would have three seasons remaining. So he quit basketball. Mostly, Parrish played blocking back while Jim Rountree carried the ball. A ferocious blocker, sometimes coaches would line Parrish up against a tackle in practice and goad him into punishing the oversized guy in front of him, as if it were on exhibition. "The coaches would say, 'Watch Parrish draw blood,' just loud enough for me to hear it."

He willingly complied and admitted to liking it at times, but still felt unappreciated. Although a good runner himself, he seldom touched the ball. One week against Vanderbilt, Bernie had a big game, rushing for 115 yards and earning National Back of the Week. The next week, he got only four carries. Somehow he felt Woodruff was never going to let him get too much attention, something that would cost his head coach dearly in future negotiations.

"I finally come along as a player. I was there, always trying to outdo the big boys from Miami and Jacksonville; but I was also showing his ass up, too. But they won't give me the ball because I was a good blocker, too. We had Rountree, a terrific runner, so the offense centered on me blocking for Rountree," Parrish said.

Teaming up with his roommates, end Don Fleming and tackle Vel Heckman—plus Rountree, Simpson, and Barrow—Parrish helped the Gators to two respectable seasons during which they lost just five total games (6-3-1 and 6-2-1). But because of that tie in '56 and a shortened nine-game schedule in '57, they never won more than six. "It was a great era for us," Parrish said of the 1955-57 football teams. "We had a helluva team."

Heckman, Parrish said, was a very consistent player with sound fundamentals. "He never missed a tackle. I was surprised when he made All-America, because he was so under the radar all the time—and he never got any publicity. But he deserved to make All-America.

"Don Fleming was as good an athlete as I ever played with. He could have been a helluva basketball player. He was a helluva baseball player. He was just a terrific football player, especially on defense, and a helluva tackler. He was always flying through the air, knocking the hell out of somebody."

Parrish and Fleming also played baseball. Together, they once concocted a scheme to rip a cast off Bernie's broken hand so he could pinch-hit in the ninth inning against Wake Forest. Fleming used a pair of pliers to break off the cast. Parrish went to the plate and scalded a pitch up the middle for the winning run.

It was about that time that major league scouts started coming by to see Bernie. With no draft back then, he could be signed by any organization as a free agent. But now that he had attained the thing he most coveted—a football scholarship to Florida—would he dare give it up for money?

He had a year of football left, but his baseball eligibility was up. The three roommates had grown close, and Parrish hated to leave them. Fleming and Heckman, both of whom also planned to go pro, warned Bernie to give baseball a serious consideration in case he became injured—there were no insurance policies for that back then. "I talked it over with them. They had listened to all the phone calls and all the scouts coming back and forth. And they said, 'Bernie, you just can't turn that big money down. It doesn't make any sense.' And they pointed out that, if I had gotten a scholarship and finished my football, we would have all been leaving at the same time."

So along came Gabe Paul of the Cincinnati Reds with a fistful of cash: $45,000 up front to sign, $45,000 to play. Parrish signed the contract. Shortly thereafter, Bernie received a call from Woodruff, asking that he come to his office.

"Woodruff offered to match whatever money Cincinnati would give me if I would stay and play my senior year," said Parrish. "Ninety-thousand bucks! I'd have been the highest paid football player in the country, by far. There was no NFL player back in 1958 making $90,000 a year. And he's got Gabe Paul on the phone! So I picked the phone up, because I didn't believe it, and it was Gabe Paul. He said, 'Bernie, I heard what Woodruff is telling you. He's leading you to believe we might not want you. We want you. You signed the contract. We don't want to let you out of the contract. We want to play for the Reds, now. And on top of that, if you'll sign a contract that says you'll never play professional football, we'll double it.'"

Parrish told Paul he planned to honor the contract and wanted to play baseball, but didn't want to sign anything saying he wouldn't play football. Although some people today doubt the veracity of that story—especially the $90,000 allegedly offered by Woodruff—Parrish sticks to his statement. At least one of his childhood friends, Gene Ritch, says he has heard Parrish tell that story a number of times. Unfortunately, both Paul and Woodruff are deceased and can neither confirm nor deny the conversation.

What amazed Parrish, he said, was that the same man who refused to give him a scholarship just two years earlier was so desperate to keep a player whom he once didn't even want. Bernie was bitter about the way he had been treated. "If Woodruff would have shown any appreciation at all, I probably would have stayed, but he didn't want me to start with. It really hurt my feelings. But he didn't. It was almost insulting. There was no sense in not giving me the damn scholarship. I have no doubt that he would have come up with the money if I would have taken it."

At Albuquerque in the minors, Parrish broke his hand. In Nashville, he broke his hand again. The really bizarre ending to the story was that Parrish also struggled with bad night vision and felt he couldn't perform up to his own standards. So he quit baseball, gave back $45,000 to the Reds, went to boot camp for the Naval Reserve, and signed a pro football contract with the Browns. He played for 12 years and became an All-Pro cornerback.

"I felt like I didn't earn the money," he said. "[Browns General Manager] Paul Brown told me I should have kept the money and said it might have been the first time any professional athlete did that." On the other hand, Brown didn't offer Parrish a bonus when he signed, either.

While playing for the Browns against the Bears one day, Parrish had a chance to meet up with his hero, the player he idolized back when he was sneaking in Gator games: Rick Casares.

"When I was a rookie, he sweeps my end, and there's just me and my old hero. And I heard him say 'Oh, s——t' just before I hit him. I hit him right in the back of the neck, and he went down hard. I *had* to do it. I just *had* to do it."

The following year, Parrish talked to Paul Brown about possibly trading for Fleming, who was lost on the Chicago Cardinals depth chart as a defensive back. They were still good friends, and Bernie felt Fleming was the best all-around player he ever played with at Florida. "He just did everything right. He was flying through the air, doing all the right things, catching the ball at the highest spot. ..."

Fleming was a starter in the Browns secondary for several years, and often Parrish would marvel at his natural football instincts. Back then, pro football players didn't make much and had to supplement their income with off-season jobs. Fleming, a lineman with a Florida power company, died tragically when he was electrocuted. Parrish was at the golf course in Aurora when his wife arrived with the terrible news.

"My wife Carol came out and told me about it. You know, I went home and grabbed the clothes that I could—I couldn't believe it—and had her take me to the airport. Because if I could get there fast enough ..." Parrish stopped, choking back tears. " ... It's hard to talk about it. He was a great guy and great football player. Florida was lucky to have him."

Jimmy Dunn, Big Little Quarterback

To paraphrase the old cliché, it's not the size of the Gator in the fight, but rather the size of the fight in the Gator—and many undersized players have played big roles at Florida. Such a player was Jimmy Dunn of Tampa, who never cracked 150 pounds as a quarterback-safety for Bob Woodruff in the late 1950s. As far as honors, Dunn didn't establish any school records or make All-SEC. About the only place you'll find his name in the history books is as the team's leading punt returner in 1958 (11 for 140 yards—a 9.4-yard average). But Jimmy Dunn was no lightweight. "Pound for pound, he was the best player I ever coached," said Woodruff, who almost didn't offer him a scholarship.

The long arm of Tennessee coach Bob Neyland reached down to Florida and prompted Woodruff to offer Dunn a scholarship, right on the field after the Florida High School All-Star Game. The Gators had lightly recruited the Tampa Hillsborough star; and though Georgia Tech had showed a mild interest in him, Tech assistant Frank Broyles believed that Dunn was too small at just 5-feet-8 and 135 pounds. Some suggested Dunn should go away to the service to add some bulk.

Florida State was interested in Dunn, who had already agreed verbally to walk on with coach Tom Nugent. If he went to Tallahassee and played well in the spring game, he'd be offered a full ride. After performing well in the all-star game, Florida assistant Dick Jones convinced him to be a Gator. Perhaps Woodrufff would've forgone the decision without the power of suggestion from his old coach.

"Years later, when I was coaching at Tennessee, I met General Neyland, and he told me the reason Woodruff offered me a scholarship is that he [Neyland] was going to if he didn't," said Dunn. "He was probably just trying to be nice."

That scholarship paid dividends for the Gators. Dunn was amazed at the ample competition due to the unlimited scholarships when he showed up to play at Florida, however, and would have to negotiate his way through a quagmire.

"One day, there were 100 guys out for the freshman team. About 40 of them left the next day—took trains and buses out of town in the middle of the night. And we also had a 'B Team' of 75 guys who didn't make the varsity, and they played games against 'B Teams' from Miami and Georgia."

Dunn looked at his name on the depth chart only to discover he was 13th-string quarterback. But the good news was that he was growing and eventually would sprout up to all of 5 feet, 10-1/2 inches, and 142 pounds. Size notwithstanding, Dunn would become priceless due to his versatility. The substitution rules change put a premium on two-way players. Other quarterbacks were bigger and had stronger throwing arms, but couldn't match Dunn's defensive skills in the secondary.

"When the rules changed, it gave me a chance to play. They had strong quarterbacks who could really throw the ball, but they couldn't run, and they couldn't play pass defense. And if you started the game, you could come back in once a quarter, but if you didn't, you could only go in once. The quarterback had to play safety."

The talent gradually dropped during Dunn's three varsity seasons, although running backs Jackie Simpson and Jim Rountree were substantial help. Once they were gone, Florida's offense no longer had the size. "I have Rountree and Simpson, both 5-feet-8 or 5-feet-9. And then I'm in there with three sophomores—Don Deal at 5-feet-8, 165 pounds; Doug Partin at 5-feet-9, 165; and Jon MacBeth, a 175-pound fullback. So we were 'ponies.' We could have won if Bernie [Parrish] had been there in 1958."

Dunn also played special teams and factored into a very large play in the Gators' first game ever against Florida State on Saturday, October 22, 1958—against those very same Seminoles who had recruited him.

Controversy surrounded the start of the Florida-FSU series when Governor LeRoy Collins strongly suggested the idea should be consummated. A veiled threat arose that the State Legislature might get involved. Finally, the deal was struck, but with the provision that all games be played in Gainesville at first. The Seminoles did not yet have an elite program, and Florida must have been at least a two-touchdown favorite. So the setting at Florida Field was tense to say the least.

"FSU had started playing pretty good in 1956," said Dunn. "Lee Corso was there then—and Burt Reynolds. By 1958, they were playing pretty good. They even beat Tennessee in Knoxville, and they beat Miami. So they were a legitimate football team. They just didn't play the schedule some teams in the South played."

Up to some chicanery, the feisty Seminoles executed a nearly perfect reverse handoff on the opening kickoff. Jack Espenship took the ball and cut across the field to Bobby Renn, fooling everybody, and suddenly Renn was running in the clear behind two big blockers with only Dunn between him and the goal. The idea that this upstart team from Tallahassee could score on the Gators so easily was incredulous. From Dunn's perspective, he thought it was going to happen:

"The defensive team had to start the game so we could be in there on the first series," Dunn recalled. "I'm the safety man on the kickoff cover team. So they take it and execute a reverse off of it. I just backpedaled, trying to buy time until somebody could come catch him with the backside pursuit. And finally I guess he got tired of waiting and didn't like his chances behind these two big slow guys, because he took off and went to the middle of the field. I had a chance to run away, too, and I tackled him. If he'd just have waited for one of them to knock me down, he'd have scored, because we didn't have that many guys chasing him."

The Seminoles kept it deep inside Florida territory and wound up scoring on Fred Pickard's run for a 7-0 lead, but at least Dunn gave Gator fans room to breathe after stopping the opening kickoff return. The Gators won the inaugural game of what would become one of the nation's premier rivalries, 21-7.

During the three years of Dunn's varsity eligibility, Florida became even more conservative. The games were not exactly track meets. The year before, when Dunn was a junior, the Gators only scored three touchdowns once. They went 6-2-1, including a 0-0 tie with Georgia Tech.

With Rountree no longer eligible to play and their best player, Parrish, gone to play baseball, the 1958 Gators limped in to beat Miami in the season finale, 12-9, but lost the Gator Bowl to Ole Miss, 7-3. The Gators had to eke out wins almost every week, exemplified best by their 7-6 victory over Georgia that year that was clinched a 75-yard Jimmy Dunn run.

"Georgia had about 19 first downs, and we had three. They were inside our goal line about four times and didn't score," Dunn said. "And they had the ball at the end of the game, throwing it around the field—Fran Tarkenton and Charlie Britt. But we won it, and we beat Georgia all three years I played."

It wasn't a banner season in 1958, although Vel Heckman did become Florida's fifth All-American, and Don Fleming was first-team All-SEC.

There were rumbles of discontent among the Gator faithful, however. In 1959, Florida was 3-0 and played Rice in Houston. But with the ball in Florida's possession near midfield, Woodruff chose to kill the clock and settle for a 13-13 tie. The damning Woodruff quote was: "I'll gamble to win, but never to lose." If that didn't spell his demise, then four straight losses to SEC teams—the last a 21-10 loss to Georgia—would.

As ordered, Woodruff did beat Georgia six out of 10 years, but it didn't save him. During those 10 seasons, he recorded a mark of 53 wins, 42 losses, and six ties for a winning percentage of just .556—the lowest of any head coach of the next half-century and perhaps beyond.

The stage was set for ramblin', gamblin' Ray Graves to arrive on the scene.

4

The Ray Graves Era

1960 - 1969

The Tennessee Connection

Pulling into the driveway of Ray Graves' Tampa Carrollwood townhouse and walking through the garage to the family room, a visitor can't help but notice the famous picture and perhaps wonder why something so significant doesn't occupy a more prominent spot in his home. This defining moment, this play, this historic decision certainly retains a place of honor in the hearts of older Gator fans.

Graves sees this photo almost every day—a black-and-white postcard reminder from his past and an epic passage in his coaching career. Snapped late in the afternoon at Florida Field on October 1, 1960, the moment serves notice that the next 10 years are going to be different. During these final seconds of the game against Georgia Tech—in his first season as Gator coach—he is about to emancipate Gator fans from a decade of dull, unimaginative, give-up football. Graves' white shirt is tucked, unwrinkled, cufflinks intact. His jaw juts defiantly, a testimony to his bold resolve. His left arm is raised, two fingers skyward. An unidentified Gator player, No. 83, gazes in awe at the new man with two raised fingers and new ideas. Indeed Graves' gesture represents a whole new day in Florida football.

Actually, Graves is holding up four fingers—two on each hand. The left hand is forming a "2" with the index and middle finger, unwittingly flashing a "V" for victory as well. His right hand is lower, waist high, duplicating the other "2," almost as a backup to support this daring maneuver.

In the photo, Graves has made the choice. Even before tailback Lindy Infante returns to the bench after scoring the touchdown to pull Florida within a point of mighty Georgia Tech, he knows he'll go for two.

Quarterback Larry Libertore sprints out right and lofts an easy pass to fullback Jon MacBeth for the winning deuce. Seismic crowd noise rocks Florida Field.

The Gators beat Georgia Tech, 18-17, earning national respect in only the third game under their brand-new coach from—of all places—Georgia Tech. Perhaps equally as important, they had buried the ghost of their archaic, stone-age football past.

Four score, five years, three months, and 26 days after that picture was taken, Graves hosted a writer for an interview on a spring day. He was asked to look at the photo and tell the visitor what he saw. "I see a chance to make football history as a winner or a loser," Graves said. "It was such a big play, and it helped our program so many ways. We were all energized with that one win."

Though Florida and Graves never won a conference championship in the 1960s, the Gators moved up in the college football neighborhood. They developed more big-name players who produced more big wins on more big plays than any period in previous history. For it, they were rewarded with big-time bowl appearances and a big-time Heisman Trophy.

So much of Florida's football heritage has stemmed from Tennessee roots, including Ray Graves. Four players off the 1936 Knoxville Central High team got grants-in-aid to the University of Tennessee, but Ray Graves wasn't one of them. In a prearranged deal with Wallace Wade at Duke, Graves went to Athens, Tennessee, where he attended tiny Tennessee Wesleyan, stashed on a "farm team" until the Blue Devils would need him. It was understood that somebody would eventually finance his scholarship to Duke. He never got there, though, thanks to Coach Bob Neyland.

"I went to Tennessee Wesleyan College on a 'Duke scholarship,'" Graves said, still amused at the notion. "My brother, who worked for J.C. Penney in Knoxville, told one of the assistant coaches at Tennessee, Harvey Robinson, 'My brother is going to Duke University.' So Harvey told Coach Neyland, who asked, 'Is he any good?' And my brother said, 'Well, he was named captain of the team in his second year.' And Neyland said, 'Well, we don't want him playing for Wallace Wade!' Neyland went down and told my dad, 'You don't want your boy leaving town.' He told daddy on me. Anyway, I went to Tennessee, which I think was a smart move."

After sitting out a year at Tennessee, Graves began playing guard, center, even linebacker for The General. He became captain of the team. Graves feels Neyland was without peer as a teacher and coach. "I enjoyed playing for General Neyland, and I still think he was the best coach who ever coached football. He had everything in the right perspective. You're never on defense,

you're always on offense—because there are more ways to score on defense!" Graves said.

The teachings of The General not only stuck with Graves, but became credo of numerous other head football coaches in the South. World War II was only months away when Graves became captain of the 1941 Vols team under Neyland. But before Ray went off to the Navy, he was able to help retain a measure of redemption for his coach. The Vols beat Boston College, 14-7, in 1941 to gain revenge for losing the Sugar Bowl, 19-13, to Frank Leahy's Eagles the previous January. From 1938 to 1952, Tennessee made the Top 10 eight times, but it was 1951 before Neyland could guide them to a national championship.

Eventually signed by the Philadelphia Eagles to play for Earle "Greasy" Neale, Graves discovered that his mentoring at Tennessee would be useful. "I knew so much more football than some of those All-Americans," said Graves. "In group meetings at Tennessee, you had to go the board and call every play we had and tell what every player did on it—the weakness or strength of that play. If you didn't do that, you didn't get to play too much. That was our toughest course at the University of Tennessee. You [had to] know Tennessee football!"

Because of his football intelligence, Graves earned invitations to strategy meetings with the Eagles coaches. Later he became captain and then an assistant on Neale's staff. Once, when the Eagles' regular center was injured, Graves had to take off his street clothes, put on a uniform, and go in the game.

Graves soon realized football would be his livelihood. So he took another part-time job scouting colleges. He was off scouting Navy for the Army staff when he received the news that Dodd was looking for a line coach. Dodd called his friend, Herman Hickman, at Yale. Hickman said he'd give Dodd a good candidate's name in exchange for a country ham from Kingsport, Tennessee. "Ray Graves," said Hickman, passing on his secret name.

Dodd hired Graves, and Hickman got his country ham. "Bobby always said, 'You came cheap, Graves—for a country ham.' But that started out 13 of the happiest years of our life, at Georgia Tech, where football was fun."

Unlike Neyland, Bobby Dodd didn't use an iron-fisted coaching technique—maybe that's why Dodd turned down a chance to become a member of Neyland's staff and went to work at Tech instead where life was easier.

"His philosophy was, 'Let's win about seven games, go to a bowl game, and play somebody we can beat,'" Graves said of his late friend and former boss at Tech. The plan worked well, because Dodd had a 57-year association

with Tech and compiled a record of 165-64-8 (.713), with a perfect 12-0 record in 1952 and a national championship. As for bowl games, Dodd was 9-4 in postseason. One of the four losses was an Orange Bowl game against his former pupil, Graves.

"He just made it fun. But one thing he insisted on was that you graduate and get your degree. Bobby never got his degree," Graves said.

That Dodd could survive in today's competitive jungle with his laid-back approach and a penchant for fun is unlikely. He believed in light practices and winning on guile—keen sideline game strategy. But would that work today?

"There's no way he would win today, because he just felt like it ought to be fun," Graves said. "Today, players may be on a football scholarship, but the schools are minor leagues for the athletes. Fifty percent of them are in school to get drafted and go to the pros. I think the last report was that 52 percent graduated. It has evolved into a business, like a lot of things have. You build bigger stadiums, more skyboxes; you've got debt service; you've got to make money. You've got a booster club that has to raise millions of dollars. And it's a big business."

Back there in post-World War II America, life was simple and football was more fun. The other upside at Tech was that Dodd let his assistant coaches innovate. As defensive coach—they didn't have "defensive coordinators" back then—Graves would go head-to-head in practice with Frank Broyles, head of the offense. During those competitive scrimmages, Graves got the idea to drop one of the two safeties into pass coverage, creating the first "free safety." And Broyles began to work on some new offensive wrinkles. Tech practices became laboratories for future head coaches.

We can thank the Great State of Tennessee for its walking horses, country music, and sour-mash whiskey, but we are also indebted for its football coaching lineage. In biblical genealogy, General Robert Reese Neyland would be the Abraham of Florida's "Modern Football." The University of Florida has imported four coaches with connections to Neyland and/or the Volunteer State: Bob Woodruff, Graves, Doug Dickey, and Steve Spurrier. Only two of them—Woodruff and Graves—played for Neyland.

Dickey played for Woodruff at Florida, but was hired away from the Vols to coach the Gators, then went back to Knoxville to be UT athletics director. Spurrier was born in Miami Beach, but grew up in Johnson City, Tennessee, where he was a three-sport star prep athlete—yet he played and coached at Florida because he preferred the Gators' T-formation over the Vols' single wing, which they inherited from Neyland. Spurrier became a Heisman Trophy-winning quarterback at Florida, then came back to coach the Gators

to their first national championship. In a negative way, then, Neyland was somewhat responsible for sending Spurrier to Gainesville.

Neyland's influence was still intact when UF President J. Wayne Reitz went looking for Woodruff's replacement in 1959. One of the first people Reitz called was Dodd, a former player for Neyland at Tennessee. Dodd had no interest in the Florida position—there were times that he had pondered it—but recommended two friends he felt were highly qualified: Ara Parseghian of Northwestern and Davey Nelson of Delaware. Graves was happy as Dodd's chief assistant and defensive coach at Tech. When Parseghian and Nelson turned it down, however, several friends recommended that Graves go after the job. Dodd agreed to speak on his behalf.

Dodd had encouraged Graves to take the Florida job for two good personal reasons:

1. Dodd's son, Bobby Jr., was already in school and on the football team. (He would play a major role in beating his father's Tech team the next season.)
2. There was excellent freshwater fishing in Florida, in which Dodd often indulged.

"He had friends around Gainesville," Graves said of Dodd. "He wanted me to go down there and find some more good places to fish—and coach his son, Bobby Jr.!"

Discussions began at the NCAA coaches meeting in New York. Once they left New York, a meeting was set up between Graves and Reitz at the Holiday Inn in Gainesville. "He told me, 'I want you to be concerned about the student interests of these players as well as coaching them.' I told him I was familiar with that. We had a nice lunch, we shook hands, and he said, 'You're going to make $19,000 a year. That's what I make. And you're never going to make more money than I make. You'll get a car, but you don't get a house.' So that was all right, even though it was less money than I was making at Tech."

The five-year deal was done. Like Woodruff, Graves was advised it would be nice to beat Georgia—except Reitz added Florida State and Miami. The 40-year-old Graves became the 14th head coach of the Florida Gators and immediately went about putting a staff together. The first call he made was to Gene Ellenson, a former Miami assistant. Graves told Ellenson he'd been offered the Florida job. "But I told him I wasn't going to take it unless he went with me. 'We'll have some fun,'" said Graves. "And Gene said, 'You've got me, Coach.'"

Of main concern was appeasing the alumni who were tired of Tennessee-style football. To run his offense, he hired the imaginative former Georgia Tech quarterback Pepper Rodgers, then at Air Force.

"I said, 'Pepper, come back—we're going to put in a wide-open offense. We're going to make the defense cover the entire width of the field. We're going to have motion. We're going to make the defense change responsibilities before the ball is snapped.'" Rodgers and Graves began to go to work on a motion offense that would require shifts by the Oklahoma-style defenses the Gators would be facing.

Meanwhile, another savvy coach, Jack Green, was added to the staff as co-offensive coordinator. Graves retained John Mauer, Jim Powell, John Eibner, Dave Fuller, Earl Scarborough, and a young graduate assistant named Jimmy Dunn as holdovers from Woodruff's staff.

The new coach reported to Florida in January. Graves would be working his way around the state and pulled his car up in front of a Fort Lauderdale hotel when the valet asked, "Are you Coach Graves?"

"That's right," Graves said.

"Well, I'm your tailback next year. I'm Lindy Infante, and I've got a job here parking cars."

"All right, Lindy … well, I'll see you in spring practice."

Little did either of them know that Infante would play a major role in perhaps the most famous game Graves ever coached at Florida.

The Stinging of the Yellow Jackets

A new-car smell accompanied the Ray Graves regime and an air of excitement radiated from the new schemes. Fans began to sniff it in the off-season leading up to late summer in 1960. Most of them still hadn't shaken off the cobwebs of Woodruff's boring offense. As optimistic and hopeful as they were, they still adopted a wait-and-see attitude about this guy from Georgia Tech with a pocketful of promises.

As advertised, Florida's offense showed some new wrinkles in the first game against George Washington. Using a two-quarterback system run by two sophomores, though, the Gators were less than spectacular in their opener. Florida won, 30-7, but with Florida State and Georgia Tech coming up next, Graves wasn't going to show his hole cards. The game was played in Jacksonville and drew a sparse 14,000.

Next week was the home opener against FSU. Bill Peterson was beginning to close the gap with his cross-state rivals in Gainesville by the third year of the series. Neither team exactly lit up the Florida Field scoreboard when

Peterson's Seminoles came to town and nearly beat the Gators on September 24, 1960.

"Peterson brought a new offense to Florida State, and I brought a new offense to Florida," Graves said of the low-scoring first two games. "It was late in our third meeting before either one of us scored a touchdown." (Florida beat FSU, 27-7, in 1962.)

Unbeknownst to Gator fans, Graves and Peterson developed a close but secret relationship. They bonded with Cuban cigars, often in a fishing boat.

"Pete and I got to be real good friends. We were fishing on a lake outside Gainesville, and he said, 'Graves, you know what we have to do, now that we're seeing each other a good bit. We've got to come out and say some bad things about each other. We don't want the alumni to think we're friends. I go back and tell the alumni how much I hate Florida.' And I said, 'Okay, I'll say some bad things about you.' If the alumni ever knew how much we were friends, they'd be upset with us."

Thanks to a 37-yard field goal by Billy Cash, Graves survived his first outing against FSU, 3-0, winning his second game. More importantly, an attempt to bribe his fullback, MacBeth, had been thwarted. MacBeth had been approached by a stranger about shaving points in the game. Graves believes the figure mentioned by gambler Aaron Wagman of New York was $5,000. MacBeth came forward and told his coach he had been contacted and offered money. Working with the FBI, the plan was for MacBeth to arrange for a meeting with Wagman. MacBeth met with the gamblers and was followed in a car by campus police and other law enforcement, but the gamblers eluded the police. MacBeth had the money dropped off and then got away, turning the $5,000 over to authorities.

(Wagman would later go to prison for his role in a New York basketball point-shaving scandal.)

If nothing else, the Pensacola fullback won the admiration of his head coach for his courage in turning in the would-be briber. "He's still one of my all-time favorite players I ever coached," said Graves. "The guts it took to do something like that! His life could have been in danger. He was just a different kind of kid, and I always wondered about what made him tick."

As if the Graves-Dodd matchup needed anymore story lines. On October 1, Bobby Dodd's Tech team came to Gainesville. Bobby Dodd Jr. was dressed out as the Gator quarterback and would share the duties with Libertore. Dodd Jr. was the passer, Libertore the elusive option quarterback.

Florida Field was at capacity with 44,000 spectators. Up in the stands, Dodd's wife made her rooting intentions known right away. "I know where my paycheck comes from," Alice Dodd told the media. But she would be cheering for her son to do well.

The Gators went into the game a touchdown underdog against the 10th-ranked Yellow Jackets. "It meant so much to me, having a chance to play against him [Dodd]. But we were ready for him," said Graves.

That evenly matched game would come down to the final ticks. Florida trailed 17-10 with five minutes to play when Dodd Jr., trying to beat his own father, came in the game and completerd a 33-yard pass to Don Deal. The Gators ran it to the Jackets' one-foot line, where Dodd Jr. fumbled the snap and recovered at the four-yard line. Fourth down. Under a minute, trailing 17-10, it was the cue for the Fort Lauderdale parking valet.

A Job for Lindy and Larry

Lindy Infante's No. 33 jersey and the Florida Field clock were locked in momentary irony, and the photo shows that 33 seconds remained as he crossed a chalky line that marked new promise in the wide-open philosophy. He was surprised to have wound up with the football in such a critical situation.

Quarterback Libertore had one last chance to score and most likely, as he took the snap and headed East toward the sideline, he would dart into daylight as soon as he saw it. At least that's what Infante thought. It didn't happen as expected, as so many other things that week. Looking back on it now, Infante—the former head coach of the Green Bay Packers and Indianapolis Colts—is still amazed at the drama surrounding the Georgia Tech game.

"You had Bobby Dodd Jr., son of the great Bobby Dodd. You had Ray, who had come from Bobby's staff. You had the rivalry with Georgia Tech, who we played home-and-home every year. So the setting was there to be exciting no matter who won or what the score was," Infante said.

The sophomore valet and his task of scoring, though, provided the first critical juncture.

"They were on the four-yard line, and the play was for Larry to either pitch it or keep it," recalled Infante. "And I was the pitch guy. I remember at the time—and I say this kidding, of Larry—thinking that, if it was at all possible, Larry was going to keep the ball. I was doing my job, keeping my eye on him as we ran to the right side of the field. And I remember it shocked the hell out of me that he pitched me the ball. I just barely got it in the end zone."

Years later, Libertore revealed that he had found Infante at the perfect angle. "He was able to thread the sidelines and just missed stepping out of bounds," Libertore told Tom McEwen of the *Tampa Tribune* in his book, *Gators*. "He was able to just miss stepping out of bounds and scored."

With the naked eye from the press box above, you couldn't tell—you could only see Infante going down with his knees inches off the ground, his right shoe almost touching the boundary as he fell forward toward the white goal line, a Tech player holding Infante's right leg, trying to wrangle him from behind. There were no pylons in those days, just red flags attached to a long spring. You couldn't tell from above until the official signaled touchdown. Then there was an explosion of jubilance, which quickly calmed into trepidation and curiosity. What would the head coach do? They knew what Woodruff would have done: play for the tie. After all, even that would have been an impressive accomplishment against vaunted Georgia Tech. What to do?

Infante remembers the exhortations of the crowd. "They were certainly cheering for us to go for it," he said of the pending conversation attempt. "I don't know what happened. I assume he had already made his decision, but it didn't take long."

Ray Graves showed zero hesitation. He was about to pass his first test with Gator fans, who still rankled over the terrible decision by Woodruff a year earlier to run out the clock for a tie with Rice. "Here we were up against a nationally ranked team with a chance to win," recalled Graves. "I couldn't face the players or the Florida fans if I didn't give them a chance to go for two and win the ball game. I knew that, and I held up two fingers right away."

The two-point was consummated with Libertore's taking the snap and running right. He faked to fullback Jon MacBeth, who drifted unnoticed into the end zone. Libertore spotted his wide open teammate—his "honest fullback," as one paper called MacBeth the next day—and lofted such an easy pass that MacBeth momentarily juggled the precious cargo before securing the ball for the two-point conversion.

Libertore later said that Graves didn't balk at the two-point conversion because they had a "hurry-up" play designed for that purpose that they had hoped to execute. Faking the same option, they'd throw to MacBeth on the end instead. Libertore was about to run it in himself when a big Tech defender appeared in his path, and out of semi-desperation he passed it to his fullback.

Graves still considers that victory over Tech—considering all the dramatic circumstances—a cornerstone to his career at Florida. Along with a huge upset of Bear Bryant's Alabama team in Tuscaloosa that would come three years later, it would rank as one his two greatest coaching victories.

"But going for two meant the most to me because it established my career," said Graves. "The Gators had come to play and could win against anybody. The fans knew that Woodruff would have gone for one and the tie. So I had a chance to give Florida fans something to cheer about."

Infante remembers the magnitude of the moment. "That was big for Ray and big for the program at that time," said Infante. "It was very special, I'm sure, because he had just left there [Tech]." Turns out it was special for Infante, too, because it was his first real notice in football, a game that would provide him with a distinguished coaching career.

Bobby Dodd learned to regret the day he told his defensive coach to take the job as University of Florida football coach. And the momentum of the win over Tech propelled the Gators to a 9-2 record that included a Gator Bowl victory over Baylor. Yet the irony of it was that the week after beating Georgia Tech in dramatic fashion, Graves would lose 10-0 to Rice. Maybe Woodruff's 13-13 tie with the Owls the year before wasn't as devastating as it seemed.

Thus Ray Graves began a successful reign of 10 years, winning 70 games, losing 31 and tying four. But it would take another six years before Graves would post that many victories again in one season. He found out the very next year just how difficult it was to repeat that success. The Gators suffered leakage of all that good will and momentum built up in the 1960 season, floundering through 1961 with a 4-5-1 record.

There would be help on the way, however, because Graves' staff had recruited well and, as a result, more All-Americans were about to arrive—as were some huge victories and near misses of the conference title. No one would know the way things began in 1962—one win and two losses—and things didn't appear to be improving.

Except for a left-handed quarterback from Miami and a crosscutting tailback from the small town of Macclenny, they might not have turned the season around in 1963. And motivational talks by assistant coach Gene Ellenson didn't hurt either.

Larry Dupree Cut Against the Grain

The Florida media guide says Larry Dupree, captain and All-America his senior year, is "in private business in his hometown of Macclenny." It must be a very private business, because he's difficult to locate. Not many people around Macclenny had seen or heard from the town's former city manager in quite a spell—not the local newspaper, not the county tax collector, nobody. Neither have his former teammates nor anybody at the University of Florida.

Perhaps it's simply Dupree's nature as a running back that makes him so elusive. That a player beloved by so many Gator fans could drop off the face of the earth was both mystifying and disconcerting to his teammates, never more so than at the annual "Silver Sixties" reunion in Crystal River.

In one of the few recent interviews with Dupree, he talked in late 2004 about his relationships with coaches, players, family, and his African-American friends. Dupree is white, but he never differentiated by skin color. He said his best friend growing up in the late 1950s and early 1960s, Fuller Reed, was black. But when it came time to go to school, segregation in Baker County sent them different ways, causing Dupree to ask: "Why does this have to be?"

Dupree told Franz Beard of *Fightin' Gators* magazine that life in Macclenny made being friends tough for black and white kids. "In the neighborhood where I grew up, there were about eight white families and 30 black families. We all knew each other and appreciated each other. I grew up playing with black kids, and they were my friends—still are today."

The father of four in his two marriages, Dupree unofficially also adopted a young African-American teenage boy, whom he coached in baseball. "We love that kid to death, and he loves us," Dupree said.

Later in life, Dupree got to know sprinter Bob Hayes, and they would often talk about foot speed. Hayes, he said, would tease Larry about being only the third fastest man on his all-white high school team. He was the fastest man at Florida until he hurt his knee. So they decided, even at their advanced age, to line up and race. Surprisingly, Dupree beat Hayes out of the box for about eight yards. "I always had a quick start, and that's why I think I did pretty well running the football," Dupree said. But when Hayes' power kicked in, "... he just hit a gear and was by me so fast."

Those who saw him as a young tailback for Baker County High marveled at his speed on long, breakaway runs for touchdowns and were curious why nobody from the Gator recruiting staff had come calling when he was a senior. Finally, with the word out that Georgia had an interest in Dupree, Florida offered him a scholarship—the ubiquitous Dave Fuller coming to the rescue to sign him.

Dupree approached the game with intense passion, yet performed with such grace and ease. He was also a popular player who was country tough, never missing a game despite a serious knee problem. He could cut back with the dexterity of an ice skater, changing of speeds so quickly that he threw defenders off balance. Instinctively, he slid back against the grain at just the right moment, then would turn straight up field to squeeze out extra yards with his forward momentum.

"He was a fabulous teammate. As a runner, he could be a slasher, but he could also cut on a dime," All-America receiver Charles Casey said of Dupree. "You think you had him and—*poof!*—he was gone. He had great moves and a great sense of where the defenders were. He was a joy to play with. And he was a super guy. He knew when to cut back and just when to go ahead for another two or three yards. It was like he had eyes in the side of his head. He would make five or six yards extra many times."

Graves was amazed at Dupree's ability to run on a straight line and score. "He was something. Running north you couldn't stop him. He made more touchdowns running north than anybody in football. He was one of those kids who would say, 'They blocked for me, I didn't do anything.'"

Nobody had a better view of him than quarterback Tommy Shannon. "Larry was just such a spectacular natural runner," said Shannon. "He would run one way and cut back across the grain. I saw the best moves in the world after I handed the ball off. He could run as fast sideways as he could forward. He could deliver a blow as good as anybody. We'd run off right tackle, and he'd cut it back left and take off down the sideline."

Shannon said he also had to be careful where he stepped because of Dupree's occasional upchucking. "Sometimes in the huddle, you could see Larry's breakfast on the ground," recalled Shannon. "A spectacular natural runner. Against Duke he ran for about 65 or 75 yards, and on the extra point he lined up on the left side. A guy came in on him, and as Larry was trying to block him, he leaped over the top; and Larry threw up right in his face."

In his first varsity season, Dupree was consensus All-SEC first team. He achieved All-SEC first-team honors three consecutive seasons, during which he rushed for the second-highest total yards in school history (1,725). His name is long ago buried in the record books because of the extended schedule, wide-open offenses, and talented backs who came after him the next 40-plus years, but Dupree became just the third player in history to make All-SEC first team three times, and in 1964 became only the sixth Gator player to make All-America first team.

Shannon, Dupree, and Casey were three reasons Florida football began to elevate in the earlier 1960s after a hiccup or two. At the start of 1962, Gator fortunes took a turn for the worse after the first three games. Being shut out 17-0 by Georgia Tech in the third game was bad enough, but the outcome of the next game was a new low.

Tommy Shannon won the quarterback job from Larry Libertore the week of the Duke game. Graves called him in after a few games and said, "I'm going to start you this week." And he replied, "Coach, I'm already the starting safety." To which Graves replied, "No, I'm going to start you at quarterback." That week Graves announced the change at a quarterback club.

"I didn't start Shannon because he was better than Libertore," he joked. "I started him because he's left-handed—and I'm left-handed."

As a southpaw quarterback, Shannon found out right away that there was a difference. Once while practicing taking snaps at Bishop Curley High School in Miami, a player from University of Miami who was working out came over to give Shannon a tip on how to receive the ball from the center more efficiently. "He noticed that I was having to take the snap and turn the laces each time," said Shannon. "And he said, 'Tell your center to put the laces the other way, toward the ground, and you won't have to change every time.'" It's something he never forgot. And, by the way, the tipster was quarterback Fran Curci—himself a lefty—who would later coach for the Hurricanes and the Kentucky Wildcats one day against the Gators.

Shannon also quickly found that he could use all the help he could get. In his first start, the Gators were seemingly breezing along against Duke without much effort, taking a 21-0 halftime lead. Duke Coach Bill Murray stood at the door of the locker room before the second half and challenged the will of his Blue Devil players. "If you believe we can come back and win this game, shake my hand on the way out," Murray said. Each player, of course, shook his coach's hand.

Deploying a "lonesome end" offense, Duke came back with a vengeance to beat Florida, 28-21, in perhaps Graves' most painful loss ever—the first time the two teams ever played and the first loss ever to the Blue Devils. Changes in the Gator lineup were imminent. (Years later, it became evident that Duke's best team in post-World War II history had beaten the Gators. With a young fullback named Mike Curtis, later of Baltimore Colts linebacking fame, and a halfback named Jay Wilkinson, son of the legendary Oklahoma coach Bud Wilkinson, Duke won the Atlantic Coast Conference title and wound up 8-2, losing only to the eventual national champions, Southern Cal, and Georgia Tech.)

All of a sudden the Gators were off to a poor 1-2 start. The next week, inspirational leader and defensive coach Gene Ellenson wrote a personal letter to the players, which raised their spirits for a game against Texas A&M.

The letter, pinned on the door of every player on Friday night before the game, said in part: "No one cruises along without problems. It isn't easy to earn your way through college on football scholarships. It isn't easy to do what academics and athletics expect of you. It isn't easy to remain fighting when others are curling around you or when your opponents appear to be getting stronger when you are getting weaker. ..."

Ellenson went on to describe the struggle of six American soldiers who were all that remained of 1,000 who had stormed the high ground in a forest somewhere near Bastogne, Belgium. He, himself, had been one of the six who survived the famed Battle of the Bulge in World War II. And then he left the players with one thought: "Self-pity is the roommate of cowardice."

An underdog Florida beat the Aggies the next day, 42-7. And Shannon began helping reverse the Gators' downward spiral with wins over Auburn, Georgia, and FSU before losing to Miami, 17-15. But it was enough for a 6-4 season and a trip to the Gator Bowl game—*again*—to play Penn State. The irony was, Duke had been invited to play in that Gator Bowl game, but the players declined, citing "fatigue," and the Gators benefited from their decision.

Going to a bowl game of any kind was still a novelty in the early '60s. Before Graves arrived, Florida had attended two postseason games. He took them to five. One was this Gator Bowl game in 1962 against ninth-ranked Penn State, winner of the Lambert Trophy for Eastern supremacy, won by Florida, 17-7. Ellenson had devised a new "monster back" scheme, which Penn State coach Rip Engle could never solve.

Although all the Florida players say it wasn't intended as a racial slur, the Gators had decided to wear Confederate flag decals on their helmets as a show of regional pride, unfortunately without realizing the cultural and racial implications at the time. For the first time a Gator team would compete against black players, including All-America end/linebacker David Robinson. Florida and the Southeastern Conference were yet to integrate. (The first African-Americans to play for the Gators, Willie Jackson and Leonard George, were signed in 1969 by Graves.)

Shannon would spark the victory and become the game's most valuable player in the win over Penn State, which garnered him national media attention. The following year, the nation's premiere preseason magazine, *Street and Smith*, would have him mentioned in the company of Navy's Roger Staubach, California's Craig Morton, and Alabama's Joe Namath as quarterbacks to watch in 1963.

Looking back at the magazine today, what Shannon remembers most is the reference to an inside story on the cover: "Will The SEC Ever Integrate?" He feels a great injustice was done to the black athletes who were denied athletic scholarships to the all-white schools—especially the "World's Fastest Man."

"Remember, Bob Hayes grew up Florida. I watched Bob Hayes run the 100-yard dash probably 15 times growing up in Moore Park when we had a track day," said Shannon, who today is the West Coast franchisee for 59 Outback Steak Houses. "Bob Hayes probably never even thought about going to the University of Florida, Florida State, or Miami. His dream was to play football at Florida A&M. So until that full effect of integration, we never had the best athletes on the best teams. We didn't know it at the time, but segregation hurt the advancement of our country and the football teams as well."

Going into 1963, the Gators had found the quarterback to run Rodgers' and Graves' "motion offense," which later evolved into the double-wideout, one-back offense, and other such wrinkles that would soon become prevalent in college football. Florida was about to embark on a run of respectability that never would've come without the event that would take place on October 12, 1963—the day thunder struck in Tuscaloosa, Alabama.

To say Bear Bryant and Alabama football were dominant in the early '60s would be like saying Elvis Presley and the Beatles sold a few records. In 1961, Alabama went 11-0 and defeated Arkansas in the Sugar Bowl to claim the national championship—the first of three Bryant would win in five years. Right in the heart of that run, Florida popped up on the Tide's schedule for two seasons.

The Gators had made a mess in the start of the 1963 by losing to Georgia Tech, 9-0, allowing Mississippi State to tie them in Gainesville, 9-9, and barely eking out a home-field win over lightly regarded Richmond, 35-28. After the Richmond game, looking down the schedule at next week's game against the nation's No. 3-ranked team, Graves admitted to the press: "We've got no chance against Alabama."

Enter Ellenson with a fairy tale about an alligator who had little or no chance in a battle with an elephant, but prevailed. The metaphor of Alabama's and Florida's mascots at war was not lost on his players—especially two-way player Allen Trammell, a halfback and defensive back from Eufala, Alabama. He still remembers how fired-up the Gator team became.

"I've never seen a group of people where 100 percent of them reacted so emotionally. We got up and left that room, and nobody said a word," recalled Trammell, now a successful Orlando businessman. "I was rooming with Dick Kirk, and we always clowned around a little before we went to bed. That night, we didn't even say good night. We got up the next morning and went to breakfast, and nobody was saying anything during the pregame meal. This group was pumped up—and especially me, being from Alabama."

Many other Gators felt the same way. Larry Dupree told Tom McEwen of the *Tampa Tribune*: "I am emotional. I was always silent in the locker rooms before a game. But all teams have loud people, and I wondered if everybody on the team cared as much as I did. I was wrong." Dupree said that, after he and his teammates saw tackle Fred Pearson, normally a jovial fellow, with a face full of tears, he knew his team was ready.

Trammell's only concern was how long this football "high" could last. He found out when guard Jack Katz took off his helmet and smashed the locker room blackboard into pieces as the team was about to run on the field at Denny Stadium, now known as "Bryant-Denny Stadium," and again on the opening kickoff, when Florida halfback Hagood Clark made the tackle.

"Benny Nelson took the ball at the goal line, and Clark hit him in the mouth at about the five-yard line. And I said, 'Oh, my goodness.' And we never lost that emotion all day," said Trammell.

Frankly, Charles Casey was scared. He had heard all about the legend of Bear Bryant and the hard-nosed football players he coached. Growing up in Atlanta, Casey remembered that one of his neighbors was Georgia Tech running back Chick Granning, whose jaw had been broken by Alabama linebacker Darwin Holt on a controversial play that eventually led Bobby Dodd to cancel the series with 'Bama. Young Charlie was there that day when Granning came home with the bandaged jaw.

"Here I was," said Casey, "a skinny little sophomore getting ready to play Bear Bryant and those kind of guys. I've gotta do everything I can just to be as tough as those guys, because these guys are liable to run right over you. It just turned out to be a fantastic football game. And I do remember a lot of guys being charged up in the locker room and being so high—and to get it from there to the field for 60 minutes was fantastic."

It was Alabama's homecoming, and The Bear had never lost a game in Tuscaloosa. That was about to change. Trammell's roommate, Dick Kirk, would play the hero.

Florida dominated, even shutting down legendary quarterback Joe Namath. One of the most famous runs in Gator history was about to unfold—and by the unlikeliest of Gators. Back then, players were still under substitution restrictions and had to play both ways. Kirk was a monster back and rarely used reserve runner. A routine off-tackle play was called, and, as Trammell remembers, the Gators were in a power-I formation set, with fullback John Feiber at fullback and at right halfback.

"I went to block the linebacker, but he was gone, so I blocked the tackle, and I could feel Kirk behind me," said Trammell. "Dick just sort of stopped there for a second and then took off running to the left. Charlie Casey threw a great block downfield to spring him for the score."

"When I sort of threw myself at the defensive back, my arm locked up with his," said Casey. "Knowing the way Bear Bryant seemed to get all the calls at Alabama, I was scared to death the officials were going to call a holding penalty on me." But the damage was done to the Tide.

Florida hung on to win 10-6. Dupree rushed for 83 yards that day, but the 42-yarder by Kirk would be the one for the history books. It went down as one of the greatest wins in school history—the first and only loss by Bryant in Tuscaloosa until his final game against Mississippi Southern.

When the Gators returned to Gainesville, even though their flight was delayed, upwards of 7,000 people and the school band were there to greet them. "We flew back that evening, and it was so great to see all those people at the airport. Everybody was still celebrating," Casey recalled. "Downtown, at the campus ... big bonfires! And I thought, 'My goodness! Maybe people here really like us!'"

The next year the Gators returned to play the Tide again at Denny Stadium. Joe Namath started the game but suffered an injury, so option quarterback Steve Sloan came on to lead the victory; and Florida's defense could never quite adjust to the unexpected change. Spurrier had rallied his team to victory in the fourth quarter against Mississippi State several weeks prior and started for the Gators, twice giving them leads over Alabama, 7-0 and 14-7. Florida, 4-0 and ranked ninth in the country, battled back in the final seconds of the game, and it looked like the Gators might pull off another upset against the third-ranked Tide, but 'Bama held on for a 17-14 win. This style of comeback play would become the hallmark of the quarterback from Johnson City, Tennessee.

The Unveiling of Steve Spurrier

Six degrees separated Ray Graves and Steve Spurrier, much as it did the connection between Florida football and Tennessee. Both sons of Presbyterian ministers—both from Eastern Tennessee—each had older brothers who influenced their athletic careers. One day, they would meet again in the Gator record books as the school's two most successful football coaches.

Steve's dad, Graham Spurrier Sr., frequently changed churches and towns. As a young boy, Steve was moved from Miami to Athens, home of Tennessee Wesleyan, where Graves had once played briefly. While Steve was in Athens, he began caddying and became interested in playing golf. He and his older brother, Graham Jr., also attended Wesleyan's football practices, and eventually Steve became the Bulldogs' mascot.

In the first grade, Steve became a huge fan of former Wesleyan star Charlie "Choo Choo" Justice, who wound up transferring to North Carolina. Justice became an All-America running back and later played for the Washington Redskins. On his radio, young Spurrier could pick up the Redskins' broadcast, never dreaming that someday he would become their head coach. Mimicking his hero, Spurrier chose to wear the No. 22 jersey in youth football, but his No. 11 would eventually he retired at Florida. (Later Spurrier "unretired" the number when he became Gator head coach.)

From Athens, the Spurriers moved to Newport, regarded as a tough town, perhaps unsuitable for raising a family. Sports for kids were limited, but pickup games were common. In anything that had a ball, little Steve excelled. It was said that at age 11, Steve scored 42 points in his first pickup basketball game, a fact that his late father confirmed in the book, *Spurrier: The No. 1 Gator* by Mike Cobb and Logan Mabe. "Basketball was my best sport," Spurrier would claim years later after he became a football coach. Golf was also his first love as an adult, and he would develop into a single-digit handicap player.

Newport, Tennessee, however, was not the place where the Spurriers would plant roots. It didn't take Reverend Spurrier long to realize he needed to accept the offer of a church in Johnson City—only a few miles from the birthplace Davey Crockett, where safety and youth sports programs had developed to a higher standard.

Not long after moving to Johnson City, Steve began playing every sport, including on his father's Little League and Babe Ruth teams. At Science Hill High School, he made all-state in football, basketball, and baseball. Steve could have had college scholarships in any of the three. The school eventually named the football and soccer fields after their famous former Hilltopper athlete.

In his senior year, Spurrier was scouted by another member of the Graves family. Edwin Graves, postmaster in Knoxville, had been dispatched by his younger brother, the head coach of the Gators.

"I had never heard of him, but my brother told me he had just beaten my alma mater, Central High School in Knoxville," said Graves. Edwin couldn't stop talking about Spurrier and sent back a glowing recommendation.

The offers poured in until it came down to Mississippi, Alabama, and Florida. Spurrier ruled out Tennessee because he wanted to be a T-formation quarterback and not single-wing tailback. It was said that Steve had breakfast with Bear Bryant, but that was later debunked. The key factors in Steve's choice would be Florida's better weather and the nearby golf course, which the university owned. So he signed with Florida, and with a single penstroke, he impacted Gator football like nothing ever before or since.

The running game was becoming less prominent in college football. Florida was among the first schools in the SEC to rely heavily on passing, thanks to the young quarterback with the unorthodox, sidearm delivery and keen football savvy. Spurrier's skills, combined with the new offensive strategy, leveled the playing field against the SEC powers—even the field in Tuscaloosa, Alabama, where the Gators would play the second of back-to-back games in 1964.

Steve Spurrier could beat you with his arm, with his toe, or with his head, often improvising on the fly. He wasn't very fast—in fact, he was slow—but he knew how to scramble to buy time. He was like a coach on the field, seldom making mistakes. But in his sophomore season, he made one choice against Alabama that he would always regret.

Quarterbacks were calling their own plays back in the mid-'60s because coaches felt it was part of the game's rhythm. Besides, nobody had conceived a good way of signaling plays into the game. This would factor into Spurrier's misread of a down-and-distance with his team trailing, 17-14, out of time outs at Alabama's 10.

"I messed that game up," Spurrier said years later to a writer visiting him in Columbia just before his first season as coach of the South Carolina Gamecocks. "I got down there and thought we were on the two-yard line, [but we] were on the seven. So I called another running play and handed it off to Johnny Feiber, who had walked it in for a score once already on that play. I just screwed up. I should have thrown the ball in the dirt. We never even threw it in the end zone. I should have thrown Casey a 'jump ball'— he'd have probably come down with it. We didn't have any time outs, but I had hit Harper and Casey on a couple of 'bang!-bang!' plays, and we're there—about the 10 with about a minute to play. Yeah, I screwed that up, no question about it."

Spurrier's faux pas caused so much confusion on the Florida sideline that the kicking team came onto the field with only 10 men. "We were running out of time, and we had to hurry," said Trammell, who was holding the attempted field goal by kicker Jimmy Hall. "To this day, when I see Hall, he always says, 'You didn't get the hold down.' And I say, 'I did get the damn ball down—you just missed it!'"

Casey recalls that Florida didn't even have those 10 men properly lined up. "We had about five guys on one side and two on the other, and Alabama went over there with them. I imagine Jimmy Hall could have run with the ball to the right in for a touchdown," he said.

Alabama held on to win, and that team was crowned national champion six games later. "It's a good thing we had that Alabama time keeper on our side!" Bear Bryant later joked about the clock.

Though Florida did not win, no one doubted this young quarterback from Tennessee was going to have a big impact. His penchant for rallying his team in the fourth quarter was matched by his excellent play-calling, punting, and decent field-goal kicking. However, he was willing to wait his turn as a starter. "Steve was a very respectful football player," Shannon recalled. "I was a senior and one of the leaders of the team, and he respected that. He never talked it down. He and I were roommates and friends. And we remain very good friends to this day."

Spurrier started just three games in the middle of that season, coming on in the second half seven times as Florida posted a 7-3 record. One of those defeats was the first loss ever to Florida State, 16-7, a black day for Gator fans. It was an especially hard day for Shannon, who would wear the goat's horns, perhaps unjustifiably, when he fumbled at the FSU goal line.

What few people know is that the fumble wasn't Shannon's fault. All-America center Bill Carr, later to become Florida's athletic director, admitted that it was his miscue.

"I never got the ball," said Shannon. "When Bill Carr snapped it, he hit the inside of his thigh with the football, and it went between my legs."

Casey says he still remembers the sickening feeling of seeing the ball loose and on the ground, but that he, too, could have worn the goat horns. "I had probably the worst game that I ever had in my career," he said. "I dropped a long pass that was perfectly thrown. It went through my hands and when it hit the ground it was still spinning, perfectly. Steve threw it, and even as slow I was, it would have been a touchdown because I had the guy beat by about five yards. And I also had my first and only fumble of my career."

FSU had taken the lead on the red-hot Seminole passing combination of quarterback Steve Tensi and receiver Fred Biletnikoff, who would victimize Trammell and the defense. When Trammell saw Tensi dropping to pass, he says he merely didn't believe the big quarterback was going to be able to throw it as far as he did. Shannon looked on in amazement at the flight of Tensi's pass, which seemed to be above the clouds as it traveled more than 60 yards. By now, Biletnikoff was well behind the Gator secondary—and Trammell.

The combination of Biletnikoff's deceptive speed and Tensi's big arm had spelled disaster. "Tensi flung that ball up in the air, and it seemed like it hung there forever," said Trammell. That Tensi-to-Biletnikoff play comes up for discussion quite often at the "Silver Sixties" reunion, when there is much jaw-jacking and storytelling. "I tell that lineman that Tensi had enough time to have a damn sandwich and a Coke back there," Trammell said.

"I was standing there on the sideline next to Spurrier when he threw that ball," Shannon said. "And when it flattened out, it went a helluva long way. And I wouldn't doubt Trammel's story, because I'll bet he threw that ball 70 yards in the air."

Given all the pregame trash talking by both coaches and some of the players, it was an especially gratifying win for Florida State. The Gators, who had not lost to the 'Noles in six previous attempts, came on the field at Doak Campbell wearing the words "Go For Seven" on their jerseys. Their other slogan was "Never FSU, Never." Bill Peterson countered with, "Never Say Never!"

Despite Florida's 16-7 loss, the seeds of success were well planted. Spurrier passed for 10 touchdowns that year in a limited role. Shannon started the final game of the year against LSU—rescheduled because of a hurricane—in which the Gators prevailed, 20-6. Florida wound up going 7-3 in 1964, but didn't make it to a bowl. However, the Gators were about to make another breakthrough into a new stratosphere: major bowl games and Heisman trophies.

Spurrier-to-Casey: Room Service

Florida football began to gain credibility on the national scene in the mid-'60s. In 1965, Sports Information Director Norm Carlson would score a major coup with five first-team All-Americans: defensive end Lynn Matthews, safety Bruce Bennett, defensive tackle (and offensive guard) Larry Gagner, receiver Charles Casey, and quarterback Steve Spurrier. Considering only six players in school history had made it prior to that, it was quite an accomplishment.

With Ed Kensler replacing Rodgers as offensive coach—and the addition of quarterbacks coach Fred Pancoast—Ray Graves' newfound passing offense flew through the air with the greatest of ease.

Until Shannon and Spurrier came along as quarterbacks, Florida's leading passers rarely cracked 600 total yards in a season. In 1965, his junior year, Spurrier passed for 1,893 yards and 14 touchdowns in just 11 games—eight of the scores to All-America receiver Casey. One reason was that Graves, Pancoast, and Kensler began to spread out the offense with more good receivers. Tight end Barry Brown, wideouts Richard Trapp and Paul Ewaldsen, and halfback Jack Harper had joined in the fun as well.

The Spurrier-to-Casey connection was still the most popular route, but because of the attention his favorite receiver was getting, opponents often double-teamed him. That didn't stop Casey from breaking all the school—and most of the SEC—receiving records. He was slow for a wide receiver, but he had soft, sure hands and a knack for finding seams in the secondary. Plus he was adaptable on routes, making curls and down-and-out patterns especially fruitful. "It was just so natural. I loved the down-and-out. Any time you came out of the break, you had a step on the defensive back, and there was the ball," said Casey. "The timing was absolutely perfect. And Steve threw the ball so soft that you could catch it with one hand—kind of like Danny Wuerffel did."

Spurrier not only knew what he and his team were facing at each moment, but where they were going next. Assistant coach Bubba McGowan remembers overhearing Steve's comments about what to do in the final minutes of the 1965 Georgia game when the Gators were trailing, 10-7.

"Georgia still had the ball, and Steve was on the sideline when I overheard him say, 'If we can get the ball back, I can throw a crossing pass to Casey and a down-and-down to Harper.' He had already figured it out. We got the ball back and, sure enough, he hit Casey on a crossing route, and [Casey] got out of bounds to stop the clock. Then he hit Harper on the touchdown, and he came off the field and said, 'Damn, we did it too quick!'"

Casey had purposely run out of bounds at the Georgia 19. "I probably could have made more yards, but I didn't want to take a chance," said Casey. Harper caught the touchdown with his back to the goal line and fell over Bulldog defensive back Lynn Hughes. With little time on the clock, Florida was able to hold on and win, 14-10.

"He knew where he had to go and what he had to do," said McGowan. Clearly, the bad experience at Alabama had taught Spurrier a valuable lesson about clock-watching.

The myth was that Spurrier would draw up plays in the dirt, but Casey said that was stretching it a bit. "He wouldn't make up the plays, but he certainly did improvise on them a lot," said Casey.

Like the time Spurrier played traffic cop. In a big game against Florida State—the year after the Seminoles had beaten the Gators—Casey got so wide open and Spurrier had so much time that he waived his wide receiver to deepen his route. It was an especially tense moment for Casey, who had dropped a pass against FSU the year before.

"Here we were losing again, and Steve took us downfield, throwing little out passes to me and Ewaldsen and Barry Brown," said Casey. "We called a simple down-and-out. He had an option of rolling out. And as soon as I come out of the break, he's waving: 'Go, go, go!' So I turned up the field, and as soon as I did, FSU's corner zipped right by me. Steve threw the ball, and the ball goes right up in the sun. My brain was saying, 'You dropped one against them last year—now don't drop this one.' But I couldn't see it. Fortunately, it came out of the sun about three yards from me. I caught it [for a touchdown]. I was a happy person. That was just one of those makeshift plays that he would do."

Spurrier recalled years later he'd known he had a free play because FSU's middle guard was offsides. If nothing else, it would get the Gators closer to a field goal and a possible nine-point lead. "With all the time I had, I kept faking like I was going to run, and so I motioned to Charlie to keep going deep," he said. More than any other, that play exemplified the radar-like instincts between these two All-Americans. Spurrier had achieved air-traffic controller instincts.

Coming back to beat FSU that year was sweet revenge. The Gators rallied late to win 30-17 in Gainesville, and Spurrier passed for four touchdowns. The boy from Eufala, Alabama, got back, too, as Trammell picked off a pass from quarterback Ed Pritchett and returned it 64 yards for a score. For the second straight year, the Gators finished 7-3, but this time they earned their biggest-ever postseason berth—a Sugar Bowl bid.

It was in a losing role that Spurrier played one of the best games. Trailing 20-0 against Missouri in the 1966 Sugar Bowl. Three times Spurrier took them in for fourth-quarter touchdowns; the coaches went for two points on three occasions, and three times it failed. Florida lost to the Tigers, 20-18, but a star was born. Spurrier became the only player ever to win the Miller-Digby trophy as the Most Valuable Player in the Sugar Bowl in a losing effort—cueing America to take a look at the Tennessee kid who would be playing quarterback for the Florida Gators in 1966.

Long before Bill Clinton took ownership of the nickname, Steve Spurrier was called "The Comeback Kid"—and with good reason. On at least eight occasions in his career, he brought the Gators back in the fourth quarter for a victory. None was more famous than the field goal he kicked to beat Auburn, 30-27, on October 29, 1966, just a week before the Heisman Trophy ballots were mailed out. The only other real threat to win the Heisman was Purdue quarterback Bob Griese, whose stats weren't as impressive.

The college football world and Heisman voters had noticed that the Gators had rolled out of the gate with a 7-0 record and boasted a No. 8 ranking. But they were tied at 27 in the final few minutes as their drive stalled at the Auburn 30. Ironically, Spurrier had missed his wide-open running back, Tom Christian, inside the Auburn 10 on a play called by the coaches. Even misfortune was going to work in his favor, though, because the play that would unfold heavily impacted his Heisman chances.

Spurrier had often fooled around after practice with various forms of the kicking game—drop kicks, punts, etc.—and because of this he had a special kicking shoe made that could be zippered on in an emergency. Even though Wayne (Shade Tree) Barfield was the regular field-goal kicker, the distance was out of his range.

Graves says on that morning of October 29, 1966, Spurrier told teammates at breakfast that he'd had a dream that he kicked a field goal to beat Auburn. Actually, he had told linebacker Wayne McCall that he "felt like" kicking one.

"The zipper part was so we could get it on in a hurry," Spurrier recalled. "But that day, we called time out just before fourth down." Graves didn't know for certain what Spurrier and the offensive coaches had cooked up when his quarterback came to the sideline. "I wasn't sure that it wasn't going to be a fake," said Graves. Opposing coach Ralph "Shug" Jordan wasn't convinced either, because Auburn hardly rushed the kicker. After all, Spurrier had only kicked a field goal in one other game during his career.

McCall was on the sideline during the timeout. "John Preston was supposed to be our long field-goal kicker, but I wasn't in the conversation on the sidelines. I believe they were discussing whether Spurrier or Preston should kick it, and Steve said, 'Let me kick it.'"

Some photographers say timeless moments are remembered best in black-and-white photo images. Indeed, something about those old still-life photos reveal more than the action. They become portraits of the athlete in conviction and determination, even more so than movie clips or color photos. In the picture of Spurrier's field goal, the ball had just left the hands of the holder, No. 10, Larry Rentz. Spurrier's right leg was nearly perpendicular to the ground, and his kneecap looked to be inches from his still-bowed head. No Auburn player was within seven yards of the play as the ball went airborne, lending credence to the theory that nobody else truly believed he would kick.

As field-goal kicks go, it was not a thing of beauty—sort of a low-trajectory, knock-down 8-iron that barely cleared the crossbar, ending maybe three rows deep into the end zone bleacher seats. Beauty aside, this single act of versatility in such a pressurized situation duly impressed the Heisman electorate. No one familiar with Spurrier's competitive spirit would've doubted that he willed it across.

Though a glorious moment, the celebration didn't last long. The next week Spurrier and his teammates got their comeuppance when Georgia knocked the Gators from the ranks of the undefeated. Spurrier took with him a valuable lesson and wrote down in his coaching manual. Just a win away from their first-ever SEC title, 7-0 Florida waltzed into the Gator Bowl stadium as the No. 7 team in America and promptly got ambushed by the Georgia Bulldogs, 27-10.

Florida was unbeaten and cocky. The night before the Georgia game, I sat at a table with offensive coordinator Ed Kensler, who was drawing play diagrams on the tablecloth to explain how the Gators would cut down Georgia's defensive rush, anchored by tackle Bill Stanfill and safety Jake Scott. The plan was foiled, though, as Spurrier was sacked and harassed all day. The Gator wide receivers were double-covered; Georgia's Scott and fellow secondary defenders knocked down the tight-end release valve; Stanfill tackled tailback Larry Smith, whether he had the ball or not.

"That was like so many dadgum Florida 'big victories,'" Spurrier said 40 years later. "We beat a team like Auburn, and we get full of ourselves and play like crap the next week. So Georgia beats us—same old, same old. So maybe that game helped us when I became the coach. We learned to keep games like the Auburn win in perspective."

(Spurrier was 11-1 against Georgia a coach.)

One other story by a Florida English professor attributes Georgia's victory in 1966 to "The Great Gatorade Hijack of 1966." Dr. Kevin M. McCarthy told the student newspaper, *The Alligator*: "The night before the game, the truck of Gatorade intended for Gators players was headed to Jacksonville. However, a group of Bulldogs fans forced the driver to pull over, and they dumped all the Gatorade out on the side of the road. When Coach Ray Graves found out what happened, he instructed that a new Gatorade truck be sent to Jacksonville with a highway patrolman escort leading the way. The truck didn't get there in time; and coincidentally, the Gators lost."

More disappointment would follow as Miami upset Florida three weeks later, 21-16. Nonetheless, many high-water marks were set in 1966. Spurrier, having thrown for 2,012 yards and 16 touchdowns that season, won the school's first Heisman. Florida football was on the map bigger than ever. Richard Trapp led the SEC with 66 catches, including six 100-yard games, and broke most of Casey's records. The Gators finished 9-2 after a victory over Bobby Dodd and Georgia Tech in the Orange Bowl, 27-12—Dodd's final game. The most famous play came when tailback Larry Smith "streaked" 94 yards for a touchdown with his pants almost falling off.

Until three seasons later, it was as good as Graves would get. In 1967, after a 4-1 start, the Gators stumbled home with losses to FSU and Miami for a lackluster 6-4. The following year was dubbed, "The Year of the Gator." Florida started 4-0 and failed to win any of the next four, winding up 6-3-1 with no postseason date. The Gators boasted several outstanding players in All-Americans Larry Smith and offensive lineman Guy Dennis, plus first-team All-SEC cornerback Steve Tannen.

What was missing was the playmaker at quarterback. After shuffling Jackie Eckdahl, Harmon Wages, and Larry Rentz into the mix, Graves made a desperate one-game coaching personnel switch that proved disastrous. Quarterback coach Fred Pancoast was in the hospital with appendicitis, so Graves moved defensive mastermind Gene Ellenson over to coach the offense and offensive coach Ed Kensler to the defense.

Hurricane Gladys brought in a gloomy, rainy day, and Georgia destroyed Florida, handing Graves his worst defeat ever, 51-0.

"To get beat that bad was one thing; to get beat by Georgia was another," said All-America lineman Jack Youngblood, a junior that season. "It was raining so hard that you could not see the top of the Gator Bowl, so I don't know if there were people up there or not."

Nobody felt worse for the coaches than Youngblood—especially for Ellenson, his defensive coach.

"Coach Ellenson was not only a coach, but he was a father figure to the kids—especially to me, being in a one-parent home. He was *the* authority, and he was the coach. He also had that instinct of how to put his arm around a kid and encourage him or correct him. I was so lucky to have him. And I had so many of those great type of human beings around me throughout my career," Youngblood said.

Florida's record that year fell to 6-3-1, the second straight six-win season without going to a bowl game, and the rumblings of trouble loomed on the horizon. The bitterness of the loss to Georgia would not wash off.

"Ray Graves' all-time worst coaching decision," remembered offensive tackle and captain Mac Steen. "We played so badly, I think it was the death knell for Ray Graves, frankly."

That single game may have served as impetus for Graves' departure. It may have also influenced offensive coordinator Ed Kensler's decision to resign. Some people believed change was in the wind.

'Reaves-to-Alvarez,' and a Whole Lot More

First impressions only happen once, so they ought to be lasting ones, which was certainly the case with the 1969 Florida Gators' quarterback John Reaves and wide receiver Carlos Alvarez. The third play of their college varsity careers in 1969 was so bombastic that cotton-candy possibilities rained on a group of starved Gator fans who'd been too long from the fair.

Reaves' 70-yard heave to Alvarez in the opening game against highly ranked Houston was the baseball equivalent of a walk-off home run in a rookie's first trip to the plate. Gator fans knew that it was no fluke by the precision of the play, and they were right—it set in motion a chain reaction of delicious accomplishment.

The magnificent "Reaves-to-Alvarez" play will be treasured forever by all Gators, because it came like a thunderbolt splitting a blue sky without warning. The 70-yard bomb served notice to Florida's opponents:

You'd better put your track shoes on when you play these Gators.

Lindy Infante had to laugh at the paradox. *Sports Illustrated* picked Houston as the No. 1 football team in the country. *Playboy* rated Florida as America's top party school. "The press had a lot of fun with that one, writing that it was a game of 'two number ones'," said Infante, who was on the sidelines as an offensive staff member that day. He and all the other coaches were quite aware that the visitors to Florida Field were armed with offensive weapons of destruction. The prior season, Houston had rolled over Tulsa, 100-6, and was capable of embarrassing a young team like Florida. That meant the Gator offense would have to put big numbers up on the board as an equalizer, because nobody had figured a way to contain Houston's vaunted Veer-T option.

"As we prepared to play Houston," said Reaves, "We watched the films—everybody in the Southwest Conference was running the ball then. We noticed that Houston was running man-free coverage, or 'cover one', as we called it. Their cornerbacks lined up five yards off the receivers, and they played man-to-man. It's almost impossible to cover anybody man-to-man from five yards off."

Especially when that "somebody" was speedy Carlos Alvarez, "The Cuban Comet."

As some of his own defensive backs had discovered in practices, nobody could stop Alvarez with one defender. Certainly not when the quarterback was Reaves, whose arm strength and accuracy would prove to be the best of any in college football during that era.

"We had a scrimmage two weeks before the first game, the starters against the freshmen and 'B Team,' and we beat them 93-0!" Reaves said. "Ninety-three to nothing! And I said to myself, 'We must have something going here, because it's hard to score 93 against the air.'"

So Reaves and Alvarez were licking their chops. For Carlos, his first game as a Gator was a virtual out-of-body experience. He was like the Energizer Bunny after a dozen cups of strong coffee. Pancoast tried to calm his young receiver, but Carlos already knew they were going deep to him on the third play, a conversation that Reaves apparently didn't hear.

Reaves had been badgering his offensive coach for weeks about throwing long early. "As we got closer to the game and watched the film, I said to coach [Fred] Pancoast, 'Coach, how are they going to cover Carlos, playing like that?' He said, 'Yeah, it looks awfully enticing. We'll just have to see.'

"So I said, 'Coach Pancoast, are we going to call the bomb the first play of the game?' That was my idea. And he said, 'No, but fairly soon.' I didn't know he was going to send it in the third play of the game."

That these first-year varsity sophomores had such an air of confidence was remarkable, but there were motivating factors. For one thing, Reaves and Alvarez had invested endless hours of practice the summer between their freshman and sophomore seasons (freshmen weren't eligible to play.)

"Carlos was a tireless worker. The summer he came up, we'd go out and run a route-tree on each side of the ball," Reaves said. "And if it wasn't perfect—if he didn't feel like the route was perfect, or I didn't feel the pass was perfect—we'd run it again. All I'm doing is taking three-five-seven steps. He is running his butt off. But he never complained. He was in fantastic shape. We got to where those routes ... man, we had them down. It didn't matter what they'd call, we thought we could hit it. We had such good timing."

This was the infancy of the team called the "Super Sophs," a bit of a misnomer because there were so many key seniors on that team, too. Among them were the solid offensive line, headed up by seniors Mac Steen (captain), Kim Helton, Skip Amelung, and Wayne Griffith (junior Donnie Williams was the other). Those seniors still felt the sting of that embarrassing 51-0 loss to Georgia the season prior and wanted to make up for it. They would play a major role in firing up the team before the kickoff. This was one a sequence of three events that had started Alvarez's motor running full tilt.

"The next thing was, once we were ready to go on to the field, the seniors took over the locker room—people like Mac Steen and Steve Tannen and Paul Maliska," Alvarez remembered. "These seniors were unbelievable! They were so emotional and fired up! It put us into an emotional high. And we were already pretty emotional because of that famous Gene Ellenson 'Impossible Dream' speech he had given the night before. Then, the third thing—to run on to Florida Field and hear, 'Heeeerrrre Come the Gators!' I know whatever my speed was for the 100-yard dash, it increased substantially. I had never had that kind of adrenaline."

Rehearsal over, the curtain was ready to rise on a majestic opening day. Florida took the kickoff in its South end zone and brought it out to the 27-yard-line, an unassuming setup for such an historic moment. Reaves handed to halfback Jerry Vinsett on two off-tackle plays to the right that netted just three yards to the Gator 30. In came the play on third-and-7: "Split left, 79 streak." Reaves says he doesn't remember how the play was called. Alvarez definitely recalls Pancoast telling him they were going deep on the third play.

Various team members involved don't agree exactly on who knew about the call. Steen says the offensive coaches came over to the defensive room before the game and told them of the plans to throw deep. Alvarez says he knew. But perhaps Pancoast kept it a secret from Reaves so that he wouldn't get nervous.

"Maybe it was signaled in, I don't remember," Reaves said. But they both have vivid memories of the play. Carlos could see that Houston's corner was playing him loose.

"I didn't see any chance of that safety coming over. ... We had run that pattern a zillion times over the summer," Alvarez added.

"They all believed that, if we got it in the air, they could catch it," said McGowan.

When Florida broke the huddle, Reaves could see money. "I looked out there and, sure enough, there they were, lined up in 'cover one.' The cornerback was five yards off, just eyeballing Carlos, not looking anywhere else," Reaves said. "The safety was way over here next to me, eyeballing our tight end. There was probably 20 yards between Carlos and any other defender because the hash marks were wide back in those days. So that cornerback was on an island. I got a little pre-snap read and said, 'Yep, this is looking good.' I took the snap, took my quick seven steps, and let it fly."

Alvarez added: "John knew my speed exactly—and he was a wonderful passer. He hit me right in stride. I didn't lose a step. I never, ever doubted that I would catch it. People have asked me that. I knew I would catch it. And the only thing I was thinking running down that sideline was, 'Don't get caught from behind.'"

He didn't. As Alvarez ran downfield, Steen was yelling, "Run, Chico, run!"

"When I finally got to the end zone," explained Alvarez, "it was like a time warp. It was like time floated—I could hear people screaming. It was a foggy kind of thing. I turned around, and my teammates were on me. I don't know how those offensive linemen ran 70 yards so fast. It was just a glorious moment."

All that practice had paid immediate dividends, Reaves said. "It was just like we'd been out there in summer practice with nobody. It just dropped right in there on the numbers. He was about eight yards behind the defender, and he didn't even break stride. And he sprinted right in with it for six. It sounded like a bomb exploded in that stadium."

McGowan treasures the moment of that first touchdown pass. "I've got the picture of Carlos running down the sidelines," said McGowan, "and I wouldn't take a million dollars for it. Of course, it's got my daughter in it, too."

From there, the two teams exploded for a combined 93 points. Said Infante, "It was a track meet. Nobody could stop anybody—up and down the field. We beat them, 59-34, and all our star players had big games. Here, we weren't supposed to be very good in football, but we pretty much destroyed a team that was supposed to be No. 1 in the country. They had scored 100 on a couple of teams the year before. It was like, 'Hold on to your seats, because here comes a team that can put 100 on you.' It doesn't sound like our defense did a very good job, letting them score 34 points, but it was a special feat."

Amazingly, Reaves had predicted in a letter to his friend, Leonard Levy, that he would throw five touchdown passes, which he did—four of them in the first half. What he couldn't have predicted was that the Gator defense would give up five touchdown passes by the quarterback of a running team, Ken Bailey, and still win. Also unpredictable was that a first-year player would start his career by setting a one-game record in reception yardage, 192 yards on six catches, as Alvarez eclipsed Charlie Casey's mark. Many more records would be set by the "Super Sophs" that year.

The game was such a huge news event that people in towns near Gainesville drove to Florida Field and bought tickets long after the kickoff. "It was the only time I remember that we were selling tickets in the second half," said Graves.

It was such a memorable play that, even today, sports fans—not necessarily even Gator fans—often recall it when they meet Alvarez or Reaves. Carlos is a lawyer who has taken up environmental causes and now mentors other lawyers on the art of compromise. His knees precluded him from playing pro football.

"Carlos was a brilliant receiver," said Reaves. "He had great hands. He was smart. He was tough. He was strong. He could bench press 300 pounds. The only guy on the team who could bench more was [Jack] Youngblood—and that was back before we had a weight room. He was like the forerunner of the modern Jerry Rice-type receivers who worked his buns off. Unfortunately, he got hurt, or he would have been a brilliant pro."

Infante, who recruited Alvarez from North Miami High, where he was a running back, was amazed at how quickly Carlos adapted to the receiver position. "From the first day, he played it like he'd been there all his life," said Infante.

The 70-yard catch of Reaves' missile against Houston may be more famous, but none ever surpassed the amazing grab Alvarez made against Florida State two weeks later. The photo from *Sports Illustrated* shows Alvarez making the fingertip catch in 1969—actually it was more like a *fingernail* catch for one of two touchdowns in that game—and it demonstrated his amazing ability to snag the ball on the dead run while fully extended. It is a study in total concentration.

"He wasn't worried about taking a shot, wasn't worried about where the other people were—just where the ball was." said Infante. "I've seen him make catches where he caught the back half of the ball. That's special. That's a gift. That is not something you coach or teach. It's just something the kid's got."

That "fingernail catch" is the only picture of Carlos playing football that hangs on the walls of his Tallahassee home. And why not? After all, it was against Florida State—a team the Gators beat that year 21-6—and the photo sometimes is in full view of his Seminole visitors.

"I remember thinking it was going to be overthrown," Alvarez said. "It was just a last-second reach with both hands and hanging on to it. I really enjoyed that moment. It was all good."

Great as the catch against FSU was—and it may have been his finest—it could still never surpass the one against Houston because of the time and place it happened.

The fortuitous timing of his arrival at Florida with John Reaves is not lost on Carlos or his biggest fans. "He was also lucky to have John Reaves throwing him the ball," said Infante. "John was a big, tall quarterback in his day, and he would stand tall in the pocket. He wasn't going to run. And he had a good sense of touch and distance—and he had a catchable ball. You can't have one without the other. They worked so well together."

After a brief pro football career with the Eagles and the Tampa Bay Bandits, Reaves went into coaching. For a while, he worked with Steve

Spurrier at Florida before opening his own real estate firm in Tampa. But Reaves still raves about the old teammate who helped him stack up 7,549 yards to break the NCAA career-passing record held by Jim Plunkett.

Many people feel Reaves had more tools than any quarterback who ever played at Florida. Tommy Shannon was one of them. "There's no doubt that John Reaves could have been the greatest quarterback in the history of the University of Florida," said Shannon. "If he'd played in Spurrier's offense, he'd have thrown for 20,000 yards." Others shared that view, including some of Reaves' coaches. Before Reaves' first game, McGowan walked up to Reaves and said, "'I really believe you're going to be a better quarterback than Steve Spurrier'—and he looked at me like I was crazy."

Those skills don't guarantee success, and Florida never won a title of any kind, despite posting the school's best record, 9-1-1, in 1969.

That first "Reaves-to-Alvarez" touchdown pass was the first kiss of a year-long love affair that Gator fans would have with their beloved "Super Sophs." They did not disappoint. They rolled through the opposition with only one defeat and a tie, establishing the best record of any Gator team ever. Losing at Auburn, however, was painful because of a nightmarish nine-interception day for Reaves. But nothing could erase the memory of that first game—and they would always have Houston.

John Reaves had one more remembrance about that day of the famous pass and huge win over Houston. The night after the game he turned on the television to watch the sports news—before the days of ESPN. "I believe it was 'The Prudential Scoreboard' back in those days," said Reaves. "The guy said, 'Houston has beaten Florida, 59-34, as expected.' And later, he came back and said, 'We have a correction here. It was Florida that beat Houston, 59-34! And quarterback Jack Reaves'—*Jack Reaves!*—'threw five touchdown passes.' I saw it myself!"

More than 35 years after "Reaves-to-Alvarez," on the week he was inducted into the University of Florida Sports Hall of Fame, Mac Steen walked by himself down on Florida Field to the spot near the 30-yard line where it had all started. He put his hand on the ground in a three-point stance, came up out of his crouch and simulated a tackle's pass-blocking move. As he stepped backward, he thought he could still hear the crowd roaring in that empty stadium and could see Alvarez sprinting down the sideline, wanting to shout out, "Run, Chico, run!"

That this group of players wound up playing against the SEC Champion Tennessee Vols in the Gator Bowl and beating the coach who later took the place of Ray Graves mere weeks later still boggles many minds.

In their final two seasons, though, the "Super Sophs" would be playing for Doug Dickey.

5

The Doug Dickey Era

1970 - 1979

A Coaching-Change Fiasco

Despite efforts to keep back-room discussions secretive about the Doug Dickey-for-Ray Graves coaching change, the word began to leak out in December 1969. Some of Tennessee's coaches had been recruiting in Florida prior to the Gator Bowl game, which would feature Dickey's Vols vs. Graves' Gators. Florida assistant coach Bubba McGowan ran across a member of Dickey's staff who leaked their impending plans. "We're coming to Florida," he told McGowan.

"I said, 'What?'" replied McGowan.

"He said, 'We're coming to Florida.'"

"And I still said, 'I ain't gonna believe this.' I just knew it wasn't so," McGowan said. "I just knew Gene Ellenson was the guy who was going to take over. Those were my feelings. He could hold us together like Graves did. They wouldn't make a change now!"

More rumors of the change began to surface, catching the media's attention, and speculative stories began to fly. The closer it came to the Gator Bowl, the stronger the rumors of Dickey's arrival became. Gator players were incredulous, and some began speaking out in favor of Ellenson.

In December of 1969, after a practice for the upcoming Gator Bowl, I asked Graves, pointblank—tape recorder in hand—"Are you going to be the coach of the Gators next season?"

His response was, "Yes, I will be the coach next season." Was Graves trying to conduct damage control and hoping to hold on to the job? Was he protecting Dickey and others? Or was it an outright lie? One printed report stated that Graves was having withdrawal symptoms at the thought of leaving behind such a talented group of sophomores. According to one unidentified Florida player, the night before the Gator Bowl game, President Stephen O'Connell told the team, "Ray Graves is the coach and will be indefinitely." Dickey, however, later told a Florida writer that, before the Gator Bowl, he had personally called Graves to ask about his intentions. "And he told me he was definitely going to resign," said Dickey. They had even met briefly in Atlanta the summer before to discuss it.

Confusion reigned, partly because Graves seemed to waffle as the Gator Bowl approached.

On a spring day in 2005, Ray Graves pulled out a copy of a *St. Petersburg Times* article written by Tom Kelly in September, 1968, to help explain his decision to quit as coach. The headline noted: "Florida's Ray Graves: Is '68 His Year To Make No. 1 and Quit?" The football program had struggled through two straight seasons; and the disappointment of 1968, predicted to be "The Year of the Gator," would be the prelude to the coaching change. Graves reportedly had tired of the coach/AD double duty. One of the names he recommended as his coaching replacement, he said, was Dickey. Nobody anticipated the reaction to the removal of Florida's most successful and most popular coach—Graves—at a seemingly inappropriate time.

Graves pointed to the *Times* article as if to say that, yes, he was planning to step up to AD following his 10th season, after enjoying a promising group of sophomores. At the same time, Graves also hinted that perhaps he was victimized by politics after the 1969 season. Having grown up in Gainesville and with a professor/father at Florida, naturally Dickey had a core of allegiance that would work on his behalf.

"There were people working behind the scenes," Graves said of the alleged forces who were prompting him to retire. Presumably Graves meant the group O'Connell had met with that summer before, which included Board of Regents Chairman Burke Kibler, UF law professor Mandell Glicksberg, and ex-Gator player and prominent politician/lawyer Jimmy Kynes.

What transpired after that is a little murky. Graves' memory is fuzzy, but he said sometime during the '69 season that he had heard Dickey's name mentioned "… because he'd just won an SEC title and President O'Connell thought maybe he could do it here."

O'Connell apparently thought he had prearranged a deal with Graves. Discussions between O'Connell and Dickey began to take place over the summer. According to Dickey, a deal was never struck, but others say the deal was already cut in principle. Dickey says he was invited to play golf by the Florida president in North Carolina in August. "'I'm probably going to make a coaching change,'" Dickey quoted O'Connell as saying. Still, at the agreement of both parties, no deal would be offered until later, said Dickey.

"We agreed to talk, but I told him that I was going about my business to coach my team and that we'd talk after the season. I told him, 'I'm going to coach my season, and you let yours run out. And when the season's over, we'll talk about it. I don't want to get involved in it any other way.'"

It was December before they talked again, when of all things, Tennessee came to Florida for the Gator Bowl. O'Connell told Dickey he could have the head coaching job. To which Dickey replied, "Let me finish this game, and we'll talk about it."

Ellenson was believed to have been preordained to succeed Graves—at least, that was the prevailing sentiment. He was loved by the players, popular with the fans, had the loyalty of the staff, and was respected by the media. His inspirational, Rockne-esque messages were part of Gator lore.

Who else better to carry on the legacy of Graves?

The cauldron of confusion spilled over in the press as Graves continued to imply he was staying. Or perhaps Graves didn't know everything. He says he can't remember the details of how he first heard the news. "They didn't come to me," Graves said 35 years later. "They went through other people, and probably some of the athletic board. I'm sure they did."

Dickey says it was his understanding that Graves was in favor of the move. But Graves waffled a bit after his young team was invited to the Gator Bowl, where the Gators beat the SEC champion Vols to further complicate things. It was sort of an unofficial SEC playoff game back before they had them, and Gator fans were ecstatic.

"It was certainly sweet," Graves said, remembering the 14-13 Florida upset.

Dickey says the deal was done right after the Gator Bowl game. If Graves had changed his mind after his "Super Sophs" upset the Vols, it was too late to turn back. A few days after the Gators' victory, it was announced that Dickey was the new coach at Florida, and Graves would be the athletic director.

Others believe it was a *fate accompli*—one of them was Mac Steen, the 1969 captain. "I think the deal was done the summer before," speculated Steen, a Deland orthodontist. "I think a group of Tampa alumni went up there and visited with Doug Dickey before the 1969 season started. It was in the wind that Ray wasn't going to be there the next year. That '68 team had shot his wad and didn't perform the way it was supposed to. I can't tell you this for sure, but I think that's one reason Coach [Ed] Kensler didn't come back. We came back from the summer, and our offensive coach was gone.

"Yet Coach Graves and President O'Connell led us to believe that Gene Ellenson had just as good a chance as anybody."

Who, why, and how the ensuing fiasco took place remains an unsolved mystery. Dickey seemed a natural fit, and even Graves admits that. Depending on which version you buy, Graves:

1. Was hijacked by politicos and forced to sign a contract as athletic director.
2. Was pushed aside in a fervent quest to attain SEC supremacy.
3. Voluntarily accepted the post of athletic director because he couldn't do both jobs.
4. Or none of the above.

When it did happen, football Camelot in Gainesville ended. More than three and a half decades later, all parties were still scratching their heads and wondering what went wrong.

"I was spending too much time in the boardroom at meetings, and I felt I wasn't doing my coaches and players right," said Graves. "With the women's program coming and with our athletic program expanding, I just couldn't do it all. And I was about the only one in the conference who had to do both. So I had to make a decision. And I told [my wife] Opal that I felt I was leaving whoever came in with a good football team with all those sophomores."

A trail of obstacles would haunt Dickey for at least three seasons, starting the day he arrived in Gainesville.

Not a Happy Homecoming

The arrival of Doug Dickey should have been a red-carpet greeting, hailed by a tickertape parade. Instead, Gator fans grudgingly welcomed Dickey as head coach in January 1970, and the fan base was divided. Dickey came in under a black cloud, as if he were an interloper. This was no way to treat a Gainesville guy who had spent eight years on the Florida campus—first as a prep athlete at P. K. Yonge High School, then four years as a three-sport competitor in college.

Dickey was the target of the wrath by angry fans who adored Graves and the "Super Sophs." Since it wasn't public knowledge that Graves had a prearranged deal, some even blamed Dickey. Facts were scarce. "I don't believe there was any way in the world President O'Connell would have offered me the job if he didn't already have an arrangement with Coach Graves," Dickey said.

There was such an undercurrent about the handling of Dickey's hiring that his program started out in a hole. Right off, the new Florida coach felt the sting when some sponsors failed to come forward for his coach's television show. Seemingly he was never able to overcome all that, partly because of bad breaks, injuries to key players, and his conservative offensive philosophy. Somehow, Dickey turned out the villain, perhaps unjustifiably.

One must wonder what prompted Dickey to leave the friendly confines of Knoxville, Tennessee, for a place that would turn out to be semi-hostile. Dickey was one of the hottest coaches in the nation at the time. It wasn't like the Tennessee coach was faxing out his resume. Florida came after him. Dickey had other opportunities to leave Tennessee, including queries from Michigan and Oklahoma, but none with the personal attraction of home. As Paul "Bear" Bryant once said of himself after returning to his alma mater at Alabama, Dickey "heard mama callin'."

"My mother and my wife's father were in Florida," Dickey explained 35 years later. "I did have a great feel for the University of Florida. My dad had taught school there. I spent eight years there in high school and college on the campus. I had a real strong feeling that was a place I could do something that hadn't been done before.

"Whatever I did at Tennessee, Neyland had already done. So it was good. It felt good. Everything was going well, but I had already accomplished what I set out to do [at Tennessee]. The national championships didn't really amount to all that much to me in those days. I didn't think about them in the same realm they think about them today. Whether you're ranked one, two, or three really didn't make any difference. The only thing that really counted was winning the Southeastern Conference championship. If you did, you got invited to some big bowl game, and that was about all there was. You had some honors for players and coaches and so forth.

"But the University of Florida had not accomplished any of those things before. I thought, 'Well, maybe I have the background and the mix that I can make that happen' ... and I said, 'All my kids will grow up in Florida, and we'll all have a long future together because of the growth of the state.' So we did that."

Indeed, Dickey brought impressive credentials to Gainesville, better than any coach there, ever. He had already won two SEC football championships—something no Gator coach had ever done once. The Vols had been successfully incorporating black athletes into their program, a process the University of Florida was slow to embrace. Dickey was twice named SEC Coach of the Year, going to five straight bowls.

If he could just duplicate what he had done at Tennessee, Dickey felt, he could bring Gator fans all their dreams. It looked like the perfect marriage. So why wasn't he received with open arms? Perhaps Dickey was a victim of bad timing. Perhaps the subterfuge and secrecy that shrouded the coaching change alienated the players, media, and fans. Perhaps the political climate of America was a factor.

College campuses were the focal point of protests with the Vietnam War going on and Watergate just around the corner. Athletes were changing. They spoke their minds about the war, social issues, and campus matters. And this controversy, along with the coaching change, was about to spark unprecedented turmoil in the Florida football program.

Jimmy Dunn, Dickey's offensive assistant, could feel the tide pulling in two directions. "It was one of those situations where not everyone wanted to make a coaching change," said Dunn. "No one could figure out why they wanted to make a change after the success they were having with this staff and players. So half probably thought that [Dickey] should be the coach and half didn't—that's not the situation you'd like to go into.

"Many situations came up that Doug had to fight through. We didn't have some of the key players they had in 1969, when they played extremely well. We lost a lot of the linemen, but we had a lot of the finesse people coming back. We had the guys who could catch and throw it, but we couldn't protect them. So it was a pretty good dilemma for Doug, how to get the most out of them."

Pretty good dilemma, indeed. Florida football fans were living large following the "Super Sophs" era and with so many good players returning, expected another banner year. As Dunn said, however, the tide had turned, and it began to feel like an undertow.

What would challenge Dickey and his staff was the immediate perception that their offensive philosophy was regressive at Florida. That's the opposite of what Vols fans worried about upon his arrival—they thought he was too progressive for Neyland country.

The Ghost of 'The General'

Regarding public image, perception is everything, and the new Florida coach received a cool reception in some quarters. Some of Florida football's close friends felt Dickey slighted them with his own ideas about how things should be run. That was probably due, in part, to the folksy, politically savvy approach Graves had taken and the number of people who felt a part of his success.

"I wasn't there to make friends," Dickey would later say following his term at Florida.

Dickey had overcome resistance to change at Tennessee. He reflected on the day he had interviewed for the Vols' head job and how he had to sell the idea of dumping Tennessee's famed single wing in favor of the T-formation.

"Coach [Bob, Tennessee's athletic director] Woodruff asked me one day, 'Why don't you fly over there [to a little town in West Tennessee]. There's a guy over there named Tom Elam, who's a country lawyer and is on our board. And he's going to make the decision [about the new coach].'

"So I flew over there and he picked me up; and we drove around for about two hours in his big ol' Cadillac. And I remember he said to me, 'We run the single wing, so how are you gonna get us in the T?' And I said, 'It's not too hard. We just take that blocking back out of the game, and we'll put a guy in there under center so he can take the ball.' He kind of thought that was pretty simple. So I guess I convinced him that it wasn't too hard."

Doug Dickey was 31 years old in 1964 when he became head coach of the Tennessee Vols. He won 46 games, lost 15, and tied four for a .738 winning percentage. He opened up the Vols offense. And eventually he did make peace with the ghost of General Bob Neyland. Dickey was not only twice the SEC Coach of the year (1965, 1967), he also put pride back in the Tennessee program in his six years there and established several proud traditions. He arrived in Knoxville on a train, and after a slow start and 4-5-1 record, he had the Vols fans jumping aboard.

Neyland Stadium held 51,527 when he got there. Five bowl games, 15 All-Americans, and two conference titles later, it was up to 64,429. He painted the end zones of Shields-Watkins Field with the famed checkerboard look. He put a prancing Tennessee Walking Horse on the field for pregame. He put a large orange, capital "T" for Tennessee on the white helmets. He had the Tennessee band, "The Proud of the Southland Marching Band," forming a "T" so his football team could run through it. Like the "Grand Ol' Opry" over in Nashville, Tennessee football was about showbiz.

That great expectations followed Dickey to Florida was no surprise, but he would soon be upstaged.

Alvarez: Voice of Reason of Treason?

On the morning after the announcement of Dickey's hiring, I met Carlos Alvarez for a late breakfast at Pumpernik's restaurant in North Miami. He was angry and said felt he and his teammates had been lied to and "betrayed" by Florida's administration. He said he was considering transferring to another school.

I wrote that story that day for my morning newspaper, *Today*, and gave a copy of it that night to my friend John Crittenden of the *Miami News*, who wrote it for his afternoon newspaper the next day. The Associated Press picked up Crittenden's story—not mine, the original—and it became national news (although Crittenden had never actually even talked to Alvarez).

These were tumultuous times, and some Gator fans considered Alvarez a traitor, especially when he used words like "betrayed" and talked of possibly leaving Florida. Alvarez says he can't remember a single former teammate telling him they disagreed with his position and isn't sorry for speaking out.

"I know that we were not told the truth. I don't know if it was done intentionally or unintentionally. It was a confusing time. Nobody expected Florida to have that kind of record [9-1-1] that year. It just didn't seem right," Alvarez said.

"I think the people in charge wouldn't have done it that way if they could do it over. Mistakes were made. Just by luck or coincidence, or the way the world is. We played Tennessee in that Gator Bowl. Who would have ever thought that Florida would end up playing Tennessee in the Gator Bowl? So that whole set of circumstances was just odd.

"I still feel what happened was wrong. And I hope that I shed some light that was not there before," Alvarez said. "I may have done it differently, but a lot of the things that I said and thoughts that I expressed I have never doubted."

Other Gator players were stunned at the Dickey announcement.

"We just wondered what those people in the front offices were thinking," said Jack Youngblood, the former All-America defensive end who spent three years under Graves before playing for Dickey in his senior season. "We heard the rumors and read the stories, and we couldn't understand why anybody would want to change a program that was winning. But when we questioned it, our assistant coaches would tell us, 'Oh, don't worry about that—it's just media hype. We're going to be back next year.'

"There was some reluctance [to accept the coaching change]. Carlos Alvarez was one of the key elements. He didn't mind, as a youngster, in voicing his criticism—of voicing *our* criticism and objections," said Youngblood.

Dickey also believes that, had the Vols accepted one of the other bowl bids, much of the turmoil about his hiring at Florida may have been avoided. But Jacksonville is where his athletic director, Bob Woodruff, wanted to go. Besides, Woodruff wasn't really convinced that his coach would jump ship.

Alvarez says he bears no ill will against Dickey, Graves, or O'Connell. He considers himself "… one of Ray Graves' biggest supporters—I love that guy, and everything that he's done for me. He means a lot to me and to any player who played for him. [Steve] Spurrier epitomizes everybody who played for Coach Graves in the 1960s. Maybe it was just confusing times. Maybe there's something that happened that can't be said because other people may get hurt."

A Word on Bob Neyland

Sometimes genealogy befuddles, but Neyland's coaching genes are very much a part of the Gators' family tree. Dickey learned them as a Gator player under Woodruff.

Neyland, an ROTC instructor and backfield coach in 1925 before becoming head coach a year later, arrived at Tennessee as an Army captain, stayed active in the service while there, and left as a brigadier general. He left twice—once when he was called by the Army to assist in the construction of the Panama Canal and once to serve in World War II. His football heritage was enriched under Scobey "Pop" Warner at Carlisle Indian School and at West Point, under Charles Daly. During that time he began to adopt material for his "Seven Maxims," which became a part of the coaching bibles of dozens of other coaches throughout many generations.

Graves still has them memorized and remembers them as part of Neyland's pre-game ritual. "He acted like he didn't know what he was going to write on the blackboard, but he wrote the same thing every Saturday," said Graves.

Those "Seven Maxims" traveled well. Graves wrote them every Saturday, as did Dickey. One of Dickey's favorite anecdotes for his after-dinner speeches is on that subject.

"If you're a Tennessee guy, you know what those are," said Dickey.

And then Dickey began ticking off those words he first heard as a sophomore at Florida: "The team that makes the fewest mistakes will win. Play for and make the breaks ...

"Coach Woodruff wrote them on the board for three years, with a little extra stuff around it occasionally, but basically, it was 'The Maxims of the Game' and how you play the game of football."

Dickey graduated from Florida and went into the Army. "And so I get out of the Army and go to work for Coach [Frank] Broyles at Arkansas. The first game, I went in there, and Frank Broyles, who played and coached for Bobby Dodd at Georgia Tech and coached with Bob Woodruff—the first thing he does is go up there and write, 'The team that makes the fewest mistakes' ... and away we went. He's writing the same stuff up on the board.

"Well, I went to Tennessee to coach, and I wrote it on the board myself. That's what you do when you're the head coach. I go to Florida and did the same thing. I came back to Knoxville, and my son was playing there for Tennessee. And there was John Majors coaching, up the board, writing, 'The team that makes the fewest mistakes ...'

"And now today, Phillip Fulmer [the Vols coach who also played at Tennessee] has them printed up on the wall."

Think of the dry erase markers they save these days at Tennessee!

General Robert Neyland's Seven Maxims of Football

1. The team that makes the fewest mistakes will win.

2. Play for and make the breaks and when one comes your way— SCORE.

3. If, at first, the game—or the breaks—go against you, don't let up ... put on more steam.

4. Protect our kickers, our quarterback, our lead, and our ball game.

5. Ball, oski, cover, block, cut, and slice, pursue and gang tackle ... for this is the WINNING EDGE.

6. Press the kicking game. Here is where the breaks are made.

7. Carry the fight to our opponent and keep it there for 60 minutes.

There is nothing left but speculation as to why the change was made. The scarlet sin was that nobody knew—players or assistant coaches. The air of deceit led to a firestorm of controversy that sparked an NCAA investigation over how the matter was handled. Florida was exonerated, but the damage was done, and bad feelings festered up.

Graves' staff wouldn't know for sure until December 29, two days after the Gator Bowl. "I didn't ask, because I didn't think it was my place," said offensive aide Lindy Infante. "Somehow or another, I guess Ray changed his mind. But we were all told everything was fine, and he was going to be back next year. We were on top of the world after beating Tennessee. Then, of course, we find out that the team we just beat—their coach is coming in to be the Florida coach. The players were on scholarship, but the coaches were all having a beer, sitting around wondering who would be staying."

Held over by Dickey were Infante, Bubba McGowan, Don Brown, Jack Thompson, and Dave Fuller. Fred Pancoast was going to Georgia as offensive coordinator. Infante was called into Dickey's office, expecting to get fired, but instead was offered a job to stay. "He said, 'Lindy, you'll probably want to think about it'—and I quickly said, 'No, I don't!'"

Alvarez laments lost opportunities, what might have been had most of Graves' assistant coaches been retained. "One of the biggest regrets of my life is that I didn't get coached [two more years] by Fred Pancoast, who was the offensive coordinator that year. The guy was brilliant—absolutely brilliant. He could really develop a great game plan," Alvarez said.

"And not just him—Bubba McGowan, who coached the wide receivers and Lindy Infante, who recruited me ... and Coach [Ed] Kensler. We had a good energy there. All those guys really, really meshed together. They liked each other, and they made the players feel that way."

Alvarez pulled in an astounding 88 catches for 1,329 yards and 12 touchdowns—records that stood for many years. Chad Jackson tied the 88 catches in 2005, and Travis McGriff broke the single-season reception yardage mark in 1998 with 1,353, but Alvarez still holds many others, including career yardage with 2,563 and total catches with 172. He is proudest of the 133 yards per game in receptions he averaged as a sophomore.

Infante still marvels at the 88 receptions in a 10-game regular season. "Back then, people weren't throwing the ball around like they are today," he said. "To have a record stand from 1969 to now—I think that's quite incredible. And we were a little bit ahead in throwing the ball as much as we did."

What happened after the magical season of 1969 stands as proof that good energy and good times should never be taken for granted. Even if the coaching staff had stayed, however, they would never see the same Carlos Alvarez, who won the rare distinction of being consensus All-America as a sophomore.

The media didn't have much positive to say. The NCAA investigation at Florida for a possible violation of "ethical conduct" was still in progress as Dickey took over. Gator fans had yet to buy into the change, and among those feeling the heat was President O'Connell, who had always been close to the athletes—especially the 1969 football team.

Later in the spring of 1970, graduated captain Mac Steen had moved out of the athletic dorm into the Tanglewood Apartments with teammates Bobby Coleman, Skip Amelung, and Robbie Rebol.

On a Sunday morning following a long night when he had consumed the legal limit of adult beverages, Steen heard a rather annoying sound. He sauntered to the front in his dirty T-shirt and shorts, peeked through the glass to see whom this early morning visitor could possibly be, and was stunned to see President O'Connell.

"He'd [O'Connell] often come down to have meals with us at the training table," Steen said. "I'd been in his office several times during the year. The team loved the guy, and he loved the team. We had given him this autographed ball about halfway through the season," said Steen. "But he had this football we had given him, and he looked like he hadn't slept all night."

Steen opened the door. "And here was Stephen O'Connell, looking forlorn and dejected, holding a ball that the team autographed and I had presented to him. And he gives me the ball and says, 'Mac, I don't think the team really wants me to have this.' I was totally taken back and tried to talk him out of it. He said, 'Nope.' I kept the thing for several years, trying to give it back to him. Finally, when they started getting this sports memorabilia going at the school, I sent it to Coach Ellenson with a note. But I think it just got lost somewhere."

The collective will of Gator fans, influenced by sportswriters' numerous critical columns, had impacted Dickey's program in a negative manner, and the fallout had begun. Dickey had dealt with resistance to change before when he was at Tennessee, but none like what was ahead for him at Florida.

Alvarez and Dickey didn't exactly hit it off immediately. As for his work ethic, Carlos said, "I think he appreciated my effort." Aside from criticizing the coaching changes, Carlos was also a campus activist and often demonstrated against the Vietnam War. That didn't bother Dickey so much, but his coach wasn't terribly pleased when his star wide receiver decided to help launch a union for college athletes, later known as "The League of Athletes."

"That got me into trouble with Dickey," he said. "I think it was misunderstood by him, and totally misunderstood by the press. After I spoke out on the coaching change, the press loved to pigeonhole me. It was always nice to say something like 'the outspoken' or 'controversial.'"

Alvarez also wished he and others would've become more involved with bringing a larger number of black students into the student population. Only two black players were on the varsity in 1970—Willie Jackson and Leonard George. There was talk of a boycott of the school. "That would have put Willie and Leonard in a heck of a situation, because they would have had to walk out. We met as a team and tried to help them out. It was wonderful to hear my teammates support them. It was very powerful and moving."

Ironically, one of the things Dickey did that helped Florida move forward was to recruit more black athletes, many of whom would become stars in the 1970s. But he was in for a decade of mostly turmoil, with the exception of the two seasons that the Gators nearly won an SEC title.

Dickey recognized Alvarez was an activist on campus. "You've always got four or five players who get involved in those kinds of things," explained Dickey. "It didn't bother me—what bothered me was he was hurt. He played the best he could for a while, but he went downhill limping and could never get back to where he was. But he was a great player when he could go."

Just the learning curve of a new philosophy, new coaches, and a new system was enough of a challenge.

"When you have a coaching change like that, unless the head coach coming in keeps the same system, then you have to go through a learning spell," said Infante, who was one of the lucky ones who stayed around for several seasons.

Chief among those changes was Dickey's more disciplined approach. The critics' book on Florida football under Graves was that his laid-back style that he adopted from the Bobby Dodd school was counterproductive to hardnosed, grind-it-out football required to win championships. Dickey's style was what one assistant called "a more combative approach."

Whereas Dickey had to convince Tennessee fans to modernize, it was the opposite sell for him at Florida. He had to go back to fundamentals and enlist player support of the running game and hard-hitting defense. It was almost the polar opposite of the "Come Fly With Me" approach of the "Super Sophs." It was a different athlete at Florida and a different time.

The adjustment just never clicked. There weren't going to be many more glory days ahead for Florida football in the early '70s. "There was a lot more discontent about everything than I anticipated," Dickey admitted. "I was young and a bit naïve about a lot of things. I'd had coach Woodruff's guidance before, but [at Florida] we had a turbulent time with Vietnam and integration. On top of that, the team we inherited had some good athletes on offense, but two of them were hurt. There were many freshmen coming in, but we'd lost some really good senior football players. But still, we managed to win seven games."

The leadership of the senior offensive linemen was gone. Crippling injuries to Alvarez and fellow wide receiver Andy Cheney further cut into the depth chart. While running track in the spring of 1970, Carlos noted his knee was swollen. It turned out to be a severe knee injury and might have been far, far worse. "It would swell up every time I ran," he said. "Ultimately, they went through a number of diagnoses. In fact, they sent me to so many doctors. One said I was going to die by the time I was 22. Another one claimed I had gout. As it turned out, they ultimately sent me to the Auburn team doctor. I drove up there in my little Volkswagen Beetle. He diagnosed it as the lining of my knee had worn out because I had an old high school basketball injury and developed a little bit of an arthritic condition."

Although he still had those splendid hands, he could no longer run like the wind. The knee injury was like the one suffered by Bill Walton, whom Carlos had gotten to know through the Academic Hall of Fame. He also would wind up injuring his other knee and having to miss two games his senior year, perhaps causing his seasonal averages to dip to nearly half of his sophomore standards.

A Florida Flop Flap

Clearly, the momentum of the "Super Sophs" had died. Florida went just 7-4 in 1970, with lopsided losses to Alabama, Tennessee, and Auburn, but still had a chance to go to a decent bowl. Miami ended those chances with a 14-13 upset of the Gators in Gainesville. There was no bowl for the "Super Sophs" one year removed—and it would only get worse.

Not all was lost. Players like tight end Jim Yancey were coming into their own and made first-team All-SEC in 1970. Youngblood also made All-America. But the "Super Soph" era was winding down. After a brilliant beginning and the consensus All-America achievement, the best Alvarez could do in his final two seasons was second-team All-SEC his final two years. Reaves got no higher than second-team All-SEC, either, but was named to one of the All-America teams.

The Gators started off the 1971 campaign by losing to Duke, 12-6. Even more difficult days were ahead. The Gators got off to their worst start since Bear Wolf's 0-9 "Golden Era" team of 1946, losing their first five games. Only an upset of Florida State kept the Titanic afloat. The Seminoles, with Gary Huff at quarterback, exploded to a 5-0 start and were a huge favorite. In one of the biggest upsets in series history, the Gators prevailed, 17-15, helping soothe lopsided losses to Alabama (38-0), LSU (48-7), Auburn (40-7), and Georgia (49-7). What had been a glorious beginning for these now-seniors was transforming, gradually, into an ignominious ending.

Alvarez had just enough left for one more hurrah. He and Reaves would not go out without some fireworks in their final game, despite a 3-7 record. Little could be salvaged, except for one record still within John Reaves' grasp. With a good night against the Hurricanes, Reaves could eclipse the career college passing-yardage mark.

"We had an open date, and Miami had an open date. So we switched defenses," said Dickey. "I told Jack Thompson, 'You know how to coach that old Tennessee Wide Tackle Six. We're going to shock them with a different defense. They've got Chuck Foreman running with the football, and he's going to run around us and kill us. I believe we can hold up better on the sweep against Foreman.'

"Meanwhile, [Miami coach] Fran [Curci] puts in the wishbone with Chuck Foreman playing spit end! Here we are … he doesn't know what to do against our six-two defense, and we don't know what to do playing defense against the wishbone. But we got eight guys up there, and we're better off than he is. So we're holding our own and doing pretty good offensively. In the fourth quarter, they tell me John Reaves needs about 40 yards to break this record, so we've got it made."

I was on the Florida sidelines as the game wound down that night. With just over a minute to go, Reaves needed 13 yards to top Jim Plunkett's record, and the Gators were getting the ball on Miami's punt. Plans went awry when the Gators' Harvin Clark fielded it and ran for a touchdown. He was horrified at what he'd done, realizing that, because he'd scored, Reaves might not get the record.

"I laughed with John Reaves and Harvin Clark about this not too long ago," Dickey said. "I said, 'Clark, you caused me so damn many headaches by running that ball back for a touchdown!' If we only would have had him fair-catch the punt, we would have spared ourselves a lot of trouble."

Meanwhile, Curci was in no hurry to give the ball back and began running out the clock even though he trailed, 45-10. Players began to plead with Dickey to let Miami score, but he wouldn't give in. I was listening to some of the players talk—if memory serves correctly, I even chatted with Harvin Clark and Doug Sorenson about the plan. It wasn't one of Dickey's favorite moments, but even he knows the value of the story about "The Florida Flop."

After Clark's score, Curci put Foreman back at tailback and began running the ball to kill the clock. "And they kept the ball away from us," said Dickey. "If they'd done that the whole game, they'd have probably beaten us."

With a little more than a minute to play, Florida called timeout, and Sorenson, a defensive back, came over to Dickey and asked, "What do you think we ought to do?" Dickey gave in and told them to allow Miami to score, but to go full speed.

"But he goes back on the field, and somebody in the huddle said, 'Just lay down.'" As Miami quarterback John Hornibrook took the snap, Gator defenders fell to the ground on their stomachs, as if they'd been struck by lightning. Hornibrook walked over for the score. The *New York Times* ran a photo of 10 of 11 defenders on their bellies.

"That didn't look good, and we got our share of trouble out of that," said Dickey. But, in fact, it *was* good because it brought symmetry and a happy ending to the "Super Soph" story.

Reaves threw to Alvarez for 15 yards and the record, then hit another three-yarder just to be sure. Reaves and Alvarez finished in the style they had begun. The celebration began as soon as the game was over. Robert Harrell picked up Reaves and tossed him in the tank where Flipper, the Miami Dolphin mascot, resided. Alvarez shimmied up a flagpole, as if to raise the orange and blue colors one more time, ending things as they began—with great joy.

That gifted bunch of "Super Sophs," who had set such high standards, could only manage an 11-11 record in their next two seasons under Dickey.

In the transition, Dickey inherited several good assistant coaches and some outstanding players. He would begin to emphasize the running game and defense, attracting a succession of excellent linebackers, running backs, and linemen. None would be any better than the defensive lineman Dickey had inherited from Graves in that 1970 season—Jack Youngblood.

The Skinny Boy from Monticello

To this day, Jack Youngblood isn't quite sure how he made it so big. But he is sure the fact that Doug Dickey retained line coach Jack Thompson from Graves' staff was a big factor in his development over the 1970 season.

Let this be a lesson for every gangly kid who has a dream of becoming a college or pro athlete: Don't ever give up hope, even when the so-called experts predict your failure. College scouts almost kissed off an All-America, All-Pro, and a member of the College Football Hall of Fame.

At Jefferson County High in Monticello, Florida, Youngblood played for a coach named Brent Hall, who won the state title that helped his players get noticed—something Hall would continue doing in Marion County years later, leading the Ocala Forest Wildcats to consecutive state chamionships in 1974-75. "A real good man," Youngblood said of his former coach, one of many father figures Jack would encounter along his journey.

For a guy coming out of Jefferson County High who wasn't even good enough to warrant the attention of nearby Florida State—just a few miles down the road from Monticello, Florida—Youngblood was a long-shot. However, his excellent football adventure defied the odds and took him all the way to Canton, Ohio. With no help, we might add, from the big-name talent scouts.

One of the NFL's legendary coaches wrote him off early. Bill Parcells was an assistant at Army when he was scouting the tall, skinny kid from Monticello. Parcells responded: "That kid will never play college football!"

It turned out to be a statement almost as embarrassing as that *Chicago Tribune* headline: "Dewey Defeats Truman." Jack Youngblood made them pay dearly for underestimating his potential.

Not until the state high school championship football game did the Jacksonville-born Youngblood receive any attention from the University of Florida.

This oft-told story is one of Youngblood's favorites, one which he frequently uses in speeches, with this precursor: "Through the wisdom of a baseball coach ..." Yes, it took a baseball coach who was also a football assistant to recognize the ability of the small-town, overly tall, underweight Youngblood. But what they didn't realize was half his 200 pounds was heart, and the other half was guts. He turned out to be the John Wayne Tough Guy poster boy of the NFL.

Baseball coach and freshman football coach Dave Fuller approached Youngblood after Jefferson County High's state championship victory and asked: "How would you like to come to the University of Florida?"

"I said, 'Wait a minute, let me think about it for a minute,'" Youngblood recalls playfully. 'Yessir!'"

A virtual fluke made Youngblood a Gator, but he turned out to be one of their all-time great football players.

Since he had grown up in the shadow of Doak Campbell Stadium and read mostly about the Seminoles in the *Tallahassee Democrat*, Youngblood didn't know much about the University of Florida, which didn't get any play behind enemy lines.

"It wasn't so much a case of not wanting to play for the Gators," Youngblood said, "as it was of being ignorant about them."

Maybe if FSU had asked, he'd have been a Seminole because he knew more about them, it proved to be a great decision for both the Gators and Youngblood. What he lacked in poundage he made up for in tenacity, toughness, and spiritual conviction—most of it learned from his grandfather.

He was farm-boy rugged. When he was playing in the NFL, he once told a writer, "I'll take a nice, plowed field to a concrete freeway any day." He knew about hard labor. In Monticello, he loaded watermelons under the searing Florida sun.

His father died when he was only 10. To survive the times, he had to call on the grit and determination he learned at his grandfather's knee while growing up in that Mayberry-like setting of Northwest Florida.

Herbert Jackson Youngblood III quotes two things about life from Herbert Jackson Youngblood Sr., the former high sheriff of Nassau County:

1. God has a plan for your life, even though you don't know what it's going to be;
2. Whatever a man pursues in life, he must endeavor to do it to the best of his ability.

"The good Lord has told us in the scriptures that He has a plan for us," Youngblood said one day on his drive from Orlando to Tallahassee. "And if you'll just seek that plan and listen—shut your mouth—you'll find out what that plan is. He will direct you in the right direction. Me being a football player to the extent that it turned out to be was *absolutely* astonishing to me when you look back at how it all pieced together."

Youngblood just didn't fit any particular position for college football, and he wasn't really thinking about a four-year school right way. His mother, a widow, couldn't afford anything else, so by his senior year Jack enrolled at North Florida Community College.

"My mother raised me and my two younger sisters," he said, "so there wasn't any extra cash laying around for me to go to a university."

Besides, he was a misfit—in football, not social life. In high school, Youngblood was a linebacker. But what position would a beanpole play in college? He was what is known as a "tweener," too tall to be a linebacker, not fast enough to be a defensive back, too small to be a lineman. He makes jokes now about his size.

"I had to eat a big supper to be 200 pounds," said Youngblood. "I was so skinny," Youngblood jested, "that I had to run around in the shower to get wet."

Apparently, he was standing sideways, where no college scouts could see him.

Armed with those salt-of-the-earth teachings, young Jack took on college. It was 1967, and the football program was in transition, just a year after Steve Spurrier had graduated and two years before the "Super Sophs" would emerge. But Florida football was in for a two-year downturn.

After a year of playing freshman ball, Youngblood was without real direction. He wanted to be a middle linebacker. Former player and graduate assistant Jim "Red Truck" Benson made Youngblood an offensive lineman at first.

"The first day I had to go through the drills with Jim Benson, it was like somebody had licked all the red off my sucker," Youngblood recalled. "On top of that experience with Benson, I was told—I think it was freshman coach Jim Haynes—I was too tall to play middle linebacker. And they had signed a high school All-American, Tom Kelley out of Tampa, for that position. I wanted to compete for it, but he was destined to be their middle linebacker of the future."

One day in the trenches with the bigger boys convinced the skinny 6-foot-4, 200-pound kid from Monticello that he needed to be stronger. That's when Youngblood embarked on a weight training program that put 15 pounds a year on his frame for the next three seasons and would eventually move him into the world-class category as a football player.

That sweat-of-the-brow commitment bulked him up to 250 pounds by his senior year and helped mold Youngblood into one of the greatest defensive ends in NFL history.

Youngblood's experience over those four years was virtually Dickens-like: the best of times, the worst of times. As a junior, he had a good seat for that magical 1969 season of the "Super Sophs." But he was also there in 1968 for the 51-0 drubbing by Georgia. He called it "… the worst butt-whipping I ever took." And he was around during all the turmoil post-1969, when Florida changed coaches.

Youngblood considered this a "growth period," and it was then he began to learn what it took to play at a higher level. What helped was the installation of the four-three defense (four linemen, three linebackers), which played to Youngblood's strengths. Graves stepped down. Dickey was hired. The players, including Youngblood, wanted the old staff, but at least his position coach, Jack Thompson, had been retained.

And eventually, the players began to accept it. This was going to be Youngblood's senior year, so he began to focus on it. He still had "no idea" he would be a pro football star—let alone an All-America, first-round draft pick of the Rams, and later an All-Pro and Hall of Famer.

Another father-figure type was his Rams teammate, Merlin Olsen, who marveled at Youngblood as a football player. Olsen called him "the perfect defensive end," and Jack looked the part. His body was chiseled, and his faced framed by a square jaw.

Youngblood's pain tolerance was incredible. If he'd been that cowboy with a bullet in his shoulder we've seen so many times in the movies, he wouldn't have even asked for the swig of whiskey before they dug it out with a hot knife. It seemed like a bazooka couldn't knock Youngblood out of the lineup—a broken leg sure couldn't.

The Iron Man of the Los Angeles Rams played in a record 201 consecutive games, missing only one in 14 seasons—that one during his final 1984 campaign. He went on to become All-Pro in 1974, 1975, 1976, 1978, and 1979, and All-NFC seven times, playing in seven straight Pro Bowls. From 1973 to 1979, the Rams played in five NFC championship games and one Super Bowl (XIV after the 1979 season).

Coupled with the heroic act of playing in an NFL playoff game with a broken fibula, this incident vaulted Youngblood's legacy to legendary status in the Halls of Canton.

Many times has the story of that day been told, and much like Achilles' adventures, Youngblood's tale has become part of NFL lore. On the day in question, the Rams we're playing the Cowboys in Dallas in the divisional playoffs. Just before the half, Youngblood's foot got stuck in the turf, and he was pinned against somebody when he felt it snap just above the ankle. The pain was excruciating, and they immediately transported their defensive star to the locker room. But the pain of missing the game was greater for Youngblood. As he was lying there, waiting for the results of the X-ray,

Youngblood screamed: "Somebody come in here and tape this damn thing up and bring me some aspirin!"

The team doctor responded: "I can't do that! Your fibula's snapped like a pencil."

"I said I didn't care," recalled Youngblood, "and he sticks the X-ray in that light board they had and said, 'Look! You got a broken bone!'

"I told the trainers, 'Tape me up!' And so they came in, strapped my leg as tight as they could. The pain was excruciating. I can't even describe it. But they couldn't shoot the bone with a painkiller—that stuff doesn't work on bone—and I got up."

By the third quarter, following a conversation with Coach Ray Malavasi, Youngblood was ready to go back in. And only one teammate knew how badly Jack was hurt because they didn't want the Cowboys to know. He already had a difficult enough chore in attempting to elude the blocks of Dallas lineman Rayfield Wright. On the first play, he pushed off his good leg in pursuit of the elusive Roger Staubach and sacked the Hall of Fame quarterback. The Rams went on to upset Dallas and make it all the way to the Super Bowl.

The pain was still there. After his ninth, Jack Youngblood lost count of the beers he consumed on the team plane back to L.A. After that he wore a plastic brace and never missed a defensive play the rest of the 1979 postseason, right through NFC title game and Super Bowl XIV against the Pittsburgh Steelers. He was inducted into the Hall of Fame in 2001.

It turned out that the skinny kid from Monticello could play a little football after all. Remarkably, even after such a distinguished career, Youngblood looks back and thinks, "I could have been better. How could I have helped us win that game which we lost?"

The voice of Herbert Jackson Youngblood Sr., or "Granddaddy," still rings in the Hall of Famer's head.

Big-Time Players, Smalltown Boys

Gainesville is situated in the middle of the Jacksonville-Tampa-Orlando triangle, and numerous Gator stars have come from those cities. But for nearly a century, some of Florida's greatest players have also been smalltown boys—Jack Youngblood being one of many.

Towns such as Brooksville, Macclenny, Mims, Longwood, Belle Glade, Live Oak, St. Augustine, Bushnell, Arcadia, Venice, Fort Walton, Ocala, Starke, Apopka, Port Charlotte, Monticello, Wildwood, Newberry, Melbourne, Fort Pierce, Stuart, Fort White, Vero Beach, Alachua, Mayo,

Marianna, Lake Wales, Graceville, Anthony, Dade City, Fort Meade, Leesburg, and Clermont have produced outstanding Gator performers.

Two such players were All-Americans Burton Lawless of Punta Gorda and Wes Chandler of New Smyrna Beach.

"I was just a small-town boy when I got out of Charlotte High," said Lawless. "In fact, when I went to Florida in 1970, the enrollment was about the same size of Charlotte County's population."

The son of a high school administrator who originally came from Alabama, Lawless drew recognition in high school as a tight end and soon had scouts from Tuscaloosa showing up at his door. Fortunately for Florida, Bear Bryant was at a low point in his career, just coming off 6-5 and 6-5-1 records in 1969 and 1970. But it wouldn't have mattered anyway. Burton's parents were Auburn graduates.

"It took me about 30 seconds to decide I was going to play at Florida," said Lawless, who now shares time between his home in Waco, Texas, and Punta Gorda. "I was born in Alabama, but I was only there about nine months. I'm a Florida boy. I figured, being from Punta Gorda, it would be easier for my parents to see me play—and they saw me play every game."

The Gators benefited from that decision, because Lawless enrolled as a freshman in 1971, went on to become All-America, and was later named to Florida's Team of the Century.

It had looked like a clear path for Lawless as a Gator, since stellar tight end Jim Yancey was graduating. "But they didn't tell me about old Hank Foldberg [Jr.]—6-feet-5, 235 pounds, waiting in the wings."

On his first practice play during a passing drill, Lawless broke his shoulder and missed six weeks. When he returned, they made Lawless an offensive tackle, later moving him to guard. "For me, it was the best thing that ever happened because I got to play," said Lawless.

By Burton's senior year, Dickey had gotten closer to turning the program around as Florida secretly put in the wishbone attack that had become so popular. They opened up 1974 with four straight wins before stumbling against Vanderbilt in Nashville, 24-10. The Gators did win the next three games before the 17-16 loss to Georgia, but were picked for the Sugar Bowl to play Nebraska. They lost, 13-10, and it remains a huge disappointment for Lawless.

"If I hadn't gone on to play for the Cowboys who won the Super Bowl, I might have even bigger regrets about that," said Lawless.

Florida went 8-4 that year, Dickey's best so far in the five seasons he'd been there.

When Hurricane Charley wreaked havoc on Burton's hometown of Punta Gorda on August 13, 2004, it brought with it an old friend. A few days later, former Gator teammate Ralph Ortega, the All-America linebacker, showed up with a generator for Lawless.

"He spent a couple of days with me," said Lawless. "It was great. Ralph and I hadn't spent time together in 25-30 years. It rekindled our friendship, and it was just like it was in college. It was a really special time. He and I have e-mailed each other and talked on the phone a number of times. When you get together with your old friends from Florida, it's just like it was when you were in school. You really never leave in your mind. But we're still kids, and we enjoyed that time being together."

That led to a subsequent summer reunion for three "Boys From Old Florida" in Punta Gorda at the River City Grill—a smalltown boy, Lawless, and two teammates from urban South Florida, Ortega and Glenn Cameron. Lawless reflected on that day and the excellence of players like Ortega and his close friend, Glenn Cameron, who had been together all the way through junior high, high school, and college together. "Heck, they even went to kindergarten together," said Lawless. Only the NFL split them up. "Glenn was drafted in the first round. Ralph was drafted in the second round," said Lawless. (Cameron went to the Bengals; Ortega to the Falcons; Lawless in the second round to the Cowboys.)

If it was possible to have "bookend" linebackers, the Gators had them in Ortega and Cameron. "They were almost identical, both about six-one, about 235 [pounds] and both of them ran about a 4.6 or 4.7 [40-yard dash]," said Lawless. "They could bench press 400 pounds. They would hit you. And they were the toughest guys to hit or get hit by on the defense. They were tougher than nails."

During that era, Ortega and Cameron anchored the SEC's No. 1 defense as inside linebackers, starting for three seasons, and each making All-SEC first team on different years. Both played in the 1975 College All-Star Game.

Together with All-America linebacker Sammy Green of Fort Meade, a year behind them in school, the Gator threesome made a formidable linebacking trio in the mid-1970s. "Sammy was built like Charles Atlas," remembered Lawless. Of the threesome, he said: "They had the size, the speed, and the toughness."

Dickey remembers how fortunate he was to have three outstanding linebackers at once. "Ralph Ortega and Glenn Cameron were just special football players physically at linebacker—Sammy Green the same thing. They were all anybody would want on any given day to play that position."

Race was still an issue for many. Green was black; Lawless is white. That only needs explaining due to the social change that was happening. Florida had begun to recruit more black players. Lawless welcomed the change. "I always had black kids on my team, so that wasn't a problem," he said.

After Willie Jackson and Leonard George had broken the Gators' color line in 1969, Vince Kendrick became the third African-American to wear the orange and blue. Kendrick teamed up with Don Gaffney, who became the first black quarterback to start for Florida, and, coincidentally, they led the Gators into Auburn's Cliff Hare Stadium and on to a 12-8 triumph that stopped a four-game losing streak and ended Dickey-resignation rumors. Gaffney also returned to his hometown of Jacksonville and helped defeat Georgia, 11-10, the following week—a team that had beaten Florida four times in the past five years. Gaffney's touchdown pass and two-point conversion pass made the difference.

Lawless grew up without prejudice. His father, a former Auburn football player, had been a central figure in the integration of Charlotte High School. In his first year as the Charlotte High principal, Burton Lawless Sr. canceled the series with DeSoto High School of Arcadia and threatened to do so with other schools that refused to compete against Charlotte's integrated team or not allow the Tarpon band to play if it had black musicians. His son knew it was wrong to discriminate.

"The four black kids who came on the team when I was there were great guys, and they were my friends," said Lawless. "And Vince Kendrick is one of the finest human beings on the face of this earth. I think the world of Vince Kendrick."

As in all athletic programs in the South, eventually some race problems would emerge. Dickey had been successful in bringing black players into the Vols football program, although he did get hate mail. He said he felt the transition was easier in Tennessee, however, than in Florida due to resistance utilized through the legal system.

"I think it goes back to the lawsuits," Dickey said. "When I got there in 1970, Alachua County was one of the counties that had gone to the Supreme Court. And it was ruled they had to integrate and could not have separate but equal [facilities]."

Consequently, it slowed down the integration process, whereas that hadn't happened in Tennessee. "People had a hard time with it at Florida. But the people in East Tennessee were not as vocally troubled by integration as they were in the state of Florida," Dickey said.

People like Burton Lawless helped make it a smoother transition.

Integration changed the balance of power in all of college football, and the state of Florida began to reap the benefits. Miami, Florida State, and Florida were the beneficiaries of that windfall. And the day Wes Chandler of New Smyrna Beach walked in the door, things got a lot better in Gainesville.

When Chandler began high school, he didn't have to overcome an obscure town like New Smyrna or playing at a small school—he faced a program in shambles. His high school team hadn't won a game in several seasons. Luckily, a new coach arrived at about the same time Chandler began playing. Bud Asher would inherit a talented group of young players Chandler's age. "And he had one goal in mind—to separate the athletes from the guys who wanted to hang on the corner," said Chandler.

(Again, because of the times, it should be noted that Chandler is black and Asher is white.)

After a slow start with only two wins in Chandler's sophomore year, New Smyrna Beach won 22 straight regular-season games, averaged a point and a half per minute, and led Central Florida in scoring. People began to hear about the small town of New Smyrna and a running back named Wes Chandler. They were going to hear about him for a long time to come. He was recruited or contacted by up to 300 colleges, but found good counsel from Asher for making his choice in 1974.

"I felt really good," Chandler recalled, "about being from this small town and this little school and going to Florida. I went there because I was very well guided by my head coach, Bud Asher."

Surprisingly, Bethune-Cookman College, an all-black school in nearby Daytona, didn't want Chandler. "Wesley Moore was the head coach, and Wesley Moore said I was too small," Chandler said. "What's funny is that we put in the wishbone [at New Smyrna] just for Bethune-Cookman College, because of my high school quarterback, Reggie Beverly, who was a helluva quarterback. We ended up in Bud's backyard running wishbone plays. But he [Beverly] was only about 5 feet, 5 inches, 120 pounds. At the time, I was 5 feet, 11 inches, 156 pounds—but I was still growing, and he wasn't! So I was really hurt that Bethune-Cookman College and Wesley Moore said I was too small to play for them."

Baron H. "Bud" Asher was a well-traveled football coach whose career spanned New Smyrna and Father Lopez high schools; the Jacksonville Sharks of the World Football League; and Orlando of the Southern Football League. He later served as a Daytona Beach city councilman and was mayor of Daytona until 2003, whereupon he joined the coaching staff of Daytona Mainland during its state championship season. Asher, working on behalf of Wes to get him into Bethune, would become Chandler's attorney, close friend, and advisor for life.

"Beginning when I played for him in high school and getting to know Bud Asher the coach and the man, we established a relationship in sports that was one for the ages," Chandler said in early 2006, while seeking employment as an NFL assistant. "We've been together for a long, long time—he knows the game very well, from high school, to college ball, to pro ball. He directed me toward Florida, being close to home and giving my parents an opportunity to see me play, along with my family and friends."

Another person who strongly influenced Chandler was Nat Moore, whose senior year hadn't been all that great due to serious injuries, but whose style and grace—as a person and a player—were impressive. Moore, later a star receiver for the Miami Dolphins, would play a large role in convincing Wes to become a Gator.

"There was a strong bond between me and Nat Moore. When I came out of high school, even though I played everything and did everything, I was a running back, and we both wore the number 33," said Chandler.

In later years, Moore and Chandler had a friendly rivalry, often ribbing each other about who was the better receiver. They both wound up as wide receivers, wearing No. 89.

Chandler was also very close to Florida assistant coach Don Breaux. "He recruited me, and he was like my best friend, in my house every week," said Chandler. "But what was good for me turned out to be good for Florida, too."

Meanwhile, during Chandler's senior year at New Smyrna, things were changing in Gainesville, and Dickey was under fire with a 16-16-1 mark after three seasons. Unbeknownst to Asher and Chandler, the Gators would be secretly installing the wishbone attack to start the 1974 season.

The heat escalated during in 1973. In the sixth game—following three straight losses—quarterback David Bowden threw the ball out of bounds to stop the clock on fourth down against Ole Miss on a lamentable play. The Rebels won, 13-10. The next week, Dickey went to a running quarterback in Gaffney, whom he used for the next two seasons. The Gators salvaged a 7-4 regular-season record in 1973, but had the embarrassment of losing to Miami of Ohio, 16-7, in a Tangerine Bowl game played before their home crowd at Florida Field. Chandler arrived the following year. David Bowden dropped football and only played baseball after that.

Then came the day Chandler had dreamed about: running on Florida Field the first time with the crowd screaming as announcer Jim Finch growls, "Heeeerrrre come the Gators!"

"I almost peed in my pants," Chandler said. "You talk about a smalltown boy! I wasn't used to playing in front of crowds like that. I played in playoff games in high school, but when you walk out in front of 75- or 80,000 screaming Gator fans at Florida Field, your hands start to sweat. I can remember the first time they were going to throw a pass to me. You know where it was going. Jimmy Fisher called it in the huddle, and the moment he said that particular play, my hands started to sweat. It was against Miami, and I said to myself, 'Oh, my goodness, he called x-post.' You talk about water being poured on your hands!"

Chandler made an immediate impact with his remarkable athleticism, acrobatic catches, blazing speed, and versatility as a running back, punt returner, and receiver. As a freshman, he was used sparingly, but learned how to play the position from senior Lee McGriff.

"What a treat it was to be tutored by a guy like that," Chandler said of McGriff. "He was a class person and a helluva player for his size. I learned a lot from Lee."

Chandler also learned quickly to watch out for the headhunters on the Florida defense like linebacker Sammy Green and safety Wayne Fields in practice scrimmages. "I was a little scared," Chandler admitted. "Wayne Fields was always out to get me. But Jimmy DuBose always kept me balanced, giving me food for thought and pep talks to keep me going. James Richards always kept me laughing."

By his sophomore year, Chandler was the team's leading receiver. Although he caught only 20 balls, five of them were for touchdowns, and his per-catch average was a whopping 22.9 yards. He was one of the keys in Dickey's best season, a nine-win year that fell just short of an SEC title by the virtue of a 10-7 loss to Georgia.

As good as his second year had been, that didn't measure up to the "Super Soph" Chandler had always idolized—that player who had once caught 15 balls in one game—Carlos Alvarez.

"When I first arrived at Florida, the first photo I saw was Carlos Alvarez, the All-America photo of him catching the ball. That has stood out to me for so long. When I look through the record books—and I look at Gator football at the records he held that stood for so long and the things he was able to do for so long as a receiver—I look, and he's a little guy! He's not a great big guy. And for him to accomplish so much was just unbelievable," said Chandler.

The light bulb didn't click on for Chandler until his junior season. On the bus rides to and from Ocala before each home game, he realized he had some special God-given skills.

"Those rides were so unbelievable," said Chandler. "Just coming back [for the game at Florida Field], wondering if I could turn in a performance that day that I had put in the week before. And so I realized it was God's way, it was God's gift. It was His will, His talent; and I was just a soldier doing his work. That's when I really realized I had to ability to play at the next level."

At the same time, his success needed to be in the same context of the team's. And he admired his coach.

Chandler and his teammates were so impressed with Dickey's physical stature (he was 6 feet, 4 inches), so much so that they imagined him even taller. "We called him 'Tall Man' because coming out of high school when you're 5-feet-10 or so—you're talking about a guy around 6-feet-6. I had nothing but respect because of the seriousness and the energy with which he approached us. And then he had that boyish smile. The man had a great smile. It made you want to go out and do whatever you could to win a football game with him."

During his time at Florida, Chandler did help win some games from Dickey—30 over the four-year stretch.

In the same genre of Richard Trapp—the lanky, rubber-like receiver of the 1960s—Chandler's zigzag running, along with blazing speed and excellent concentration for catching the ball, fooled defenders. As a senior against Auburn, he demonstrated those skills in the 24-19 win over the Tigers, going 44 yards with a pass from Jimmy Fisher for a touchdown. He followed up with an 84-yard run described by Jack Hairston of the *Gainesville Sun* as, "… a breakaway run by Chandler reminiscent of Richard Trapp's long touchdown reception run against Georgia nine years ago."

Even more spectacular was the one-handed catch Chandler made against Georgia in 1977, almost beating the Bulldogs single-handedly. He hauled in the toss from quarterback Terry LeCount with his left hand, somehow managing to stay in bounds. In the second half, Dickey lined him up at running back, whereupon Wes scored from 18 yards out in the third period and then wrapped up the victory with another touchdown run in the fourth.

"Probably the best all-round player I had while I was there was Wes Chandler," said Dickey. "He could make more happen to change the course of the game than anybody. He made the some of the greatest catches and runs … just really fast, and probably the best athlete I coached."

In those four years at Florida, Asher stayed out of Chandler's personal affairs until it was time for more counsel about pro football. And when his pro football career was over, Wes then followed Asher's advice— and his footsteps. "He never got into my thoughts about pro football until my senior year was almost over," said Chandler. "He wound up coaching at Father Lopez. Ironically, when I got through playing pro ball, I became his offensive coordinator. And after that, I became the head coach and athletic director of Father Lopez."

On rare occasion, Chandler daydreams about what it would have been like playing for the Gators when the forward pass was king. "There's so much about Florida football that I admire, if I'd just had a chance to play for Spurrier when they were playing Spurrier ball. I had my chance to play [for San Diego] when I played in the 'Air Coryell' system, where all they did is play 'catch.' And so I know what that was like. But to relate it back to Florida football with what Spurrier did …"

And then Chandler caught himself.

"… I really can't say it, because I'm so happy to have played when I played and the people that I got to know." Like Lawless, Chandler treasures the relationships he built, the moments off the field with his friends and teammates at Florida just as much as the ones playing.

"Just the camaraderie at Yon Hall, hanging out with the guys, talking and getting to know them as people meant so much to me. Your college years are the best years of your life, it's often said. If you've ever gone to college, when look at the people you've met and the cordiality among friends … it's unbelievable. Those friendships will last you a lifetime," Chandler said.

Since that time, athletes no longer live in one facility. However, Gator players of various eras have begun bonding at various functions.

"I never knew Carlos Alvarez," said Chandler. "I never met Carlos Alvarez until we had that [Team of the Century] anniversary. Just having a chance to sit down and talk to this man! Because in Florida football, this man was 'The Receiver'. Just talking about football was so great. He was so down to earth … said he would like to give more credit to others than himself."

Chandler also talked of meeting other former teammates he has seen along the way.

"Burton Lawless, when I was coaching with the Cowboys; Emmitt Smith—of course, I've known Emmitt a long, long time. The memories of Gator football is all of that, but more importantly, when I was there it was the locker room, the camaraderie—the Yon Hall concept of team who became family. Just watching television down in the lounge. You never watched it in the room when everybody was in the lounge. I was playing bumper pool, or pool, or ping-pong, or watching television, or playing cards … we were just that close. We went to the Rathskeller, or the [Student] Union. We all went together. And it was always fun, no matter who you went with.

"I also marveled at watching my teammates. To see them display their talents was a real treat for me, and I guess my inspiration and my motivation outside of my family … the guys that I played with, watching their efforts and their energy."

It motivated Chandler to become one of only eight two-time All-Americans at Florida. One could only dream about how many records he would own today if the Gators hadn't gone to the wishbone. He also had quarterbacks who were run-first, pass-second. In his senior season, Chandler even had Collinsworth, an All-America receiver-to-be, under center for a few games.

That motivation also carried over into his NFL career as a wide receiver for New Orleans Saints (1978-81), San Diego Chargers (1981-87), and San Francisco 49ers (1988). As the third player chosen in the draft, Chandler went from ridiculous to sublime, first playing for the New Orleans "Ain'ts" before being traded to San Diego to play for Don Coryell in the "Air Coryell" offense. He was named to the Pro Bowl three times, and in 2000 was picked as a member of the All-Time Chargers team. He was also named as the NFL's Receiver of the Year in 1982.

In his college days, Wes would drive home to New Smyrna in the off-season and, after making All-America his junior year at Florida, he'd take a little side detour on the way. "I made it a point to drive through Daytona on Second Avenue, right down the heart of Bethune," Chandler said with a big laugh. "As a matter of fact, I often stopped to go see my good friend and high school teammate, Reggie Beverly."

He wanted to make sure Wesley Moore didn't forget about him. After all these years and Chandler's success, there's no danger of that.

Afterword

Different eras present different challenges for coaches. Dickey took over for a successful and popular predecessor and also had to coach in a difficult climate. Although Dickey's teams improved in the mid-1970 and came close to winning SEC titles a couple of times, his overall record never matched what he did at Tennessee—nor did it surpass that of Graves. In fact, Graves won 13 more games and had a better winning percentage than Dickey, .686 to .573. The 9-1-1 record of Graves' 1969 team captained by Mac Steen and Tom Abdelnour was better than any of Dickey's, including the 9-3 record of the 1975 club captained by Jimmy DuBose and Sammy Green.

Dickey went to four bowls and won none; Graves was 4-1 in post-season. Dickey's 1974 team had lost four straight before becoming the first Florida team to beat Auburn on the road—followed by wins over FSU, Georgia, and Miami in the same month. Graves was 7-2-1 against Georgia. Dickey was 3-6.

Giving credit where it is due, however, Dickey brought in a rookie quarterbacks coach in his final season to spice up his offense. His name was Steve Spurrier. Both of them were fired the next year after losing three of the last four games and finishing 4-7. Both of them would wind up in the College Football Hall of Fame one day, taking different routes to get there.

In retrospect, the Dickey-for-Graves swap was probably a hasty decision for everyone involved. The manner in which it unfolded accounts for part of the bitter aftertaste, although nobody appears to have held a major grudge after nearly 40 years. But it surely cannot be measured as one of the University of Florida's shining moments.

"Doug just never got close to his players," said one former Gator who played in the NFL, but didn't want to be named. "He was just not very personal. And we had some great players. I think that one of the things that did Coach Dickey in was when one of the big papers in the state—I forget which—ran a story listing all the Gators who had gone on to play in the NFL."

Dickey acknowledges the wealth of talent. "We had some really outstanding players who I really enjoyed coaching," he said. "Guys who were terrific kids and wanted to do their best for Florida. I think we all felt good that we were doing that, and all of a sudden it seemed the world got down on us. We couldn't really get it done in recruiting anymore because they [critics] said, 'You can't win the championship. You missed it by one play or by one game there, and that's not good enough. You've had your chance. Seven or eight years is enough. And you don't get another chance.' And that was kind of the way it went down. I pretty much accepted that as the way it was. Public opinion of us got down, and the players wouldn't come."

Ironically, like Graves and Spurrier, Dickey feels dreaded Georgia and his friend Vince Dooley played a role in his demise. In 1975, the Gators were 7-1 and unbeaten in the SEC when they played the Bulldogs but lost 10-7. Although Florida dominated the game, Georgia's tight-end-around pass from Richard Appleby to Gene Washington proved to be the backbreaker. Quarterback Matt Robinson handed it to Appleby; then the tight end pulled up and threw to a streaking Washington behind the Florida secondary.

The following year, after losing the opener, 24-21, to North Carolina, Dickey's team rolled up six straight wins before losing to Georgia 41-27 after leading by 14 at the half. One play, referred to now as "Fourth and Dumb", seemed to take the air out of the Gators, who had their fastest backfield ever in Earl Carr, Willie Wilder, and Tony Green, with Terry LeCount at quarterback. Dickey, sensing Georgia's swelling momentum, decided to go for it—on fourth-and-2 from his own 30. "With the wind against us, I didn't think our punter could kick it very far," said Dickey. "We ran an option play, and Earl Carr made about a yard. The safetyman [Johnny Henderson] came up and made a great tackle. If he doesn't make that tackle, Earl Carr goes 70 yards for a touchdown."

Those games weren't forgotten. By 1978, they had culminated into a final straw against Dickey, who was fired.

After a brief stopover in Colorado with Chuck Fairbanks, Dickey got out of coaching and went into private business. When Bob Woodruff called and offered Dickey a job to succeed him as Tennessee athletics director, Dickey accepted. He retired in 2006 and planned to move back to Florida.

Football is only part of the legacy for coaches and players. Perhaps off-the-field relationships between Graves and his players left the most indelible imprint on the program: providing the opportunity for educational advancement.

Aside from Graves' success as a coach, he was also revered by his players for embracing them as students, always making education available, even if they couldn't play. Thus he endeared himself to people like linebacker Wayne McCall, a prominent Ocala attorney.

"One of the reasons the graduation rate was so high was that, if you signed with the Gators, you were guaranteed the opportunity to graduate. If you got hurt the first day, you got the opportunity," said McCall. "If you didn't graduate in four years, you got the opportunity. If you wanted to go to graduate school and got it, you got the opportunity. You might work as a manager or as a graduate assistant, but you got the opportunity.

"When I started, there were graduate assistants who were in law school. I thought I wanted to be a college coach. I went into the Army because of my two-year commitment through ROTC. I planned to come back to law school, work as a graduate assistant, and then choose. Meanwhile, Doug Dickey came in and discontinued the program, which, of course, was his choice."

Every year at the "Silver Sixties" reunion, lawyers, doctors, dentists, educators, politicians, engineers—a diverse group of men who benefited from Graves' enlightened position—come together to celebrate and commemorate much more than mere football.

Big-time college football, however, is all about winning and raising money—and by that count, the next coach would be the best in Florida's athletic history.

Some, though, say Charley Pell might have done that a little too well.

6

The Charley Pell Era

1979 - 1984

The Patron Saint of Lost Causes

Charley Pell was a man of many colors, and he loved them all—the crimson of Alabama, red of Jacksonville State, orange of Clemson, and the orange and blue of Florida. He played or coached at all those places, wore their colors proudly, and demanded the same loyalty that he professed from the fan base. Pell also loved the color green, as in money—not for himself, but to pay for the bricks and mortar. If each coach from each era represents a cornerstone in the development of Florida football, Pell's legacy was an entire brick wall. His fundraising acumen provided the infusion of cash needed to upgrade the program, and his enthusiastic vision forged a template for future success.

Pell could have been perceived as anyone from Bill Gates to Robin Hood. But how will he be remembered? Is his legacy threatened by a Watergate-like purgatory of misdeed? No, according to many friends and former associates, who insist Pell was *not* Jesse James—*not* a crook. He was also not totally innocent. He did wrong. He paid. He gave far more than he got; and what little he got, he left behind. His loyalty-up, loyalty-down philosophy was admirable but ultimately led to his demise when the NCAA demanded a sacrifice. In that sense, Pell was a tragic figure.

Pell refurbished Gator pride with loyalty oaths and currency. He governed through the pioneering of Gator Clubs, which have since gone global. All of this translated into success on the field as Pell brought Florida into the national championship arena. And he even rebuilt that arena, expanding Florida Field right away, improving all the facilities without using a dime of the school's money. He built it—they came.

Back in the mid-1990s, I took a random sampling of influential Gator fans and key members of the media, asking them to name the three biggest reasons behind the Gators' success. An estimated 80 percent said Charley Pell was one of them. This came about 10 years after he had been run out of Gainesville with a list of 57 NCAA infractions stuck to his head like a target. In the straw vote, though, Pell was mentioned right up there with Steve Spurrier and Ray Graves. Without Pell's enthusiasm, solicitation of funds, and organizational skills, Gator football might yet be light years behind.

Upon arriving via Clemson in late 1978, Pell knew right away his challenge would be mammoth. The task of pumping pride back into a flagging program that had been below .500 the past two seasons was far more strenuous than he could have fathomed. Had he realized the depth of disarray, perhaps Pell would have never left Clemson. The damage went far beyond the on-field losses.

Pell came with a reputation as a consensus builder, motivator, fund-raiser, recruiter, and disciplinarian from the Bear Bryant school of coaching. He had just put Clemson on the map with an 11-1 season (8-3-1 the year before). Life was good. The Pells had been living in their dream house for a mere month when the University of Florida began courting the two-time Atlantic Coast Conference Coach of the Year.

It all came about so fast, unfolding in a semi-secretive manner. Charley had been contacted by Florida through Dallas Cowboys Player Personnel Director Gil Brandt. Without cell phones in those days, reaching coaches during the recruiting process, when they were on the road, was impossible; therefore, Charley's wife, Ward, took most of the messages and relayed them to her husband whenever he finally surfaced. Perhaps she wasn't completely forthcoming with the Florida big shots, but she wasn't wild about being uprooted like a vagabond again either.

"Here we were at Clemson, things were going wonderfully well, it was a great program with wonderful facilities," said Ward, Charley's widow. "The only thing they had as a negative was they hadn't been able to win in football. Now all of a sudden they are winning in football. Things were great. We finished construction on our dream house that we had planned to build two years prior. I loved it. Carrick [their youngest son] loved it. Everybody was happy. We moved in that house and we lived in it one month and one day. Then the University of Florida called."

How could Charley possibly turn down one of the best college coaching jobs in America? "It wouldn't have been difficult for me to turn down. I loved Clemson," Ward said. "There was no place any prettier than Clemson and Lake Hartwell."

Pell was not a man to linger in his decision-making. Though he claimed that he informed Clemson of his interest in the Florida job, athletic department officials acted like scorned lovers and accused him of dealing behind their backs. Florida was on a fast track to replace Doug Dickey, and Pell received a full-court press.

Charley had already been scheduled to speak to the Jacksonville Beach Quarterback Club, but was headed to Georgia for a recruiting trip on December 4, 1978. This would be a fortuitous meeting for Pell and Florida, because it would eventually play a big role in the foundation of the Gator Clubs. "He ended up in the baggage department of Eastern Airlines at Greenville-Spartanburg Airport," Ward said. "And that's where they did the interview." And the deal was struck right there in the Eastern baggage department.

"Charley called Clemson, and they attempted to keep him, but Charley was going to sign with Florida," Ward said. Pell succeeded Dickey for the 1979 season. Florida needed that effusive Charley Pell Type-A personality at that time, somebody with fresh enthusiasm. Little did they know they were also getting an obsessive-compulsive whose attitude would be good for the Gators, but bad for his own personal health.

Pell showed up in Gainesville for the job sight unseen. After inspecting the tattered athletic dormitory, noting the absence of a first-class weight room and observing the early austere décor of the football offices, Pell actually became physically ill. The orange plastic sofa with duct tape plastered on it in his new office became a symbol of despair.

"What slum lord lives here?" Ward quipped after seeing the sofa. "Well *that*," Charley said in mock protest, "happens to be in *my* office."

"I almost left him," said Ward. "I just looked at him and said, 'You have got to be the dumbest man ... I cannot believe I'm in love with a man so dumb. I guess that makes me the dumbest woman, so what are we going to do?' It was just deplorable."

They took the challenge and began digging themselves—and the Gator football program—out of the hole. This was the Charley Pell way: adopting a bunker mentality, issuing the call for allegiance, and then going on a crusade for funding. Such a mode was critical to his success, because Pell always seemed to wind up landing jobs where winning had been on a sabbatical and facilities needed a visit from one of those television home-makeover experts. First Jacksonville State, then Clemson—now Florida, where contributions were sparse, and the athletic facilities had become among the worst in the Southeastern Conference.

To say that Charley Pell was "The Patron Saint of Lost Causes" for college football would not be too strong in Ward's estimation.

"If it was downtrodden, with a lack of funds, with everyone else writing it off as a no-win situation," Ward said from her Alabama home, "then Charley was there with arms open to hug it."

Things didn't get much better after a few months. While walking the route of Tampa's Gasparilla Parade in February of 1979, Pell noticed that, out of the thousands of people, hardly anybody was wearing attire with "Florida" on it. Pell knew right then he had a tough sell. He needed fan loyalty. He needed football players. He needed new facilities. And he was going to need money—lots of money.

The money wasn't for him. Pell never made more than a five-figure salary at Florida in his final college position. "In our day, they didn't pay them $2 million," Ward said. "He made $79,000 [at Florida]. And at the same time he was doing that, Jackie Sherrill was making $250,000 at Texas A&M."

When it came to asking for the money to support football, however, very few people could close the deal like Charley Pell. If he'd have chosen Wall Street or investment banking, the man may have been a billionaire. "Yeah," Ward said cynically in agreement, "instead of a broke football coach."

Few coaches had the ability to prompt a checkbook-whipout at a Gator gathering like the former Alabama lineman. Pell realized early in his coaching career that he needed a money-green thumb. His gift for raising money would put Florida football back in the game. "The gift was not so much being able to ask for it [money]," said Ward, "but being able to convey to the people the love and loyalty they could show to the University of Florida—and the need of their school. Plus, they could have pride because of their contribution."

Pell immediately built a more inclusive network of people around the state, healing some of the wounds created by the cracked fan base by broadening the circle of Gator Club membership. Up until 1979, Florida football booster membership had consisted mostly of white-collar graduates, almost all in the state of Florida.

As late as 1978, a Florida alumni group met regularly in Jacksonville, sometimes at Brewmasters, and its members were constantly fighting among themselves. "On one side, it would be pro-Dickey and the other side would be anti-Dickey," said Jacksonville attorney Bill Dorsey, himself a former scrappy defensive lineman from the 1960s. "We'd watch the film. It was very divided, especially toward the latter part, when they were really spiraling downhill. We all wanted to do something to bring us together."

The Jacksonville Beach Quarterback Club had already booked Pell while he was Clemson's coach. By the time he reached the Turtle Club for the speaking engagement, he was already the head coach at Florida. That's when he struck up a relationship with Dorsey and four other concerned Gators.

Five Jacksonville men would help change the power base of Florida football forever—Dorsey, Marty Edwards, George Garcia, Bill Gulliford, and John Seroyer—when they huddled up with Pell to conceive the strategy for Gators Clubs.

"And there was a feeling among some of us, 'What about "Joe Lunchbucket?"'" Dorsey said. "What about the guy who never went to college, much less Florida? He's just as big a Gator fan. Where's his place in this whole thing? Charley was the one who brought all that together."

This was a pivotal moment in the birth of "The Gator Nation," and it immediately swelled the ranks. The model came from Clemson. "Charley sat us down and told us about 'IPTAY,' which is what they had at Clemson," Dorsey said. "That was 'I pay 10 a year, I pay 20 a year, I pay 30 a year' … and at some point, 'I pay thousands a year.' He was just such a motivator and a leader. And he told us we needed to do something at Florida to bring everybody together. One of his famous sayings was, 'Florida's worst enemy is us'; and that anytime we complained about ourselves or our coach or our team, we were just feeding the enemy what they wanted to hear. And if we would stick together, there was nobody that could stop us.'"

Pell sold them on the fact that the IPTAY included people who may not have attended Clemson but supported everything the university did—not just football.

"So we decided we were going to start an organization called the 'Gator Club,'" Dorsey continued. "We got rid of that silly, goofy Gator on the logo and got something more fierce and ferocious. So we came up with this old Gator that had big teeth and eyes about to pop out."

The five men also agreed that their mission should be togetherness and bringing in more people from different backgrounds. For his part, Pell sent defensive line coach Dwight Adams and other coaches to tell stories and show game films to the Jacksonville enthusiasts. In no time, the membership grew to nearly 500 on a weeknight. There was no more bickering. "It just got bigger and bigger," said Dorsey, "and we got really involved in the Florida-Georgia game. We raised a ton of money. We were still getting beat by Georgia, but we had a good time."

A year later, Pell asked Mike Shanahan, then a 20-something offensive coordinator, to drive to Jacksonville and speak to the Gator Club. "I had just come there from Minnesota and was expecting maybe 50 people or so," Shanahan said, "and there were over 1,000!"

Pell took Florida football to the masses and made it public domain. "And that's what Charley wanted. People needed to have a sense of belonging," Ward said. "The first couple of months, we went to some alumni functions, and it was all strictly Florida alumni. They had not been trained to give to athletics. There had not been any capital improvement in the athletic department for football since 1959. Bob Woodruff was the last coach who had done anything to improve the facilities."

Everybody could get a piece of Florida football—or could buy an even bigger piece. Loyalty got you in the club, literally. Money advanced your standing. "All they had to be was a Gator," Pell once said. "Nothing else." Once in that circle, however, there was a financial obligation to support the cause.

What Sam Walton was to retailing, Pell had become to Florida football. The idea grew like crab grass, and as it began to spread, the University of Florida Alumni Association decided to take over the Gator Clubs. "There were some mixed emotions," Dorsey said of the UF alumni takeover. "We did it all—and we were Charley's boys."

The impact of Pell eventually went global. Among the countries today where Gator Clubs meet regularly these days are France, Taiwan, Bermuda, Peru, The Netherlands, England, Hungary, and Mumbai. And, oh yes, there is even a Korean Gator Club in Gainesville.

At first, though, it was small advances. Badcock furniture, thanks to the local storeowner Carl Ellis, donated some bedding for the oversized beds with thicker mattresses and longer frames for the big athletes. The family of the late Q. I. Roberts, owner of a nearby dairy, donated part of his estate toward building a new dining hall, which was called the "Q. I. Roberts Dining Hall."

Linebacker Scot Brantley, a senior holdover from the Doug Dickey era, remembered how bad the conditions were in the athletic dorm. "We were on concrete floors in our dorm rooms and had the worst-looking facilities you could have," Brantley said. "We didn't even have central air-conditioning—Charley had window units put in. It was horrible. It was almost like being in prison."

One of the first checks came from the late Dave Thomas, founder of Wendy's, whose daughter was in school at Florida. The $50,000 in bacon-cheeseburger money went for a new weight room. That was a nice start, but Pell felt he needed much, much more. That's when they first told him about the rich man in Polk County.

Getting to Know 'Mr. Ben Hill'

As in football, fund-raising gurus need a go-to guy or go-to girl. What Charley Pell needed was somebody who could transform Florida football with the single stroke of a pen. Such a man was Ben Hill Griffin Jr., the wealthy pioneer of Polk County whose fortunes were made in citrus, phosphate, and real estate. Or, as the Pells called him, "Mr. Ben Hill."

"Charley asked, 'Who among the friends would have the wherewithal and the leadership ability to step forward, make a statement, and challenge others to come forward?'" Ward recalled. "They said, 'Ben Hill Griffin Jr.—but you'll never get a dime out of him. He's a great guy, but people have talked to him, and he's just not going to give any more.'"

They just hadn't sent the right man yet. No cultural divide existed between Florida's new football coach and one of Florida's richest and most powerful citizens, Ben Hill Griffin Jr. He and Charley Pell understood each other immediately, like only two small-town country boys could. Both were fiercely independent thinkers, hard-driving businessmen, and workaholics. Each valued the concept of grassroots networking. And they understood the importance of money and the obligations that came with it. They also loved catfish, collard greens, black-eyed peas, cornbread, fried chicken, and sweet tea.

Charley understood the Southern way of life. He was born as the second son of a working-class family and raised just up the road from Boaz and east of Arab—so far north of Tuscaloosa that he never hardly paid much attention to all that fuss about the Crimson Tide. He didn't play football until he was a senior in high school because his brother had gotten his nose broken as a player. His mother, Cleo Shirey Pell, only consented after she heard that the new coach, Bobby Golden, was a Baptist Deacon.

When a 'Bama assistant came to town to recruit the Albertville High quarterback, he wound up signing the slight six-foot, 169-pound running back instead. But only after "Mamaw" Pell was persuaded this playing football thing and getting a college education was on the up-and-up. Charley arrived in Tuscaloosa, driven by his mother and father (M.L. Pell). They waited in the car while Charley went in to ask assistant coach Jerry Claiborne if he could have a copy of his scholarship so his mother could see it. "I'd never been asked that before," Claiborne later said, somewhat befuddled.

The slight boy from Albertville soon became a three-year, two-way starting lineman for Bear Bryant, and a member of his first national championship team in 1961.

"Mr. Ben Hill" was born during a hurricane in Tiger Bay near Fort Meade, Florida, in 1911 and built a 10-acre citrus grove—a wedding gift from his father—into a $300-million empire. He had attended the University of Florida for three years. A conservative Democrat, he was an eight-year member of the Florida House of Representatives starting in 1956 and later lost a bid for governor against Reubin Askew. He lived mostly in Frostproof, spending much of his time at his Peace River fish camp.

They started with phone conversations. Then the Pells visited the Peace River fish camp. "When you went to Mr. Ben Hill's, you sat out on the porch and you ate. He just loved good home cookin'. It was just fun," Ward said. "Charley and Mr. Ben Hill developed a mutual admiration for each other right away."

They would sit and rock, and talk, or sometimes not. A tactic Pell learned from his grandfather was practicing the art of silence. "He taught me that sometimes you need to have the sense to keep your mouth shut," Charley once said. "He [Griffin] would ask a question, and it might be three or four minutes before he'd ask another one." Then one day, on just the second visit, Griffin said, "Whatcha need?"

The deal was done in just two visits to Polk County, and apparently the gift was offered before the naming rights were promised. Florida Field would bear the named "Ben Hill Griffin Stadium."

"Charley told him he thought that would be a great legacy to the Griffin family," Ward said.

Reportedly, Griffin said: "That'd be good, too."

The amount of the check written by "Mr. Ben Hill" is in question, but it was somewhere between $20 and $25 million—changing everything about Florida.

Griffin and Pell were a team. Contrary to rumors, Pell did not carry around a blank check in his pocket with Griffin's signature on it. "The check he had in his pocket from 'Mr. Ben Hill' was his heart and his generosity," Ward said. "And if we needed more of something else done, 'Mr. Ben Hill' could be depended on."

That Forgettable Season—1979

In the assemblage of his new staff and team, Pell made at least one—and maybe three—unfortunate choices of assistant coaches or administrators that came back to haunt him. This, coupled with the brazen zeal for supremacy, spelled the downfall of the Pell regime.

To say that the Pell era started out from scratch would be an understatement: 0 wins, 10 losses, one tie. While he had been busy raising money, things had gone from worse to awful. "That first year, so many things had to be done that the actual coaching was neglected to a great degree," Ward said.

Of all the ugly times endured by Florida football fans, never had there been a season like 1979. Since the Gators began playing a full regular-season schedule had they gone winless just once—that 0-9 campaign in the "Golden Era" of 1946.

Some 26 players would be kicked off the team, and others were demoted. In sorting out players, decisions had to be made on the injured and who may or may not be able to perform up to expectations without permanent harm to their physical being. Such a case was Scot Brantley, once one of the hottest prospects ever to come out of the state of Florida.

A two-time All-American at Ocala Forest when the Wildcats won back-to-back state championships in 1974-75—and *Parade Magazine*'s Defensive Player of the Year—Brantley been recruited by the likes of Woody Hayes, Bear Bryant, Vince Dooley, and all the premier schools in the country. That rarely happened to an athlete from Florida. His decision to become a Gator under Doug Dickey was a hugely popular one that was fostered, in part, by his fondness for defensive coordinator Doug Knotts. Scot also had a burning desire to carry on the legacy of excellent linebacking by players like Ralph Ortega and Glenn Cameron.

Brantley was proud to represent his hometown as well. "There were so many great Gators from Ocala," said Brantley. "It's indescribable; to know that you sat there in the stands watching them run on the field when you were a kid, and now you are doing it. I thought of some of the older players—Fred Montsdeoca, Red Mitchum. They went there, and they loved that school. There were so many that I wanted to write them all down, because I wanted to become like them. I knew since I was 16 years old that I would be at Florida. In a sense, you were representing them when you put on that uniform. And they said, 'Hey, that's the boy from Ocala!' I wanted all that."

One of the Gators from Ocala was his brother, John. That Scot was able to play for three seasons on the same college team with John, a quarterback, was very also meaningful. Scot and John had been playing contact football since they were seven and eight years old in a South Carolina midget league. When their father, John Jr., a bridge-builder, moved to Ocala in 1970 and found out there was no midget league program, he immediately helped start one.

"And that was one of the main reasons Ocala Forest won those back-to-back state championships," said Scot. Thirty-seven years later, the youth football program in Ocala also produced John Brantley IV, grandson of the bridge-builder and son of the ex-Gator quarterback, who would go on to star for Kerwin Bell's Ocala Trinity Catholic state championship team, but ultimately chose Texas over Florida as his college.

A hopeful feeling abounded that five-star recruits like Scot Brantley would make the difference for the Gators. Many people felt that with Brantley and other young defensive stalwarts on the way, Dickey might be able to turn the team around. Early expectations were met as the 1976 season started with six wins in seven games. Things fell apart against Georgia in a 41-27 loss, after Florida had led at the half. "I can't help but think back to that Georgia game," said Brantley. "We were going to win our first SEC title. We were taking ring sizes at halftime. And I will never forget seeing Erk Russell [Georgia defensive coordinator] come out a halftime. He was staring across the field, and you could see the blood streaming down his face. He had beat up on a locker at the half."

Despite that, the Gators could claim a piece of the SEC by beating Fran Curci's Kentucky team, which they failed to do. They lost to the Wildcats, 28-9. Still, Florida posted a respectable 8-3 record and played in the Sun Bowl, losing to Texas A&M, 37-14. For Dickey, it never got any better.

The 1978 season began badly as the Gators went 1-3, ending with a thud as Dickey's team was thumped by Florida State, 38-21, and lost a heartbreaker to Miami, 22-21. Dickey was fired before the Miami game, but coached anyway, and posted a 4-7 record

For three years as a starter, Scot lived up to his billing, twice being named All-SEC. Brother John started a few games in 1977, switching off with Terry LeCount, and by 1978 had won the job. In 1979, John beat out Tim Groves, Tyrone Young, Johnell Brown, and 5-foot-8 Larry Ochab before getting injured (Young went onto be a very good receiver. Brown became a running back; Groves a safety; and Ochab stayed at quarterback.)

Along came Charley Pell and all his enthusiasm. Scot was a fearsome All-SEC linebacker with All-America credentials. The dominating 6-foot-1, 230-pounder was already one of the leading all-time tacklers in Gator history when he was injured in the second game against Georgia Tech. (He wound up eight tackles short of the career record.)

In the early 1970s, Dickey had converted Florida Field to artificial turf. "Doug's Rug," as it would be known. This would factor in Brantley's serious head injury. As he was about to make a tackle, he slipped on the turf. "I remember it was a muggy, humid day at Florida Field, early in the game, when they [Tech] ran a fullback-lead play," Brantley said. "I got kneed upside the head, and that's the last I remember."

Trainer Chris Patrick and Pell came running out on the field with concerned faces. Brantley was kept in Shands Medical Center overnight for observation. When they did a cat scan, they found a bruise about the size of a small coin. At first Brantley was told he'd miss a game or two. "It was like a bruise on your arm," Brantley said. "I said, 'Hell, I'll be back for the Alabama game.'" Alabama was two weeks later. Scot Brantley never came back. He was called to a meeting in Pell's office. He knew when he saw his mother and father, brother John, Pell, and the trainers in the room the news wasn't good.

"'We made a decision,' they told me," Brantley said. "'You're going to have to miss the season.' I said, 'Lord of mercy, you must be kidding me.' And that's the way it went down."

Ironically, John was injured in the same game as his brother, ending his career as well.

With the loss of the starting quarterback and an All-SEC linebacker, the fortunes of Gator football also took a downturn. The next week, they lost to Mississippi State, 24-10—just the beginning of a year without the taste of victory for Charley Pell.

"I loved Scot Brantley," Ward said. "But there is no game worth [depriving] a young man of his capability outside football; to be injured and it be a permanent damage or possibly fatal. And he had a history of head problems. When he went down and went out, Charley did that out of pure parental love. Because he would have wanted somebody to have done it for his son. Charley said, 'He is *not* going to die on that football field.'"

Brantley, of course, did not die. His brain injury healed, and he was able to go on and play eight years for the Tampa Bay Bucs, and then became the team's radio color analyst through 2005. He now does pregame radio for the Gators as well.

The loss of Brantley personified the first-year gloom, because he was going to be the first of many stars in Pell's superb, hard-rocking defense. But he was not Pell's last player to be lost via injury.

Probably no other game symbolized the frustration of Pell's first season than the loss to Florida State, a team he would eventually beat in each of his last three seasons. On November 24, 1979, however, the Seminoles boasted a 10-0 record against Florida's 0-8-1. A win here would have been the greatest upset in the history of the series. The cards seemed stacked against the Gators. FSU needed what is deemed by most observers as a one-hop interception to kill off Florida's rally and win, 27-16.

Team physician Dr. Pete Indelicato experienced some tough times with Pell, but none tougher than the day the Gators lost their 10th game of the 1979 season in Miami, 30-24. As they were walking off the Orange Bowl field together, Pell turned to "Dr. Pete" and said, "Well, Doc, now you know what it feels like to be on the bottom."

Indelicato, longtime team physician at Florida, still holds Pell in highest esteem. "He was a special coach to me," said Indelicato, "a man's man. He'd smoke that cigarette, and he'd look right through you. You didn't b-s him. He didn't fumble around with words. He wanted a direct answer in as few words as possible."

The bottom, however, was yet to come. This was just one more blow for Pell, who had also encountered drug issues with players, theft among teammates in Yon Hall, and racial disharmony. The loss of Brantley's leadership was huge.

On the heels of that bleak 1979 season would come a ray of sunlight. A young assistant coach from Oklahoma, Northern Arizona, Eastern Illinois, and Minnesota would arrive to provide an offensive spark that would vault Charley Pell's team into the limelight. With Mike Shanahan came a package of new surprises and the convergence of football talent the likes of which Florida football fans had never seen. One of his surprises almost derailed Georgia's hopes of a national championship.

The Two Sides of 'Run Lindsay'

Even while their team lost, Gator fans continued to fill up Florida Field. Despite the winless 1979 season, Pell's stadium initiative would increase the seating capacity to 72,000. Fan loyalty also accelerated, so the bricks and mortar were beginning to bond. After a disastrous start, better players began to jump aboard. Among them were wide receiver Cris Collinsworth (the Gator's 23rd All-American); linebacker David Little (24th); and All-American-to-be, defensive tackle David Galloway, who'd be chosen after the 1981 season.

The fruits of Charley Pell's labor began to pay off when he landed some prized recruits. One of the first to commit was James Jones, a sure-handed tight end who would convert to running back. "James Jones was given to Charley for his birthday by his mama," Ward Pell said. "We had a birthday party that was scheduled for Charley that first February we were there. Mama Grace [James' mother] decided she was going to wait until Charley's birthday. Charley was due in the day before, and Mama Grace asked him to stay over, which he did. And they made the announcement the next day. So James was a gift. Mama Grace used to come every weekend and help recruit after that." It was a gift that would keep on giving.

Offensive coordinator Mike Shanahan provided more help for the 1980 season. Soon to follow was quarterback Wayne Peace of Lakeland, who was such a hot prospect that Bear Bryant dispatched Joe Namath to have lunch with him. Namath told Peace he had been miserable the night before Super Bowl III—in which his Jets would upset the Baltimore Colts. "He said he felt unprepared, and he was nervous and scared to death," Peace said in the late spring of 2006. Peace would encounter a similar experience in his first season when he was pressed into action after an injury to starter Bobby Hewko during the LSU game. The following week, Peace was picked from the rotating group of freshman quarterbacks. "It's funny how things happen in life, but who knows—I may not have touched the field at the University of Florida if Hewko didn't get hurt."

Among the four losses in 1980 would be one to Georgia in what is now called the "Run Lindsay" game. Freshman quarterback Peace struggled with the new offensive game plan in practice and suffered a sudden loss of confidence. "Shanahan was such the master motivator—he expected so much of you," Peace would say years later. "He would work your tail off. But at the same time, he would treat you with such dignity and respect. He was just a phenomenal guy. But I remember having to get up in front of the team every game, and I had to recite the starting lineup of their defense, the height and weight and what year they were, what their tendencies were, what the defense would run."

Frank Frangie of ESPN 1460 in Jacksonville, then a student at Florida and about to become a sports writer for the *Florida Times-Union*, remembers the "Run Lindsay" game and all its backstories. "Charley Pell found a hotshot offensive coordinator who installed a state-of-the-art, four-wide receiver spread offense for that game only and almost won it," Frangie said. "That young hotshot was named Mike Shanahan. ABC also had a bright, young play-by-play guy calling the game. His name was Al Michaels."

Shanahan remembers that Florida's four-wide-receiver set caught not only Georgia by surprise, but Michaels and his color analyst as well. "The announcers kept saying, 'Obviously they'll have to change, because they're not going to stay in this set the whole time,'" Shanahan recalled from his Denver Broncos office. "But they beat us and won the national championship."

That Shanahan could convince the conservative Pell to try such a radical approach in a big game seems incredible. In Peace, however, the Gators had the ideal short-passing, West Coast-type quarterback. And the Gators wanted to offset Georgia's superior defensive manpower by spreading out the Bulldog defense.

"There had to be some convincing, because it wasn't in his blood to use it," said Shanahan. "But he was strong enough to say, 'Go ahead.' The one thing that we continued to do was to change things up each week so that the defense wasn't preparing for the same thing they'd seen the week before— especially against some of the teams we saw in the SEC."

For some reason, Peace just couldn't grasp this new four-wide-receiver offense that Mike was installing for Georgia. "Practice was terrible that week, and I was really nervous about the game because my preparation was so bad," said Peace, who found a sense of himself as he exited the tunnel.

"Seeing all the fans, all the commotion, I remember the players around me were just jumping and screaming and hollering," Peace continued. "And yet I could hear nothing. It was surreal, such a calming influence on me. It made me settle down, relax, go have fun, and play the game. It turned out to be a great game for me and for the Gators."

Great game for Peace, too, who passed for 285 yards against the Bulldogs—but not so great an outcome for the Gators. As he stood on the sideline in the final minutes with James Jones and Tyrone Young, preparing to celebrate knocking off unbeaten Georgia, a freak play occurred to reverse the game's outcome and rock the Gator world.

Coincidentally, it was also one of the all-time greatest moments in Georgia history, recognized with a slanted account on the University of Georgia website, along with such other famous historical moments on November 8 as the re-election of Abraham Lincoln and the birthday of *Gone With The Wind* novelist Margaret Mitchell.

Here is an abridged version of the account, from the UGA perspective:

> "Florida took a 21-20 lead. With just over a minute left, the Bulldogs were faced with third down on their own 8-yard line. Hopes for an undefeated season now seemed doomed. Then the miracle happened! Quarterback Buck Belue dropped back. Rushed by a Florida defensive lineman, he rolled to his right. Suddenly he saw wide receiver Lindsay Scott breaking open in the middle of the field. Lobbing the ball over a defender's outstretched arms, Belue saw Scott make the catch, hoping it was enough for a first down.
>
> "Scott came down with the catch, simultaneously turning to look for room to run. He slipped, put his hand on the ground to catch himself, then sprinted for the sideline, hoping to get out of bounds and stop the clock. But his slip forced the Florida defenders to over-commit, and Scott found the sideline, outrunning all defenders to the end zone for a 92-yard touchdown! Legendary Georgia radio announcer Larry Munson abandoned all pretense of objectivity and bellowed, 'Run, Lindsay! ... Lindsay Scott! Lindsay Scott! ... Lindsay Scott!'"

"I remember every detail," Frangie said. "Mike Clark almost getting to Belue, David Little reaching up for the ball, defensive backs falling down. And the telling stat is in this trivia question. How many TDs did Lindsay Scott score that year? *One!*"

That was also the day that a freshman named Herschel Walker rushed for 238 yards, 72 of it on one play for a touchdown. And a young wide receiver named Tyrone Young caught 10 passes from freshman quarterback Wayne Peace.

The 1980 season ended with the union of coaches and players, plus a 35-20 Tangerine bowl victory over Maryland. Peace had another big game, passing for 271 yards to emerge as a starter for the next three years. Collinsworth bowed out brilliantly as the Most Valuable Player in the bowl game with a 56-yard touchdown grab. He also led Florida in receiving for the third straight season, posting 14 career touchdowns and nearly 2,000 yards, and was named All-America.

"Cris was our captain and the leader of the team," Shanahan said. "A guy like Cris, you didn't have to coach. He'd coach you. Especially a young coach like me. He had a great feel of all the positions, being a former quarterback. You didn't think a guy like that could run like he could. But more importantly, he was the catalyst for the football team."

What Shanahan liked about being at Florida was the open-mindedness of his boss. Though it wasn't in Pell's nature to play a finesse game, he gave his coordinator full rein. Shanahan said of Pell: "Charley was going to let people coach if they knew the Xs and Os. He made sure everybody was doing what they should do to give his team a chance to win. If you weren't on top of your game, he'd embarrass you. So he made it very tough on guys who maybe weren't very organized and maybe weren't as tough as he'd like—he made it to the point where it was almost unbearable. And that was his mind-set—but he was never that way to me. Charley's mind-set was he was going to let his coaches coach. And if you could prove to him you knew what you were doing, he was going to let you go."

The improvement from 0-10-1 to 8-4 was the biggest turnaround in NCAA football history. Obviously Shanahan knew what he was doing— in one year he took one of the worst offenses in the nation and made it top 10, going from a Power-I formation to a wide-open passing philosophy. "I believe we were dead last in the NCAA in total offense the year before," Shanahan said. "Charley asked me what we could do. I said I thought we could be in the top 10. He sort of laughed and said, 'You mean top *half.*' Ultimately, we wound up in the top 10."

Because of the cutting-edge offense, Shanahan began to get phone calls from places like Texas and Notre Dame. Finally, he asked how they knew about him.

"Bobby Bowden," he was told. The FSU coach wanted Shanahan out of Gainesville. "I considered that a big compliment," said Shanahan, who after 1983 accepted a job as an offensive coach for Dan Reeves and the Denver Broncos, going on to become head coach there and win two Super Bowls.

Wilber Marshall: One-Man Wrecking Crew

As Florida's newfound offense began to attract national attention, so did Joe Kines' defense, thanks in part to the arrival of Wilber Marshall. Once he switched over from tight end, Marshall became one of the most feared linebackers in the game. Pell was able to sign the blue chip linebacker-to-be because Marshall was impressed with the straight-shooting coach and looked to him as a father figure. Plus, Wilber enjoyed hanging around the Pell household.

Like Jones, Marshall was a star tight end in high school. Charley promised Wilber he'd play tight end at Florida, which he did on a limited basis as a freshman. Meanwhile, he was terrorizing opponents on special teams with bone-jarring tackles. With so much talent at the tight-end position—including future NFL head coach Mike Mularkey—Pell needed help at other positions. An injury to a weak-side linebacker created a void and a tough choice for Marshall, who nearly quit rather than switch to defense.

"I went home and thought about it," Marshall said from his home in Washington, D.C. "I was going to leave, but I said, 'I don't really want to do this.' So I changed my mind and said, 'I put my foot in that pot, so I'm just going to go ahead.'"

Ward Pell remembers that Wilber was a special player to Charley and his family. Marshall was a three-sport star from Mims near Titusville, where he looked up to his elder Astronaut High graduate, Cris Collinsworth.

"Wilber was quiet and shy," said Ward Pell. "His quietness and shyness often gave him the reputation for being aloof and arrogant, but he really was not. He was genuinely shy. During the time he was recruited, we would have recruits in the house on Sunday morning for brunch. While the rest of them were back playing pool, Charley would have one of the recruits and the parents come visit him."

But there was something different about Wilber.

"This one particular Sunday morning, Charley comes in from his TV show and came into the kitchen, saying, 'I've got one player that's going to come over and eat breakfast with us at nine o'clock. I think he would enjoy being just with the family.' But Carrick had spent the night with a friend, and Charley said, 'You've got to go get Carrick.' And when I got back, Wilber was already there and sitting at the breakfast bar, glancing at the newspaper. Charley was cooking. And he was looking at me and pointing like, 'Would you talk to him?'

"Carrick came sauntering in the door, and before I could say anything, he stuck his little hand out and said, 'Are you Wilber Marshall?' And Wilber grinned—he had the most infectious grin—and answered, 'Yeah.' And

Carrick said, 'Let me ask you one question. Are you as good as my dad says you are?' Out of the mouth of babes! ... From that day, he and Carrick developed a friendship."

Marshall, a self-confessed "introvert," would eventually become a volunteer babysitter for the Pells. He confirmed the story, saying, "There's just something so honest and innocent about children."

The year was 1982. Coming off a mediocre 7-5 season that ended with a Peach Bowl loss, 26-6, to West Virginia, Pell's Gators needed a statement game. The South end zone was expanded, luxury boxes were added, and a new weight room was unveiled. Along with stadium expansion under A.D. Bill Carr, the financial impact of those capacity crowds virtually saved the program, bailing the athletic department out of the red and solidifying the future. Former Gator player Gene Peek, a Jacksonville attorney, the former president of Gator Boosters, Inc. who currently serves on its board, said flatly, "Without Charley Pell, there might not be a North end-zone expansion; or South end zone, for that matter, at Ben Hill Griffin Stadium."

At the refurbished Florida Field, No. 10 Florida got that chance against No. 11-ranked Southern Cal September 11 on ABC's national game. Marshall was a one-man wrecking crew of quarterback Sean Salisbury in one of Florida's biggest wins ever, 17-9. ABC would name Marshall "National Defensive Player of the Year" the next year.

USC's offensive scheme pulled the guard and left the backside linebacker unblocked. The Trojans underestimated Marshall's speed, who was able to run down the tailback from behind. Said Marshall: "When they ran 'student body' [right or left], they usually pulled guards on the weak side to come around, and they didn't have any backside protection. With my speed, I wasn't going to let them get to the line of scrimmage, and no one was going to block me. I just lined up and played, regardless if it was USC or anybody else, I used to get around the corner playing in that three-four [defense]."

Shanahan watched in awe at some of the athleticism displayed by Marshall. "They ran the pitch sweep in that game and they knocked us off the ball with one of the great offensive lines. But Wilber Marshall caught everything from the backside," Shanahan said. "If they would have run at Marshall, we probably would have gotten beat by 28 points, but they ran away from him. If you watch the film, you will see Wilber make plays at the line of scrimmage, that if he doesn't make that play, their running back is going the distance. He went unblocked, because they didn't think Wilber could chase them down. Wilber was such an athlete that he made—I think—10 solo tackles from the backside. He was the type of guy who would do things, and you'd say, 'My God!' He wasn't a very big guy, but he'd rush the quarterback, and all of a sudden, he'd jump over a guy. You'd say, 'Wait a minute, did you see that? He just jumped over that running back to get to the quarterback!' He had such great leg strength and such great agility that he could do unbelievable things. I heard he could dunk the basketball when he was a freshman in high school."

While USC was memorable for Marshall, he'll never forget his last home game. Looking back fondly, Marshall reflects warmly on his final day at Ben Hill Griffin Stadium, when he and the Gators slammed FSU, 53-14. Pell wanted to give his first class of seniors a good sendoff, so he took them off the field in style. "They took us out of the game and gave us a chance to address the crowd and see the appreciation to fans who loved football," Marshall said. "I've never seen a crowd like that support the players like that, and it made it very easy to play."

Marshall was a fan favorite, though his statistics didn't really bear out some of the play-making ability that he could pull off as a defender, whether intercepting a pass, running down a back, leaping over bodies, or knocking defenders over in King Kong fashion. Because teams double-teamed him and ran away from his side, the stats don't reflect his contribution. Although he led the team in tackles for the 1981 and 1982 seasons, Marshall is only ninth in career tackles and seventh in sacks. However, he's No. 1 in career tackles-for-loss with 58 and still holds the season record of 27.

Marshall was two-time consensus All-America—and a finalist for the Lombardi Award in both 1982 and 1983—and was chosen by the *Gainesville Sun* as Florida's Defensive Player of the Century. He made All-SEC first team three straight years.

Once he finished playing NFL football, Marshall became a diehard Gator fan again. He had rarely returned to the campus after going to the NFL to become a star on the 1985 Super Bowl Champion Chicago Bears and the 1991 Super Bowl Champion Washington Redskins. A dispute followed an all-star game after his senior year when he found out that he was classified as a professional because he was paid. But he still rooted passionately for anything Gator. "I always pull for them," said Marshall, who came back for the Letterman's Club Golf Tournament in the spring of 2006. "I watch everything—golf, baseball ... I watch it all."

He still cherishes his life as a student at Florida and looks forward to being part of the program again. "When you're part of it, the atmosphere at the university is great," Marshall said. "At the time, basketball was just starting to get good, and you went to the games. We had a great swim team. We always had track. There was always something to do to break up some of the schoolwork."

These days, with pro football well behind him, Wilber is free to make trips back to Gainesville again, and he welcomes the chance to help his alma mater. "If they need some help recruiting or whatever around there, I'll offer myself," he said.

In Urban Meyer, Marshall sees a little bit of his old coach. "He's a good motivator. I've seen him talk to the guys, and he has a part of Charley in him. He knows how to communicate with the players. You've got to have a player's coach." Wilber appreciates directness in a coach, as he did when Pell gave him his weekly list of tasks.

"The way Charley put it in front of me was, 'This is what I need from you. This is what it takes for you to have a good game. I need this kind of pressure. ... I need this many sacks.' We'd talk at the hotel, and he'd tell me what it would take. 'If you do this,' he'd say, 'I can't be disappointed.' I always went to my coaches and asked what it would take to win. Not just the plays that I would make, but motivating the other guys, keeping the other guys in the game."

Charley asked it of him, Wilber accomplished it, and together they achieved some lofty goals.

The Period of Prosperity

Pell's second year brought fresh air and fresher results: eight wins, four losses, and promise for the future. The Gators were headed for three more bowl games, but another year of seasoning was required before the star recruits would impact. After losing a tough opener to Miami (21-20), Florida also suffered SEC losses to Mississippi State, Auburn, and Georgia. Yet along the way, the Gators picked up running backs Neal Anderson, John L. Williams, and Lorenzo Hamilton—as well as receivers Dwayne Dixon and Spencer Jackson.

James Jones had led the Gators in rushing for three straight seasons, and may have earned his scholarship on one play in 1982 to beat Miami, 17-14—when he hauled down Peace's pass with a falling-down-backwards, one-handed circus catch for a 17-yard touchdown. Peace began his junior year with such an impressive performance that *Sports Illustrated* featured "The Peace Corps" on its cover, with No. 15 scrambling against Miami, a team which he threw for 220 yards against on an 18-for-24 performance. One of them was Jones' 17-yard touchdown catch.

Thus, Peace was on his way to an outstanding year, setting national records for completion percentage (70.3 percent), good for fourth in the nation for passing efficiency (143.4 percent). He would become the SEC's No. 2 all-time career leader in yards (7,206) and total offense (6,946). When he looks back at his time at Florida, however, Peace's memories aren't filled with stats.

"People ask me all the time if I miss playing football at Florida," said Peace, the owner of a Lakeland insurance agency. "I don't miss it at all. What I miss is the relationships—friends. You miss being in that huddle with your teammates. People think you stay in touch with all of them, but you really can't. I've got four kids, and I coach all their sports and do things in my community, but it's not like you talk to these guys all the time. So you go back to your memory bank. It was just such a marvelous experience and a great time in my life."

The star players kept on coming, and the Gators kept on getting better. Over four seasons—from 1982 through 1985—Florida would win more football games than in any 48-month period in its history with records of 8-4, 9-2-1, 9-1-1, and 9-1-1. That coincided with the arrival of some outstanding running backs like Anderson. To get him, Pell had to go head-to-head in a recruiting battle with his mentor, Bear Bryant.

Anytime The Bear came to town created big news, but when he came to tiny Graceville in Northwest Florida—just across the state line—he might as well have been the Pope. Growing up near "L.A."—or "Lower Alabama," as quarterback Kenny Stabler called it—Anderson's favorite team was the Crimson Tide. Yet there was something more important than playing football for Neal and his parents. "When we went to visit a school, my parents would want to know what kind of journalism school they had, because 'My baby wants to major in public relations,'" Anderson said of his mother.

The Anderson family was of modest means, but wanted no special favors. Instead of getting gifts or cash as some recruits demanded, Neal's mom spent money to fix up their home in anticipation of all the special guests that would arrive at the front door—like the ones from Tuscaloosa, Gainesville, and Auburn. "We went into debt because we bought some new silverware and plates," Anderson said.

Considering whom the Gators had signed already, that Anderson chose Florida was surprising. "Most people thought I was crazy," Neal said. "They already had Lorenzo Hampton starting, and he was only going to be a sophomore. And they had already signed John L. Williams, one of the top-three running back prospects in the country. So I was about fifth string on the depth chart for the pre-season and the first game—until I was able to get into the lineup later and show what I could do."

His breakthrough game was at Kentucky, when he started while Williams was suspended and Hampton was suddenly injured. One other back went over to defense; and yet another had quit. "And they were left with me," said Anderson. "Coach Pell decided I was so raw that he was going to go to a one-back set and let James Jones, who was a great player, handle all the running-back duties. I was very disappointed." So disappointed that he told coaches he was going to transfer because he wasn't getting a fair shot.

"I didn't understand at the time that you don't stick a freshman in that kind of game," Anderson admitted. "But grudgingly, I did get the start. I had 197 yards and three touchdowns—from that point on, things worked out." He would lead the team in rushing the following three seasons as Florida football shot to the top of the charts.

The passionate quest for an SEC title was so intense that it brought out the best in some, the worst in others. Shanahan remembers when such an accomplishment was a mere dream. "People discussed whether Florida could ever win the SEC, Charley Pell, or whoever was the coach, would definitely be the hero because of such loyal fan support. You knew when it happened that it was going to be very special in Gatorland."

It did happen, there was a short-lived hero, but it wasn't Charley Pell.

'A Shakesperian Tragedy'

Sadly, in his zeal to excel at Florida, Pell pushed the envelope too far. He crossed the line himself and allowed others to overstep boundaries, failing to monitor his staff members' indiscretions. When the NCAA charges came down in January of 1985, among the 107 violations were giving players money, use of slush funds, and spying on opponents. Florida received a two-year ban from television and would not be allowed to participate in bowl games. The Gators were stripped of their only SEC title as well and lost 20 scholarships. Pell would admit later that he had lied to the NCAA, but made a mistake in not fighting for himself. Ward feels her husband was betrayed by some of his own people.

By now, Shanahan was gone, and the new offensive coordinator was Galen Hall. That Pell fell on his sword was not unexpected. "It doesn't surprise me at all that he took the fall," Shanahan said.

Ward said her husband was ruined by the prejudicial collaboration of his enemies.

"With the NCAA, you're not innocent until proven guilty. You're guilty," she said. "If they can get two people to corroborate a story, then guess what: it's true. It doesn't matter how sleazy the people may be. That doesn't have a thing to do with their ethics. So they came in, and they really didn't find anything, except on the one coach we had released. And he ended up being the one that blew the whistle on everything. And then he got another guy who really wasn't a coach. Charley gave him a job because he felt sorry for him since [Clemson coach] Danny Ford wouldn't keep him."

The "one who was released" was Mike "Ice Cream" Brown, a former Clemson manager and student assistant/gopher and the apparent "Dirty Tricks" operative for certain members of Pell's staff. Brown was friends with line coach Mike Bugar and recruiter Sonny McGraw, among others. According to Jacksonville Gator Club member Dr. Frank Jenkins, Brown was a "… nondescript, chubby guy who blended right in with the students" and used to spy on other teams for one of the assistant coaches. "He'd go to someplace like Mississippi State and run around the track and keep a mental idea of what they were doing."

One former staff member described Brown "… as sort of a mole who hung around the dormitory." After both Brown and McGraw were fired, they allegedly vowed to get even with Pell by feeding information to the NCAA. "I guess that was their idea of revenge, so they did their thing," Ward said.

In most places those days, alumni were heavily involved in recruiting. At many other schools, money flowed and sometimes landed in the pockets of recruits or their families. Mostly at Florida, according to Jenkins, it was nickel-and-dime pocket money for meals or helping athletes sell their football tickets—a practice that was widespread, but remains illegal and frowned upon today.

Jenkins, a maxillofacial surgeon who now lives in Atlanta, acted as a go-between for Florida during the Pell era and helped Adams recruit Jacksonville. In those days, recruits were often feted to dinner. Among those Jenkins visited at a camp for high school prospects was All-SEC running back John L. Williams, for whom he bought a shrimp dinner after a friendly wager about the time of his 40-yard dash.

"I took him to a restaurant and got close to him; and I would go down and visit him. At that time, everybody was doing it [taking players to dinner, etc.]," Jenkins said. "And it wasn't quite as improper. Now it's downright illegal. Back then, they wanted somebody that could get close to the kids and help them out if they were in a bind. I used to give them pocket money for gas, etc." Jenkins said his purpose was to encourage them to come to Florida and to help find them summer jobs, "… because the kids didn't have any money and didn't have any jobs."

This sort of concierge-for-athletes concept was apparently widespread in college football during the 1980s. "Everybody was doing it. I knew who my counterparts were," Jenkins said. "In fact, Charley sent me up to meet some of the guys in Alabama that Coach Bryant used." Jenkins said there were about a half-dozen of these alumni "helpers" in key spots around Florida. They were not so much bagmen as they were lobbyists. Cheating was rampant in college football, especially in the South—a half-dozen huge-profile coaches were sanctioned or slapped on their hands between 1978 and 1985.

Personal relationships with key boosters began during recruiting and lasted through college—and sometimes beyond. Once the players signed to play at Florida, these "helpers" kept in contact and would provide services like selling the four tickets each player was allotted. The label bearing the players' name was stuck to the ticket envelope. By tearing off labels of star players and inferring to the buyer that they came from a Wilber Marshall or Wayne Peace, Jenkins was able to get higher prices for some of his players. "And I'd give them the extra money. I didn't take any of it," Jenkins said. "I didn't need the money."

It was illegal, of course. Money for players, however, was otherwise nonexistent. The NCAA had already taken away the stipend that athletes received for laundry, so to counteract that Pell put washers and dryers in the athletic dorm.

"Some schools were flat out offering money to sign," Jenkins said, and he named several SEC teams, as well as one other in the state of Florida. "We never put large bundles of money on a kid to sign. But we'd get close to them and make them a part of our family. They'd come over and meet the wife and kids. We were extended family. So when people from other schools would come along and offer them money, we'd tell them, 'That's not where you ought to go. You need to go to a good school where you can get your degree.' We became like a second parent—and they still stay in touch. They still call up and still come to see me. Some are lawyers, some are doctors."

The NCAA's crackdown on selling tickets, buying meals, and transportation spelled trouble—especially since the former Pell staff member was there to sing. It all fell at Charley's feet, who did nothing to deflect the wrongdoing. That Pell loyalty oath became a double-edged sword. "Essentially, if Charley would take the hit, then all the other coaches would be saved," Ward said. "If you knew Charley Pell for 12 minutes, you'd know he wasn't going to let anything happen to his coaches. That was part of his makeup, which we later learned when we went through counseling—that he felt a great need to be responsible. That was fine, but it destroyed his coaching career. But he was a big man. He shouldered a whole lot of things."

Only 13 of the charges named Pell directly, but clearly he had known about some of the other activities. However, when NCAA investigator Doug Johnson walked into the room, Pell told him he was responsible for everything. In later years, Pell spoke of a handshake deal with Florida president Marshall Criser that, if he took the blame, the coaching staff would remain intact until the end of the year, then Charley could step down. Criser, a former attorney, denied that deal was ever made. Others say the deal was contingent on the NCAA not raising any more severe violations. Reportedly, their severity was revealed in certain communications by Pell and his staff, which came to light because of Florida's Sunshine Law, and Criser had no choice but to act. Pell had trusted Criser to live up to his half of the agreement and felt betrayed when he didn't. In the end, partly because he was not able to separate himself from that stigma and shouldered blame for everything, he was branded as a cheater.

"Charley Pell was not a crook," said Dorsey. "He was almost a Shakespearian tragedy. He deserved a lot better than what he got. When the house started falling apart, he took the blame. He didn't name people, but he opened himself up to some things. One of his assistant coaches did something bad, and Charley fired him. He got very vindictive with Charley and opened up a lot of that stuff. Unfortunately, he [Pell] didn't have control over all the things that were going on."

Dorsey says he will always remember Pell as the builder who laid the foundation of the Gator House that is the underpinning of today's program. "He took us from a team that was sometimes a laughingstock to a national power," said Dorsey. "We were a divided nation until he came along. Charley was the guy who created 'The Gator Nation.'"

Jenkins remembers Pell as "… a most honorable man who was a great father figure to a lot of people—but like the general, he took the blame because he was in charge of the troops. When it all came out, Charley took the blame for everybody," Jenkins said. "Everybody was involved in doing that stuff. I mean, *everybody!*"

Steve Spurrier didn't know Charley well, but recognizes Pell's contributions toward rebuilding his alma mater. When South Carolina started its first-ever capital campaign in 2006, he had a new appreciation for Pell's ability to rally pocketbook support of alumni. "Charley Pell was the first true fundraiser at our school," Spurrier said. "He got some booster people with big money to give substantial amounts to the University of Florida. Unfortunately though, something in his background or whatever, [for him] bending the rules and fudging was just part of coaching—to him and so many people who have come from the state of Alabama. Maybe he was just a product of his coaching environment."

Wilber Marshall saw Pell as a good family man and somebody concerned for the welfare of others. "He was a great father who spent a lot of time with his kids and wife and would go out of his way to do anything within his power for anyone," Marshall said. "He could make a person have that same confidence that he had in himself. That was important—to get guys to believe in themselves."

As for Pell's troubles, Marshall prefers to think of it as the result of overzealous alumni. "You can't control what the alumni do," Marshall said. "You can't control everybody. So when he took the brunt of everything, my belief is that you can't do that. You can't stop a parent or a player from doing anything. That's on them. And he always told me, 'Never take anything from anyone. You want to make it to the next step. You've got to keep yourself in line.'"

Charley was also very important in Marshall's personal life. "He knew I was a very introverted person, which is pretty much why I spent so much time around him, because he was more of a father figure to me than a coach," Wilber said. "He spoke to my parents and said, 'He'll be just like one of mine. I'll take care of him, and I'll keep him on that straight line.' And that's what he did."

At first, Ward and Charley took the firing in stride, moving to Northwest Florida and discovering there was a life after football. Ward remembers what it was like having time together as a family and the joy they took in even the smallest of pleasures.

"It was just another adventure," she said of their life after football. "It was difficult, but there were some good times. One of the most wonderful nights of the year—I guess it was 1985—Florida and Miami were playing. And while the game was going on, Charley and I were walking on the beach in Gulf Shores. I thought, 'Gosh, this is how real people live.' It was really kind of cool."

Football people began distancing themselves from Pell as if he were a leper. As the investigations wound down, the university's call for compliance intensified, and an air of suspicion hovered over the athletic department. Talk even arose of an "NCAA mole" being planted amongst the rank-and-file employees. Charley Pell's friends were scarcer and scarcer.

"Mr. Ben Hill," his true friend, remained loyal. Hill was honored with a dinner while the head coach was still Galen Hall, who took the reins from Pell after three games in 1984. Arising and stepping up to the lectern, "Mr. Ben Hill" opened his comments with: "I'm a Charley Pell man." Griffin died in 1990.

Two of Pell's biggest regrets were allowing Florida State to pick off prized recruits after the probation hit the Gators and not being more selective about some of his assistant coaches. But he had bigger problems than that. Despite their adjustment to private life, Charley bore deep scars, and his emotions began to fester up nearly a decade after his firing. That's when he planned his suicide—the Charley Pell way, of course, in infinite detail. Just as he planned practices at 4:30 every morning, Pell began the process of planning his funeral. He made a list of his pallbearers, shopped for caskets, wrote letters to friends and loved ones.

On February 2, 1994, one day after his 25th wedding anniversary, Pell drove his car to a remote spot in the woods near Jacksonville. He'd left suicide notes to Ward and a close friend, who was a Florida state-trooper. He swallowed some pills, took straight shots of whiskey, and ran a hose from the exhaust pipe to his mouth. The combination of the whiskey, pills, and carbon monoxide made him nauseous, and as he was about to vomit, he opened the door so he wouldn't soil his Buick. Instead, he slumped onto the ground where he was found later, still alive, by his good friend, Trooper Malcolm Jowers. His penchant for neatness had spared his life.

"It's a miracle I'm still alive," he said that day.

His perfectionism, when combined with the combustible bitterness he harbored from his firing, produced a volatile explosion in his belly years later. He took the blow, but the pain eventually resurfaced. After checking into the New Vision Center in St. Simon's Island, Georgia, counselors said that Pell had repressed his pain much like a trash compactor eliminates excess garbage. As part of the treatment, Pell and other patients walked around several days in the treatment center with teddy bears. Once he completed treatment, Pell became a spokesman to people suffering from depression.

Charley never got another college coaching job. He tried his hand at a brand-new high school, Lake Region (Florida) High School near Lakeland, but after a 1-9 start, he couldn't bear to keep going. He came close to getting the head-coaching job at Louisville, but apparently the school changed its mind at the last minute and gave the job to Howard Schnellenberger.

While Pell was in Lakeland, he had a few occasions to visit with Peace, his former quarterback. "When I played for him, about half the time I wanted to break his neck, and I'm sure he wanted to break mine," Peace said. "But I was fortunate to play for him. I just had so much respect for Coach Pell because he looked you in the eye and told you what he wanted to tell you. You get in the world, and there are so many false people out there. You know what? Coach Pell taught me if you've got something you want to say, look a man in the eye and tell him what you want to tell him."

Ironically, one of the people who wrote a letter of recommendation on Pell's behalf was Doug Johnson, the NCAA investigator. "There are coaches coaching today who have done far worse than Charley, and have paid significantly less or not at all," Johnson wrote. "As a coach of football, Charley has had few peers. ... He has paid more dearly for his mistakes than others have for similar mistakes."

Cancer came soon thereafter, spreading from his lungs all over his body. In January, 2001, upon learning he was dying, Charley and Ward began entertaining friends every week. Ward told him, "Charley, you've taken on football programs with less chance. We can whip this, too."

Charley Pell passed away on May 29, 2001.

"It's hard to believe that it's been five years since he died," she said, just two days before Memorial Day on May 29, 2006. Pell wanted to be cremated, then taken to Albertville, but Memory Hill had no facility for that. Ward told him she'd take him home with her until that time. "So he is in his home," Ward said.

There was a memorial service in Gadsden, Alabama, 20 miles from Albertville, with 27 private planes from the state of Florida parked at the local airport. Sports columnist Jimmy Smothers of the *Gadsden Times* called it one of the 10 biggest sporting events of the year.

History is vulnerable and often victimized by revisionists. Sometimes the limited knowledge of a person or event leads to omission or even distortion of facts. The measure of a man is more than his mere shortcomings, of course, or we'd all be remembered merely for our mistakes. Charley Pell's positive contributions need not be forgotten, even though they weren't necessarily passed down to the next generation, as Ward Pell found out one day on a plane to Chicago.

"There was a young man standing there with a Gator cap on," Ward said. "I said to him, 'Son, I really do like that hat.' And he said, 'Well, thank you ma'am. Are you a Gator?' And I said, 'I am.' And of course he started talking … how great it was, da-dah-da-dah. And he said, 'You know, we have the greatest facilities,' da-dah-da-dah, and 'The school does all this,' da-dah-da-dah. I just looked at him and grinned and said, 'You *sure* do.' And I just walked off. And I said to myself, 'Bless your heart. You don't have a clue.'"

7

The Galen Hall Era

1984 - 1989

The Grand Plan—He Didn't Have One

Galen Hall just never looked the part as a quarterback or a head coach—no strapping physique stuffed into skin-tight uniform, no dashing heroics on the field, no long, wavy hair or toothy-white smile, no spiffy wardrobe or sideline grimaces to attract the cameras. When he led the Penn State Nittany Lions to successive bowl wins, Hall was already well on his way to a receding hairline. He was a blue-collar guy, and among other reasons, he chose Penn State—just 30 miles from his home—so he could be close to his family.

On scholarship at Penn State, he honed his football knowledge under Rip Engle and a position coach named Joe Paterno. He had no real plans to coach—he'd later say, "I just sort of fell into it"—but Hall seemed destined to be around the game. After a brief fling in the American Football League for the Redskins and Jets, he showed up at the Nittany Lions' doorstep once again. This time, he was looking for a job. Rip and Joe recommended him for a job in West Virginia, beginning Galen's newfound chase of becoming a coach. "My hometown was so small, I don't even think we knew who coached colleges," Hall said. "We didn't know. So, my goal starting out was high schools. This was before the NFL was anything—the Super Bowl hadn't even started yet.

"You've got to be at the right place at the right time," Hall said, acknowledging his good fortune in becoming Florida's coach. "I don't think I had planned out that I wanted to be the head coach at the University of Florida."

Of all the Gator coaches in the last 50 years, Hall probably gets less credit than anybody—he is perceived as the man who inherited the wealth of Charley Pell. After all, he was the beneficiary of a Pell powerhouse that he merely maintained, critics say. But you could win a bar bet by asking somebody which coach won the first SEC title at Florida, posting the first back-to-back 9-1-1 seasons. That would be Hall in 1984. His 1985 team was ranked No. 1 briefly by the wire services during the season, finished first in the SEC again, and finished as the *New York Times'* No. 1 and The Associated Press' No. 3 at season's end.

Just like everything in Hall's uncharted life, the big break at Florida was totally unanticipated. He arrived in Gainesville as offensive coordinator after 18 years as an assistant coach at Oklahoma following Shanahan's departure.

"I'd just gotten remarried, and I figured it was time to move. So I moved to Florida with Coach Pell, who was let go in the middle of the year, when I was named interim," Hall recalled. Three games into the season with a 1-1-1 record after a loss to Miami, a tie with LSU and a win over Tulane, there was an open date during which the administration reacted to the findings of the NCAA and dismissed Pell. Hall reflected back on the sequence of events.

"I got home from work on Sunday, and I got a call from [Athletics Director] Bill Carr saying he wanted to talk to me. I really didn't know what was going on, because I was new there—I had just gotten there in the spring, and I didn't know how involved the investigation was and all that. And I went in, and he said, 'Hey, I want you to be the interim coach.' And, you know, I was sort of shocked and everything. And I said, 'Well, if I am, I want a chance to be the head coach also.' And they said, 'Well, we'll have to see how the season goes.' I'm sure they weren't thinking of me. But we went on—and we won, and won, and won—so it all worked out."

"It was time when the athletic department didn't know what to do," Hall continued. "They stepped up and did whatever they did to Charley— whether that was right or not, I don't know. But I was still a part of that previous program. You come out of nowhere and [they wonder] 'Can this guy manage to take over the whole thing?' I think there were a lot of doubters, probably."

Most of those doubts were quickly erased when the Gators went on an eight-game winning tear, won the SEC title, and Hall was named the Associated Press Coach of the Year, earning the head job. As the coach at Florida, they said Galen didn't fit the pretty-boy image needed for recruiting. He spoke softly with a slight lisp and didn't play to the cameras. Some said he was too nice a guy. But they forgot about his supple mind and his competitive heart. The man could coach. He also happened to coach some excellent players, specifically eight of whom made All-America: offensive tackle Lomas Brown, offensive guard Jeff Zimmerman, linebacker Alonzo Johnson, linebacker Clifford Charlton, defensive back Jarvis Williams, defensive back Louis Oliver, defensive tackle Trace Armstrong, and—perhaps most importantly—running back Emmitt Smith.

They also had a walk-on quarterback from Mayo would put his hometown on the map.

The Boy from Mayo: Kerwin Bell

Top NFL picks were growing in Gainesville like Plant City strawberries by the mid-1980s. By the 1984 season, five future NFL No. 1s were already in the mix—receiver Ricky Nattiel, fullback John L. Williams, running backs Neal Anderson and Lorenzo Hampton, and offensive tackle Lomas Brown. In those halcyon days for state prospects, high schools overflowed with so many good players that many of them couldn't get a scholarship. Fortunately for Galen Hall and the Gators, in 1983 a boy from Mayo named Kerwin Bell walked on and made the squad. By the fall of 1984—after losing backup after backup—Bell moved all the way up to the No. 2 slot on the depth chart.

Pell was known for his hard-hitting practices, much as they were at Alabama under Bear Bryant. "He used to run some unbelievable practices," recalled Dr. Pete Indelicato. "Like they used to say about Bryant's practices, whoever they played on Saturday wouldn't hit as hard as they played against in practice."

At the beginning of the 1984 season, just as the Gators began to take shape, more bad news came from Indelicato—there was another costly injury. Pell knew Dale Dorminey, the starting quarterback, was out, but he had yet to hear all the bad news: that the backup was also hurt. Pell was down to Bell, his redshirt freshman walk-on. Charley walked in, cigarette dangling in his mouth; the backup walked out of Indelicato's office and Pell asked about the health of his second-stringer. "What's the bad news?" he asked his team physician, who replied, "Coach, he tore his ligament, and he's out for the season."

Pell removed the cigarette from his mouth and put it out in a cup, Indelicato recalled, then said: "I'm sorry, Doc. I wish I knew a better way of getting these guys ready to play. But I don't. This is the only way I know."

Fortunately, Pell had Bell, who would inherit the starting job for the opener against the defending national champion Miami Hurricanes. Who knew that, when the Gators lost to Miami 32-20 in Tampa, it would be their only loss in 1984? Charley was fired just three games later. The loss of their coach made it hard for the players to focus on the tasks at hand, and when the bad news hit, such a pall was cast over the team that some players considered leaving.

"It was tough," said Neal Anderson. "So many players were [confused] … wondering, 'Is anybody going to transfer or change schools?' I had people trying to contact me and ask, 'Are you going to stay on with University of Florida?' The NCAA investigators were at the school so often. But the weird thing about that whole thing is, they were investigating everybody. One thing I was very proud of is that I was supposedly the 'star' player, but the NCAA never even talked to me."

The 1984 team's mission was to hang together and get through the dark days, which players like Anderson and Bell helped accomplish under Hall. "When Galen got there, he was such a likeable person, and he knew he had a great offense," said Anderson. "He didn't come in and say, 'Do it my way.' He just kind of said, 'Okay guys, we're doing good—let's just keep doing it.'"

Anderson remembers the players for their resiliency, depth of talent, and attitude. "We were a team that was borderline confident and cocky," Anderson said, "which is what you need to be successful in football. We had guys that, when we got the ball down at the 5-yard line, everybody wanted the ball because everybody thought they could get it done. Sometimes you get down there, and nobody wants the ball in their hands. But we had the opposite—players on both sides of the ball like Wilber Marshall, Tim Newton—and so many good defensive backs [Tony Lilly, Jarvis Williams]. We could beat you a lot of different ways. We could throw the ball, and we had Frankie Neal and Ricky Nattiel on the outside. And we had very capable running backs."

The 1984 Gators were as good as any team in history, especially given that they played under a cloud of uncertainty for two different coaches without the promise of bowl-game exposure. They began to creep up in the polls, starting with wins over Mississippi State and Syracuse. They were 18th in the AP poll when they beat Tennessee, 43-30, and 13th after beating Cincinnati, 48-17. In one of those weird college football seasons when the top teams kept getting bumped off, the Gators shot up to the top 10 after a 24-3 win over No. 11 Auburn. Thumping eighth-ranked Georgia 27-0 broke a seven-year losing streak to the Bulldogs—something very sweet for Gator fans. It was the second-largest victory margin ever over Georgia and vaulted the Gators to No. 5, setting the stage for the game Florida fans had been waiting for since 1933: a chance to win a Southeastern Conference title.

On November 18, 1984, at Commonwealth Stadium in Lexington, Kentucky—just hours after Galen Hall had been officially named the head coach by Florida—the Gators took the field to exorcise all those past demons that had thwarted their SEC dreams. Those demons made a strong run with 90 seconds left, propelling Kentucky into the end zone; but the eight-yard touchdown pass from Bill Ransdell to Joe Phillips was called back on a penalty. Florida sophomore safety Adrian White intercepted Ransdell's subsequent attempt for the end zone. Two Kerwin Bell kneel-downs later, Florida had secured the game 25-7—and captured the championship ... for a while. That a walk-on would be in charge of leading a multimillion-dollar cavalcade of future pro players was quite ironic, but perhaps he was the Golden Boy with the Golden Touch.

"Everybody knows that everything Kerwin does turns to gold," Anderson said with a laugh. "It's not luck. He's a hard worker and a very dedicated person. When he puts his mind to something he's not going to leave any stone unturned. And he had quite a bit of athletic ability, although I tell him differently sometimes. He was able to find a way to win. I think his parents were going to name him 'Ker,' and then they added the 'Win' to his name because, in everything he does, he's a winner. It is not a coincidence. And I aleays used to tell him that he had the easiest job in the world—just hand me the ball.'"

Even in his high school years at Mayo, Kerwin quarterbacked his team to 24 straight victories and a 13-0 state championship season in his junior year (1981) as he passed for 24 touchdowns. Overall, the Hornets were 32-3, losing three times on the road. Despite those numbers, nobody came calling, and Mayo maintained its record of never having a Division I scholarship athlete. "Nobody really took me seriously," said Bell. When Valdosta State failed to deliver on a scholarship as promised, Mike Shanahan invited Bell to walk on. Instead, the Gators signed Derrick Crudup.

Bell would start his redshirt freshman year at the bottom of the depth chart and work his way up during Pell's "Monday Night Football" scrimmages.

"I remember going up to the depth chart and seeing it," said Bell. "Eighth string!"

Shanahan watched those scrimmages and had his eye on the kid from Mayo. "Look out for Bell," Shanahan told the other coaches before departing after the 1983 season. "He's going to be the key quarterback for the future." He was right.

In his first year, Bell would lead the Gators to a 9-1-1 season, and an SEC title that would later be stripped for NCAA violations. A star was born, though, and he would become an All-SEC quarterback and winner of the Forrest "Fergie" Ferguson Award, which goes to the senior most exemplary of leadership, character, and courage. Pell had seen those qualities in his fellow small-town boy. So despite Florida having this interim coach and a redshirt freshman walk-on quarterback, the dream came true.

The bad news came five months later, on April 4, 1985—here is the *New York Times'* account of the situation:

"The presidents of the Southeastern Conference schools voted by 6-4 today to strip the University of Florida of the conference football title it won last fall, the first in the school's history. The action came during the closing business session of the league's annual spring meeting and brought an angry reaction from the Florida president, Marshall Criser, who called it 'extraordinary and unprecedented.' Florida won the championship last November after compiling a 5-0-1 record in the S.E.C. The team was barred from representing the conference in the Sugar Bowl, however, because of impending N.C.A.A. probation. L.S.U. represented the S.E.C. in the Sugar Bowl after finishing second in the conference with a 4-1-1 record. The decision was made, however, not to recognize a champion for 1984."

"We were a heck of a football team. That 1984 team was maybe the second-best football team I've ever been around," said Hall, the man who coached eight of those victories.

Although Anderson and his teammates were disappointed when they couldn't keep the championship, he says they had the satisfaction of knowing in their hearts that they were champions. "In my opinion and the opinion of many other football people, we were the best team in the country," Anderson said. "And that was enough for me. We wouldn't be getting any rings, but at the time—and even now—it really didn't bother me. BYU won it that year, and I played with a guy in Chicago who was on that team. And even he— although he got the ring—admitted we were the best team in the country."

How good were the 1984 Gators in comparison to the 1996 national champions? "I would take that team we had and line it up against any team that ever played at the University of Florida," Anderson said with pride. "And I would like our chances a whole lot. The '96 team that won the national championship was a great team. But I would love it if somehow we could all get out there and play. I feel pretty sure we'd beat them. We were a lot more physical."

The following season, the Gators opened with a huge victory over Vinny Testaverde and the Miami Hurricanes. Wilber Marshall beat on Bernie Kosar like a rented mule in a 28-3 smackdown of the national champions-to-be that year. After a shocking tie with Rutgers, Florida ripped off five straight wins and a No. 2 ranking. The following week, the Gators beat Auburn, 14-10, on the same day No. 1 Iowa lost to Ohio State, and the Gators became the nation's top-ranked team by the Associated Press. They owned the school's first No. 1 ranking in history for a week before losing to Georgia,

24-3. At least Hall's Gators had another milestone. The 9-1-1 was bittersweet, though—once again Florida won an SEC title it couldn't keep.

Hall remembers getting the bad news from President Marshall Criser. "The whole thing looked pretty good, except when the sanctions came out. I remember being in President Criser's office, and he said, 'Well, the sanctions aren't real bad, 10 scholarships a year.' And I said, 'Well ...' I looked at it, and it's 10 off a total of 85, not the original 95. We were allowed [to sign] 30 a year at the time. ... And that means we could have signed 40 athletes. We [Florida] were the only one that ever had scholarships taken off the total. You were allowed 30 a year to a max of 90. And then they said, 'Okay, you guys can give however many scholarships you want to up to 30, but you can only have 85 on scholarship—and the next year you can only have 75.' It ended up we gave 11 scholarships one year and 14 the next."

This was the virtual death knell for a Florida program that had jumped into a dominant role in the mid-1980s. The Gators would defeat FSU six times in a row (1981 through 1986), often by big margins like 35-3 ('81), 53-14 ('83), and 38-14 ('85). There was talk in some circle that the blow to FSU's program may have placed Bowden's job in jeopardy. As for Miami, Florida also won three out of four against the Hurricanes from '82 through '85—a period when Miami was regarded as the nation's best.

That's when the other two of the state schools began to gain ground on the Gators. "Florida State and Miami were signing 30 a year," Hall said. Even though it would not have a happy ending, as the talent began to fall off and Florida slipped to 6-5 and 6-6 in 1986 and 1987, the Gators were not without excellent players. In addition to the aforementioned players of All-America status, the first-team All-SEC players were offensive lineman Zimmerman, outside linebacker Charlton, defensive tackle Keith Williams, and defensive backs Jarvis Williams, Louis Oliver, and Adrian White.

Bell said his four-year experience was a positive one. "I think we proved that we could handle everything," Bell said. "The pressures of a major college football program, going out and meeting the people and getting them behind the university, etc. I enjoyed it. I enjoyed meeting the people and going out and trying to recruit with our hands tied behind our backs. It was a challenge, but we got through it."

When asked how a small-town boy without a scholarship could walk on to a major college football program and become one of the stars of an SEC champion team, Bell said it was pure stubbornness. "The one thing I had was perseverance," Bell said. "I believed in myself. Even when people said I couldn't do something, I just continued to believe and never lost faith in myself. And on the football side, everything came real easy to me. I can sit down and watch a couple of game films and come up with ball plays on how

I want to attack a defense. I sort of used that as my strength—the mental side of the game—and used that to make my decisions."

His head coach saw some of the same qualities. "Kerwin was intelligent, and he wasn't afraid of anything," said Hall. "And those are two good qualities to have in a quarterback. And in his own way he had some leadership skills, because he was tough enough to take the hit, get back up, sort of laugh about it, and go on."

Throughout the record books, the name Kerwin Bell still pops up: sixth in career touchdown passes with 56; among top five in career efficiency for a season and for completions in one game with 33; among the top four in career-passing yardage with 7,585. At the time, his career touchdown passes and total yardage were the all-time best in the SEC.

For gallantry, Kerwin and sidekick Ricky Nattiel were No. 1 in the win over Auburn. Kerwin was injured and out for two weeks, but dressed out on November 2, 1986. What turned out to be one of the most exciting days ever at Florida Field certainly didn't start out well. The No. 5 Tigers jumped to a 17-0 lead on a hapless band of Gators with an awful 3-4 record. Coming off the bench in the second period, Bell put together three straight scoring drives.

Bell was suffering from a torn ACL, but few people knew the severity of the shoulder separation to Nattiel, who had been advised by the team doctor not to return to the game. Dr. Pete Indelicato said that back in those days he hadn't yet begun the practice of taking a player's helmet to prohibit his return to the game. He told Nattiel after his injury, "'That's it. You can't go back in. It's way too painful. God forbid if you catch a pass. You won't be able to hold it. You may fumble. You may make it worse.' He just looked at me like I had two heads. We got the ball, and he just ran out on the field. Two plays later, he caught about a 50-yard pass over his shoulder. I mean he couldn't raise his right arm because it hurt too much. So the only way he can catch a pass over his shoulder is with his hands down around his legs. He caught it like on the Auburn 15 and stepped out of bounds."

Shortly thereafter, Bell tossed a five-yard scoring pass to Ricky Nattiel to pull within one point, 17-16, with just 36 seconds left.

"I was just hoping I could get there," Bell told reporters. "It seemed like it took me all day. But I was running as fast as I could."

Nattiel was the intended target for the winning two-pointer, but was covered. Seeing this, the gimp-legged quarterback took off hobbling, sidestepped an Auburn linebacker, and fell in for the winning margin, 18-17.

Even today, Indelicato says that was his favorite game. "It was the most exciting and one of the most personally rewarding games that I've ever attended," he said.

Later it was learned that Hall had invited former defensive coordinator and inspirational speaker Gene Ellenson to give a pregame talk. In the parking lot before the game, on a visit to see Florida play while he was in between coaching jobs from the USFL and Duke, Steve Spurrier had told Jack Hairston of the *Gainesville Sun* that he expected an upset. "Big Gene's speech has got them fired up," said Spurrier, who, in three more seasons, would be coaching the Gators himself.

Run Emmitt, Run

After two lean seasons for Hall, he finally found the fruits of many treks to Pensacola.

Not since Larry Smith (Tampa Robinson) or Scot Brantley (Ocala Forest) had there been a more highly pursued Florida product than Pensacola Escambia's star running back, Emmitt Smith. And he did not disappoint. The balance, power, and vision of Emmitt offset any lack of speed that his critics may have noted, but he was by no means slow, of course. Emmitt was so quick off the ball that a sneaky burst often propelled him past linebackers to reach the defensive secondary before the lineman saw him touch the ball.

Over three seasons at Florida, the durable back carried the ball 700 times. In his first start (as a true freshman nonetheless), Emmitt made a huge statement with 224 yards on a school-record 39 carries—a performance good enough to lead the Gators to a 23-14 victory over Alabama in Birmingham. Two years later, Smith would break his own record, amassing 319 yards in a game. Before his career was finished, Smith had rushed for 3,928 yards—Errict Rhett was the only Gator with more (4,163). His final, junior year, Smith would blossom to lead his team in rushing for the third straight season, collecting 1,599 yards on the ground and scoring 14 total touchdowns—both stats that attracted NFL scouts.

Meanwhile, Hall's players began to flex their muscles again after an opening loss to Ole Miss, winning four straight. The last one was over LSU in Baton Rouge, 16-13. Galen knew before kickoff that it was his last game as head coach of Florida and his last time coaching players like Emmitt. Once again, the long arm of the NCAA had reached into Gainesville, and people were implying that this time the so-called "death penalty" could be in play for Florida's program.

"You knew and couldn't tell your players," Hall said. That's why Galen was so teary-eyed in the locker room after the game.

More reports of impropriety had surfaced, including one that the NCAA says involved the payment of money to Jarvis Williams, who needed to catch up on his child support to his child's mother in Palatka. It was never proven that money was involved, and many people—Steve Spurrier among them—don't think there was cash in the envelope as alleged. With an insider's help—Director of Athletics Bill Arnsparger was pipelining directly to the NCAA—a case had been made against both Hall and, in a separate charge, basketball coach Norm Sloan. Both were fired. To this day, Hall hasn't talked about it, and he clams up when the subject is broached. He says there was a lot he didn't know, and he declines to point fingers at anybody.

"I don't think anyone knew—with the whole turmoil going on at the university—President Criser leaving, the interim, Bob Bryan, coming, and the AD we had [Arnsparger]. Could I have been saved? I don't think I could have been saved. The job had already been done inside." He backed off again. "Oh, it's not something I want to get into. It was an unfortunate situation I had to put my family through. I felt it was unfair. I didn't know everything that was going on that maybe I found out a little bit later. Anyway, that's something that happened 15 or 16 years ago."

Perhaps the double-edged sword, too, had thrashed Hall, who lost his job in the same manner that he'd acquired it. One man's bad luck is another man's good fortune. In this case, it would be Spurrier to benefit, although he never thought he'd have a chance to coach at Florida when he was first hired at Duke.

"It happens all along," said Hall. "And you've got to be ready to seize the opportunity, and you've got to be prepared when it comes along. If Steve hadn't been prepared, he wouldn't have done what he did—and Steve did a great job."

Hall later became a football globetrotter, crossing the continental United States in the college ranks before traversing to Europe and coming back to America. He coached both indoor and outdoor football, and became a very successful coach at nearly every professional football level known to the game—the NFL, NFL Europe, the AFL (Arena Football League), even the XFL.

Hall held the reins steadily after Pell left, handing them over for the final seven games of 1989 to defensive coordinator Gary Darnell. Having garnered bits and pieces of knowledge along the way—from the Oklahoma Sooners to the Florida Gators, from the Rhein Fire to the Charlotte Rage and the Dallas Cowboys—Hall showed up in Happy Valley just in time to help Penn State win the Big Ten title and likely extend Paterno's career. Paterno lured Hall off the golf course and back in the film room to help complement quarterback coach Jay Paterno, his son. Many credit Galen for the rebirth of offense and the maturity of quarterback Michael Robinson, who led the Penn State resurgence under Paterno when it appeared that the wolves at the door might be more ferocious than the Lions on the field.

You've heard the old cliché about the last guy leaving being asked to turn out the lights. As the person asked to hold the reins for seven games until a decision was made on the new head coach, Darnell had control of the light switch. What very few people know is that he almost didn't let go of it. Darnell was defensive coordinator at Wake Forest when—through contact with Galen Hall, whom he knew at Oklahoma, and former Kansas State coach Jimmy Dickey—he was hired on at Florida.

"I didn't go there to be the head football coach," Darnell said. "I didn't even know if I was going to be a head football coach. Circumstances turned out that you couldn't have packed more experience into one human being over 24 months. One minute, I was a defensive coordinator in the Southeastern Conference. Then, the next minute, I was the interim head coach handling all kinds of problems, coaching in a bowl game."

Even though Hall knew he'd been fired before coaching against LSU, nobody on his staff did. That led to an intriguing encounter for Darnell following the win over LSU.

"I was walking around after the game, it was such a huge win," Darnell said. "Our wives were with us, and I asked [Athletics Director] Bill Arnsparger if he knew where the wives were. He said they were on another bus, headed for New Orleans. And he said, 'By the way, I need to see you tomorrow.' I said, 'Oh, no!' So I saw Galen, and I said, 'Coach Arnsparger wants to see me tomorrow.' Galen said, 'Well, I need to see you tomorrow, too.' I got on the team plane and went home. The next day, I got a phone call at 7:30, and it was Jimmy Dickey, with whom I coached. And he says, 'Why didn't you tell me!' And I said, 'I don't know what you're talking about.' And he said, 'You really don't know? You're the head coach!'"

After a 4-1 start under Hall, the Gators beat Vanderbilt and New Mexico, then things started to slide. After a 7-4 regular season that concluded with a 24-17 loss to FSU, Florida went to the Freedom Bowl in Anaheim, California, where Washington pounded the Gators, 34-7.

Darnell actually signed a contract to be the next head coach at Florida—just in case Spurrier didn't take the job. "At the time, Steve was also messin' with a couple of NFL teams," Darnell said. "I signed a contract. I was the next head coach. I met with the president, and he said, 'I don't know anything about football. I defer to Mr. Arnsparger.'"

It never was the same for Emmitt after Hall or under Gary Darnell, who was 3-4 as interim coach. And it wouldn't be under Spurrier, either, because Emmitt wouldn't be around.

Smith had once said he thought he could win three Heisman Trophies, though the best he ever finished was seventh. On another Florida team at another time, he may have gotten his Heisman, but in his three seasons as a

Gator, they never ranked higher than 10th, with records of 6-6, 7-5, and 7-5. In Emmitt's junior season, his last, he was consensus All-America and SEC Player of the Year. He broke 58 records and rushed for nearly 4,000 years and 36 touchdowns in just three seasons and was selected to Florida's All-Century Team. Through 99 years, Smith held the record for the longest touchdown run from scrimmage—96 yards against Mississippi State. After being picked No. 1 by the Dallas Cowboys, he played 15 years in the NFL, retiring as game's all-time touchdown scorer (164) and leading rusher.

In 2006, Smith became the seventh player or head coach from the University of Florida to be named to the College Football Hall of Fame, joining Dale VanSickel (inducted 1975), Spurrier (1986), Jack Youngblood (1992), coach Charles Bachman (1978), Coach Ray Graves (1990) and Coach Doug Dickey (2003).

"Emmitt Smith was a great ballplayer," said Darnell. "I've been around a lot of great ballplayers, but I learned to appreciate both sides of Emmitt."

Maybe it was because another NCAA probation was coming, or maybe Smith just didn't warm to the new coach headed for town, but Emmitt would be heading to the NFL. Spurrier said he never knew exactly why Emmitt didn't come back, but he'd heard Emmitt was unhappy that the new Gators coach hadn't approached him.

Smith chose to move on—in his book, *The Emmitt Zone*, published in 1994, he wrote that the probation and no bowl game were factors in his choice, but money wasn't the main issue. "Before making up my mind, I wanted to talk to Steve Spurrier," Smith wrote. "He would be my coach if I came back my senior year. We had never met, and I wanted to see what impression I got of him. I also thought I should find out if he *wanted* me to stay. But Spurrier never asked me to stay at Florida. He never said, 'Let's work together. Let's make this a great situation.' He never said, 'I want you to stay, but I'll understand if you go to the NFL.'"

Emmitt seemed to get the impression, right or wrong, that Spurrier wanted his decision quickly. "Spurrier basically told me he needed me to make a decision because there were guys he was recruiting who may be on the fence," Smith's book said. "Maybe I was wrong, but I took that to mean: 'These high school guys are runners, and they won't come to Florida if you stay; so I need to know what to tell them.' This left me with a cold feeling inside. I also thought it was strange."

Spurrier claims that he had no intention of pushing Emmitt aside.

"I just told Emmitt he had to make his own call," Spurrier said. "All the other Gators were expecting him to stay. And I think that was what he didn't quite understand. Hopefully, he does now. It worked out for Emmitt, to go to the Cowboys and become the all-time leading rusher. If he'd have gone to a bad team, it may have been different—it's hard to play on bad teams."

So although Emmitt missed out on the start of something big, it worked out best for all parties, as Steve would say later.

Afterword

During his pro football career, Smith took the time to return to Florida academics and fulfill a promise to his mother by getting his degree. Later on, during Urban Meyer's first season, Emmitt came back into the Gator football family and spoke to the team, giving a 10-minute speech about the importance of being able to rely on your teammates. Meyer, who is choosy about whom he allows to make those kind of talks, called it a "... strong, strong moment."

Hall wound up with a record of 40-18-1 at Florida, tying Ray Graves for the highest percentage of any coach (.686) until Spurrier's arrival. Over three years, 1983 to 1985, the school had its greatest run with a 27-4-3 mark. During those three seasons, Florida became the only team to be ranked in the top six each year.

8

The Steve Spurrier Era

1990 - 2001

The Truth About the Ol' Ball Coach

Let's play, "Do You Know Steve Spurrier?" If you feel that you may have insight into Spurrier's style and personality, please pick the best adjectives to describe him from the following columns:

Column A	Column B
Passionate, brilliant, honest, ethical, demanding, perceptive, creative, crafty, funny, fun-loving, bold, proud, relentless, loyal, inspiring, disciplined, fearless, committed, thoughtful, handsome, grateful, generous, confident.	Evil, vicious, devious, cunning, vindictive, arrogant, phony, lazy, stubborn, selfish, childish, petulant, unsportsmanlike, unprofessional, overbearing, mean-spirited, spiteful or untruthful.

Oddly enough, nearly all of those terms have been used in one way or another to describe the "Ol' Ball Coach" over the last 30 years, which tells you a little about people's schizophrenic perceptions of him. Having known Spurrier more than for 40 years and studied him closely as a person, athlete, and coach, I can tell you that, while he's unpredictable and very outspoken, he has just one personality—and it has changed very little. Perhaps people have so many different opinions about Spurrier due to the wide swath he cuts through the game of football. How one views him depends on which side of the field that person is sitting.

When he's on your side, you pick from Column A. When he's not, it's Column B.

He's the perfect blend of the hero and nemesis. For instance, Spurrier inspires a whole range of emotions for fans of South Carolina and Florida.

Gamecock people are learning to love the man they used to hate. Gator people, while respecting his impact on their program, remain divided between those who fear and loathe Spurrier for betraying them and those who'd allow him to murder their grandmothers and go unscathed. Yes, it's true—a few Florida loyalists pull for him, no matter the opponent.

Whatever you think of Spurrier, college football is far more interesting now that he's back in it. Football needed him as baseball needed Albert Pujols after the steroid scandal, as television needed Johnny Carson and Milton Berle. Say what you will about Spurrier, but he makes the game fun for everybody—players, coaches, opponents, writers, broadcasters, fans, and even little old ladies. It's because he has fun taking jibes at others, teasing his coaches, players, and writer friends, all while continuing to put an entertaining product on the field. Spurrier is a walking, talking quote, pitching colorful remarks right into the media's wheelhouse. At the same time, he wants to score as many points as possible on the field and, if he can, totally humiliate his opponents.

Upon his hiring at South Carolina, legit media folk were appalled at the indulgent applause Spurrier received when he was announced as Gamecocks coach—a courtesy not extended to Urban Meyer a few weeks later at Florida. One writer from Florida, who had covered Spurrier as Gator coach and was in Columbia for his press conference, quipped: "Hey, if he'd have come back as Florida's coach, even I would have given him a standing ovation!"

Spurrier's razor-sharp wit and constant needling keep people on edge—all of it part of his swagger, which is part of his own brand. He doesn't teach the swagger, yet his players model it with the pride of a battlefield promotion. Perhaps the Spurrier brand is more of a panache, which the *American Heritage Dictionary* describes as "a distinctive style." That panache causes some coaches to cringe at the very sight of Spurrier as if they've just heard fingernails scratching a blackboard. Yet, Spurrier's Gator teams inspired other coaches such as Urban Meyer, who openly admitted he admired everything about them—from the way they played, to the way they walked, even the way they dressed. However, to those who opposed him, Spurrier's Gators were the very essence of Carly Simon's words, "You're So Vain."

On occasion, his own wife, Jerri, has called him "a brat," although lovingly. One of his best friends, who shall go nameless, calls him " ... a pain in the ass at times." SEC coaches lambasted him for refusing to pull back when his team was winning by 30 or 40 points with only a few minutes left to play in the game. Georgia fans will never forgive him for coming to Athens and ringing up 52 points to avenge all the pain they inflicted on his coach, Ray Graves—not to mention getting even for the day they knocked off Spurrier's undefeated Florida team and denied his only chance at a SEC title as a player. Miami fans hate him for announcing his resignation on the same day their beloved Hurricanes won the national title, getting bigger play in most Florida papers. Alabama fans hate him for blowing the whistle on their coaches for cheating. Tennessee fans hate him for growing up in their state, leaving it to become a Heisman Trophy winner at Florida, and coaching the Gators to a national championship. (And, yes, abusing Vols coach Phil Fulmer both verbally and mentally.) If that's not enough, then some people just hate him for being handsome, rich, and playing a lot of golf ... well.

The television cameras love to catch Spurrier in a moment of angst on the sideline. Yet, for a guy who was branded as a visor-tossing, sideline-ranting, fire-breathing coach in tense situations, Spurrier could be cooler than a cup of Gatorade over ice in certain situations—even when the news was bad.

In 25 years as Gator team physician, Dr. Pete Indelicato experienced a variety of reactions from coaches receiving bad news about injured players and the seriousness of their ailments. Though reluctant to say too much about private conversations, Dr. Pete still marvels at how unpredictable the coaches' comments might be.

"Coach Spurrier never really appeared to get upset over the bad news," said Indelicato, who also has worked with the Miami Dolphins and New York Giants medical staffs. "Some of the previous coaches tend to 'shoot the messenger' a little bit."

As a freshman, star quarterback Danny Wuerffel suffered a knee injury that, in a morning exam, Indelicato had determined to be a tear in the ligament. Dr. Pete wasn't able to tell the head coach until later, just before afternoon practice.

"I thought, 'Well, I gotta go tell him the bad news,'" Indelicato recalled. "So I walked out on the practice field, and when I got a moment to talk to him alone, I said, 'Coach, Danny has a torn ACL.' Whereas some coaches would go pale, he just looked up in the sky, where over the practice field there flew a formation of birds—40 or so in number—and he said, 'Doc, where do you think those birds are going? Are they going south for the winter?'

"I said, 'Gee, I don't know, Coach.'

"He said, 'Well, thanks, for the help.' And he walked away."

Although legend may suggest that Steve Spurrier pulled the sword from the stone to inherit his rightful place as Gator football prince, the fact is: he almost didn't get the job. Forces at work were slow-dancing with each other, perhaps due to a suggestion that a selection committee member wanted the position for himself. Were it not for the no-nonsense approach of interim University of Florida President Bob Bryan in 1989, "I never would have gotten the job," according to Spurrier. "Talk to Dr. Bryan, put him in the book," Spurrier suggested.

Bryan's swift action ensured that Spurrier was hired, since Athletics Director Bill Arnsparger seemed to be dragging his feet. Pressing Arnsparger for an answer, Bryan finally asked: "Bill, do you want the job?"

"He said, 'No,'" Bryan responded; but on the other hand, Arnsparger wasn't asked a second time. Instead, the two of them took a private plane to Raleigh-Durham with Dr. Nick Cassissi and gathered in their new coach. "It was already a done deal by then," Bryan said.

Looking back on those times, Bryan recalled he was being pressured by alumni to hire Spurrier. Four prominent boosters took him fishing on a Boca Grande, but all of them became ill and had to return to port. Once they were back, Warren Cason of Tampa reported said in jest: "We were going to take you out into the Gulf of Mexico and tell you to hire Spurrier, or we were going to throw you overboard."

They didn't have to. Once he was hired, nobody could have guessed that Spurrier would bring home five SEC championships in his first seven seasons and achieve the national title in the seventh. Nobody, perhaps, save Spurrier, could've made it look so easy. He merely had to take over a team on probation, change the outlaw image of his alma mater, unite the fractured fan base, improve the program's third-place standing among the state's "Big Three," and unearth a quarterback who was buried on the fifth string.

His previous pretty-boy image and country-club, clean-hands reputation was quickly overcome.

Shane Matthews and the Quarterback Factory

When Spurrier started spring practice in 1990, everybody asked him who out of a five-man scramble would emerge to become the Gators quarterback, and he told them, "Whoever it is will lead the SEC in passing next year"— a prediction that would come true. Spurrier found Shane Matthews, a bottom feeder on the quarterback charts, and made him the big fish in a pond that would soon become "The Swamp." Actually, quarterbacks coach John Reaves probably "found" Matthews, but Spurrier empowered Shane as a starter and educated him on the nuances of playing quarterback at the highest level.

Quite honestly, Shane grew up living and breathing Ole Miss in Pascagoula, Mississippi. "I followed Ole Miss football all my life," Matthews said. "My dad was a former player there, and my mom was a cheerleader. Every Saturday afternoon, I was watching Ole Miss football wherever they were. After every high school game on Friday night, we would pack up and go wherever Ole Miss was playing."

When it came time for college, Shane wanted to play at Alabama, partly because of the Tide's winning tradition. "I'm a uniform guy, and I loved their uniforms," he said, "but they didn't show an interest in me." He thought about FSU, but his mother was against that idea. So he chose Florida, where Galen Hall was the head coach. It was while he was in his redshirt freshman year that trouble found Shane, who had this ticket problem—not football tickets—parking tickets. Every week he was scratching around for cash, trying to keep his car out of hock. Some guys at a fraternity had a way to make some easy money with football parlay cards, so Matthews and three of his Gator teammates decided to help peddle them. They got busted and suspended for a semester.

"I used to average about $100 a week on parking tickets on campus. That was killing my checkbook," said Matthews, "We got in trouble and paid the price for half a year."

While at home, Shane began to consider his options. "I thought about transferring to Ole Miss. But my dad always had a rule in the Matthews family: 'Once you start something, you finish it.' So he was not going to let me."

Despite the tug of alma mater on Bill and Peggy Matthews, the parental urge to have their son do the right thing was stronger than the desire to have him come home permanently. Then came the news about Florida's coaching change.

"I didn't know who Steve Spurrier was. I remember being home when Spurrier coached his last game at Duke against Texas Tech in the All-American Bowl. After my dad and I watched it together, I said, 'I could run that offense.'"

Even though the Blue Devils lost that day, 49-21, Matthews had gotten a glimpse at his future. First, though, the shy, soft-spoken kid from Mississippi had to get himself out of the doghouse and back on the squad. When the spring of 1990 rolled around, Shane was back in pads and competing with four others for a job under quarterbacks coach Reaves and Spurrier's watchful eye. At the first meeting, Spurrier told the team, "Nobody has any jobs, everybody is going to be given open competition, and we'll see who can play."

"A lot of coaches just say that as a token saying, but he meant it," said Matthews, whose roommate, Kyle Morris, was atop the depth chart at the time.

Behind Morris were Brian Fox, Lex Smith, Donald Douglas—then Matthews. Douglas decided to transfer to Houston. Brian Fox broke his ankle. Meanwhile, Spurrier worked with Shane on his throwing motion. Bill Matthews, a high school coach in Mississippi, trekked down to Gainesville and saw that his son was struggling for playing time. So he decided to speak to Spurrier, coach to coach. "I wasn't getting a whole lot of reps," Shane recalled. "[My father] just introduced himself, said he was a high school coach and said, 'My son, he can play if you give him a chance. He's not going to say a whole lot, and he won't say anything to you; but if you give him a chance, he can produce.'"

Apparently, Spurrier listened, because Shane would get his chance. "They divided the teams for the Orange and Blue game," Shane said. "Reaves was the head coach of the Orange team, and he said, 'I'm going to start you.' He liked the way I played and handled the offense. We had to play that spring game in the Gator Bowl over in Jacksonville because they were renovating our stadium. Things worked out well. I played well," he said in typical understated fashion. He was actually named the game's MVP. "I threw three touchdown passes, and I guess the rest is history," he said.

When fall practice began, Morris was listed first string, though Matthews had excelled in the Orange and Blue Game. A week before Spurrier's debut rolled around against Oklahoma State at Florida Field, the job was Shane's. Declining a suggestion from his coach that he should throw a screen pass on the first play to get rid of his jitters, Matthews went downfield for 26 yards to the only player Spurrier ever named a play after, Ernie Mills. That completion to Mills would be the first of many, as Florida scored on a six-play, 70-yard drive in less two than minutes, with Dexter Mills running it in from two yards. The Gators clobbered Oklahoma State, 50-7. Matthews was brilliant, completing 20 of 29 passes for 332 yards without an interception. It was a new day for "The Gator Nation."

Florida's deep-post routes would become known as "The Mills Play." Ernie became one of Matthews' and Spurrier's all-time favorites. "He was a great wide receiver," Shane said. "A lot of people said he couldn't catch the ball. But once he got into a passing game, and Spurrier and Dwayne Dixon worked with him, the guy ended up having a tremendous career and went on to play eight or nine years in the NFL. He got a play named after him he caught so many post routes. His senior year, I think, he caught 12 touchdown passes from me, and I would say eight of those touchdowns came off a deep post. So after he graduated, Coach Spurrier called that play 'The Mills Play.'"

"The Mills Play" lives in perpetuity because of the hand signals used to call it as an audible. Spurrier always signaled in the play by cupping his hands around his eyes, making fake binoculars. "And that's because Ernie Mills wore glasses," Matthews said. "Any time we wanted to throw that pass, that was the signal to Ernie. I know that when I played for the Redskins we used the same signal. He probably still uses it at South Carolina."

Success came early. In the second game of Spurrier's inaugural season, the Gators made their bones in Alabama. Many still consider that 17-13 road victory in Tuscaloosa as a key component toward building a reputation as a champion. Florida had to bounce back from a 10-0 deficit with a Matthews-to-Terrence Barber touchdown pass and an Arden Czyzewski field goal. But the game was won on three interceptions by defensive back Will White and Jimmy Spencer's blocked punt, which Richard Fain fell on for a touchdown. Defense and special teams bailed out the offense that day.

"It proved to people around the country—and to the Florida football players—that we could win titles here and win big games on the road," Matthews said. "That's one thing he [Spurrier] emphasized when he took the job: if you expect to compete for championships, you've got to win in tough environments, on the road, in the toughest conference. Florida always had tremendous players but could not win games on the road. But Coach Spurrier said, 'If we're going to take the next step, we've got to find a way to win these games.' We struggled offensively, but the defense kept us in the game. We hit a couple of big plays offensively against Alabama and won a close game, and that started the snowball effect and it went on from there."

Spurrier wrote in his book, *Steve Spurrier Gators* (with Norm Carlson), that the events of that triumphant day in Birmingham gave him great hopes: "We were going into the unknown where we could beat good teams and have a chance to win the championship."

The next week, however, the probationary sentence came down hard. The announcement that the NCAA would prohibit the Gators from playing in a bowl or keeping another SEC title in 1990 infuriated Spurrier, because he felt his players were paying for the sins of a past regime. The one single violation had occurred in 1986—alleging that Florida coaches gave money to Jarvis Williams for child support five years prior—when none of these players were even around. But the Ol' Ball Coach used that as a motivation for his players and had them playing with a chip—no, a boulder—on their shoulders. He knew that, if they could mount a championship run—even if they didn't get to keep the trophy—it would set the standard for all future Spurrier teams. That would prove, once and for all, that the Gators' image as losers could be changed.

The win over Alabama on the road, Spurrier wrote, broke the bad habit of losing big games. He called it " ... the turning point for our success at Florida over [the period of] those championship seasons."

After a crushing 45-3 loss to Tennessee, Florida began chopping down big rivals as if they were tiny seedlings—LSU, 34-8; Auburn, 48-7; even Georgia in Jacksonville, 38-7. Georgia was always on Spurrier's mind—always had been since he was a player—and he made the Bulldogs a priority when he took the Florida job. He delivered on a promise to the alumni that he would try to reverse the curse of Vince Dooley, who had a decided 17-7-1 advantage over the Gators that he started in 1964 and upheld until his retirement as coach in 1988. Spurrier would own the Bulldogs at the end of his 12 years in Gainesville, losing to them only once.

The 1990 Gators finished the SEC season with one loss, claiming the title in their minds only, coming back from Lexington, Kentucky, with a 47-15 win for their ninth victory. Perhaps they celebrated a little too much and forgot what was next, because when the mythical SEC champions rolled into Tallahassee, FSU hammered them, 45-30. Lesson learned? Never celebrate until the task is complete, even though the goal was attained. One never could have predicted that Doak Campbell would become a graveyard for Spurrier, whose teams would never win there—even his national champions.

Spurrier felt that his team, ranked as high as sixth nationally that year, had achieved a breakthrough, setting a new standard for the future. Yet, he would never let anybody else claim the spoils of a virgin champion. "When they [the '91 players] tried to give us the story, 'First Ever,' I'd say, 'Hey, we're just trying to do what last year's team did, same thing, no difference—win the SEC. If they don't want to recognize us this year, fine; they don't have to. But last year's team won it, and this year's team will try to win it.'"

That is why recognition of the 1990 team has remained one of Spurrier's missions; why that Gator team is inscribed as "Best in the SEC" on the facade of the Florida Field south end zone; why he counts six SEC titles in his first seven years instead of five. It's not for his personal aggrandizement. "The 1990 team will always be recognized by me, but whether or not the university will, I seriously doubt it," Spurrier said from his South Carolina football office. "In a way, the '90 team winning the SEC made it easier on me and the coaches, relieved the pressure brought by, 'The Gators can't take the pressure—can't win the big one.'"

The mold for the Spurrier Quarterback Factory was ready for clay, as Matthews was chosen 1990 "SEC Player of the Year," the first of two for him. More accolades began rolling in as defensive tackle Huey Richardson and free safety Will White became the first of 21 to be named All-America during the Spurrier years.

Florida's championships began unfolding when the 1991 Gators finally realized their dream: an SEC trophy to keep. Who knew it would almost become old hat? Equally as important, these new Gators had a positive self-image, too. This time, they got Alabama at home and trashed the Tide, 35-0, and Matthews threw for three touchdowns passes. They blew past 10 teams during the regular season, stumbling only once—against Syracuse, 38-21. Spurrier blames himself for trying to coach more calmly on the sidelines in that loss to the Orange, as suggested by some friends and a letter-writing fan, but he immediately went back to his visor-throwing self the next week in a 29-7 whacking of Mississippi State. Florida clipped off seven successive wins, including those over LSU, 16-0; Tennessee, 35-18; Auburn at Auburn, 31-10; and Georgia, 45-13.

That old war-story-telling firebrand, Gene Ellenson, rallied the team with the code words "Another Level," which were worn proudly on their lapels the night before the FSU game. The Gators received a 14-9 deliverance from Bobby Bowden's Seminoles on a thunderous night of cheering at Florida Field, and the '91 squad became the first in school history to win 10 games. That 10-win number would become the standard over the dozen years of the Spurrier Dynasty. Spurrier later told his old Duke buddies that he never thought he'd win a game by the low score of 14-9. Finally, when Spurrier's team made it to a bowl, they ran into a battering ram—Notre Dame's Jerome Bettis—and lost the Sugar Bowl, 39-28.

Florida had its SEC title, and the flush of success must have prompted Spurrier to strut boldly in the name of tradition, to come up with a nickname for Florida Field that would set it apart: "The Swamp." During a conversation with media czar Norm Carlson, Spurrier learned that Florida President John J. Tigert sought out the current site in a marshy swamp. The word "swamp" triggered Spurrier's imagination, and he replied, "'The Swamp' is where Gators live." It stuck.

Winning begets winning and elevates the quality of play, attracting the attention of other winners. A record 10 Florida players made All-SEC first team in 1991, totaling 19 over Spurrier's first two seasons. Defensive tackle Brad Culpepper was picked as the school's 37th All-American and won the Draddy Trophy as the nation's top scholar-athlete. Running back Ericct Rhett became a force in the so-called "Fun 'N' Gun" offense, almost forcing them to change the name to "Fun, Gun 'N' Run."

As far as Matthews is concerned, Rhett was one of the best running backs to ever play at Florida. "And he was also one of the craziest guys you'll ever meet," Matthews said. "He was one of the toughest players I've ever played with. I remember handing the ball off to him or throwing it to him—*man*! The punishment he took week in and week out, every play. I couldn't understand how he could get up from that. I seriously think he could run 100 miles per hour into a brick wall, and it wouldn't faze the guy—he was that tough."

Culpepper and Matthews formed a strong bond as pioneering, new-breed Gators. "I played with some great players," said Matthews. "Brad was the vocal leader for the defense and a tremendous player. Not very big at the time, but he was a fiery competitor who found ways to make plays—the same way with Jerry Odom, our starting middle linebacker. Not a very talented guy, but he was a guy who played with tremendous heart and desire who would fire up the team with his inspirational play."

Florida football was in a championship mode, but early in 1992, there was a 31-14 drubbing at the hands of the Vols in Tennessee, and a misstep in Mississippi resulted in a shocking 30-6 loss to Mississippi State. That's when Spurrier realized that he'd better learn to rely more on the running game. Rhett was there to comply, and the senior tailback finished the season in style. He romped for 11 touchdowns on nearly 1,300 yards to lead the team in that department for the fourth straight season, and Florida won seven in a row before losing in Tallahassee, 45-24.

A semi-freak play and grand piece of larceny in the '92 SEC championship game by Alabama defensive back Antonio Langham—a villainous name that shall live forever in the hearts of Gator fans—denied Matthews three straight seasons of playing for the SEC team with the best record. Earlier in the game, Langham had made his first interception and turned it into a 28-21 Tide advantage. Then, as Matthews was taking his team on what looked to be a certain tying—or winning—drive, Langham came out of the shadows to intercept Shane's pass, ending Florida's hopes for victory. "If I had one play in my career that I wish I could do over," said Matthews, "that would be it."

Shane has only one other regret. "I wish we could have played for a national title, because that's everybody's goal when they tee it up for college football," Matthews lamented. "But it was nice to win the first 'official' SEC in 1991. That was a great, great moment. In '90, '91 and '92—Spurrier's first three years—we laid the foundation for him to build the dynasty he had here and for them to win the national championship."

Matthews was 28-8 as a starter with one real SEC title and one mythical one.

"I wouldn't be where I am today, with 13 years under my belt, if it wasn't for Steve Spurrier," Matthews said. "He taught me the little things about how to play quarterback, the little things about how to prepare for games, and just the little things that make you successful. The way I do things today in the NFL are totally different than the way other guys do it. A lot of others say—I don't want to say they 'stress out'—but things that come so naturally to me. He taught me so much about the passing game and the concept of different routes and things, that once I see it, I don't have to look at it but one more time, and I've got it down—whereas some guys sit there and look at their playbooks six or seven times. It's just the way he teaches you to play the position."

For those wanting to play quarterback for Steve Spurrier, purchasing earplugs and perhaps a suit of armor may be wise. That education would be to quarterbacks what an MBA from the Wharton School of Business is to entrepreneurs. That being said, surely quarterbacks wish to retreat from Spurrier's diatribes whenever possible. Spurrier's quarterbacks are scolded and embarrassed, if not outright humiliated on the sidelines. Not the kind of physical abuse, say, that a Bobby Knight dishes out to his basketball players; or even the coarse cussing out those NFL rookies receive from Bill Parcells—but certainly a tongue lashing.

Some of them can't take it. Shane Matthews was one who could.

"You can either take constructive criticism, or you can't," Matthews said. "And that's a job of a coach, I don't care at which level. They have to correct your mistakes when you make them, and if you're not getting the job done, they've got to make a change. I played for my dad in high school, and that's harder than it ever was playing for Spurrier. You're going to catch, 'The only reason you're playing is that you're the coach's son,' even though you may be the best player. So I was prepared playing for him. I just took it as constructive criticism. Sometimes I listened; sometimes I didn't. I'll be honest with you: sometimes I let it in one ear and out the other, trying not to let it affect the way I was going to play. He would chew your butt out on the sideline, throw his visor, yell, scream. But then the next minute he's patting you on the back. It's just the way you handle it. Some guys can; some guys can't."

Not only did Shane take it, he dished it out, completing 722 passes for 9,287 yards and 74 scores—all school records that would be broken by two members of the next generation of Spurrier quarterbacks. Meanwhile, Matthews' Machine was rolling as Rhett ran for nearly 3,000 yards of his career, a record-breaking 4,163 over three seasons, and Willie Jackson pulled in 18 touchdowns over the '92 and '93 season. Rhett was named All-America—as was kicker Judd Davis, who also won the Lou Groza Award.

Spurrier's style of offense was a magnet to players like Danny Wuerffel and Chris Doering. The former came aboard as a much-ballyhooed high school All-American. The latter walked across the street and onto the field without a scholarship.

Wuerffel for Dean, and In Between

Spurrier's high-octane offense began impressing the nation, but who would be Matthews' successor in 1993? Many people thought it might be a promising redshirt freshman from Fort Walton Beach named Danny Wuerffel, who would throw for 22 touchdown passes his first season but later suffer a knee injury.

One of those TDs was the game-winner to Chris Doering at Kentucky with three seconds left—"Doering got a touchdown!" yelled announcer Mick Hubert—clinching the 24-20 comeback victory.

"That was sort of a coming-out party for both me and Mick," said Doering, who had scored his first career touchdown earlier in the fourth quarter. It was also the first step in a long relationship as teammates and friends for Doering and Wuerffel. On that same day, Doering had learned that Florida was putting him on scholarship. After Terry Dean's four-interception effort, Wuerffel earned the start the next week, and Florida beat Tennessee, 41-34, before a record Florida Field crowd of more than 85,000.

Spurrier's very first signing upon arrival in Gainesville, Terry Dean had waited his turn, which he would receive in 1993. Replaced by Wuerffel after his four-pick game against Kentucky, Dean came off the bench against Georgia to engineer a 33-26 victory. His career moment came in the SEC Championship game—played in Birmingham, the city of his birth—where the 28-13 licking of Alabama would earn Dean the game's MVP. The next season, just as he appeared to be the next in line of superstars, his world would crumble. He set a record with seven touchdown passes in the first half against New Mexico State and finished the game in street clothes. He was so close to stardom after a brilliant performance in Knoxville that he was already moving in the direction of the early lead of the Heisman Trophy race. Except every time Spurrier heard or read the names "Heisman" and "Dean" in the same sentence, he was overcome with apoplexy. Dean's performance in the 31-0 lashing of Tennessee was flawless, however, and he was too good to ignore in a season where there were no hot Heisman frontrunners. Dean, unfortunately, turned out to be one who couldn't take Spurrier's heat.

However, the kid from Fort Walton Beach, Wuerffel, *could.*

In what would be one of the biggest games ever played at Florida Field, the No. 1-ranked Gators hosted No. 6-ranked Auburn—a team that had won 17 in a row but continued to serve probation and was unable to achieve postseason status. Someone figured out that Coach Terry Bowden and his dad, Bobby, were 4-1 against the Ol' Ball coach, about to be 5-1.

Spurrier was already mad at the way his team and his quarterback, Dean, had played in a 42-18 win over LSU. He was most upset, probably, with all the "No. 1" talk and the fact that Dean was, at that moment, the top candidate to win the … well, you know the name. A vocal confrontation between quarterback and coach erupted before the Auburn game, in which

Spurrier gave Dean the ultimatum: focus, concentrate throughout the game, or he wouldn't finish out the season as the starter.

One game later, Wuerffel was the starter, and Dean was done for his career.

After the game, Dean went public and made it known that his head coach had put extra pressure on him with the ultimatum. "I've never experienced anything like that," Dean told the media. "My knees were shaking."

Perhaps he had rolled over on his coach because Dean never played another meaningful series the entire season—a season in which another SEC crown was captured.

"That was just a culmination of many things for Terry," Wuerffel said. "It was a high-pressure game; we were No. 1 in the country; and I think he threw his fourth interception in that game." Wuerffel and Dean remain friends today.

In 2005, Dean came to a Gator Club meeting in Southwest Florida, where he told Franz Beard of GatorCountry.com that he felt somewhat redeemed. "I think my story is a little bit different than most of the guys who played at Florida; I felt like the black sheep of Florida football for a long time," Dean said. "I've not been involved in Florida football for 10-plus years, but Coach Meyer came here and things changed. I met him a couple of months ago, and he has done so much to recruit the former players to bring them back."

Though the '94 Gators would end the season with a 10-2-1 mark and a conference title, they suffered perhaps the all-time worst fate in a game they didn't lose—called the "Choke at Doak." Leading 31-3 as the fourth quarter began, the Gator defense totally collapsed, allowing FSU to rally for the 31-31 tie. Bobby Bowden said he'd "… never had a tie feel so much like a win." Spurrier never had one feel so much like a loss, but pretended to look past it and pointed toward the SEC Championship. All Gator fans were grateful that Bowden had not elected to go for the two-point conversion, because quarterback Danny Kannel was so hot, he no doubt would have made it.

The next week Florida won the SEC for the third time officially, beating Alabama, 24-23.

The Gators had to overcome Dwayne Rudd's interception runback, though, catching up with Alabama on an 80-yard drive that culminated with the winning two-point reception by Chris Doering. Spurrier pulled out his bag of tricks, and the Gators faked an injury to Wuerffel, who limped off the field as backup Eric Kresser came in the game and proceeded to complete a 25-yard pass to Ike Hilliard, followed by a two-yard scoring pass from Wuerffel to Doering. The Ol' Ball coach also dusted off the Emory & Henry formation—after the school of the same name—which features clusters of receivers and offensive linemen bunched wide on each side. On the play, Florida ran a double pass, with Wuerffel throwing to Doering, who then connected with Aubrey Hill. The Gators won the SEC, and their reward was a trip to the Sugar Bowl, where they lost in a rematch with FSU, 23-17.

End Kevin Carter became Spurrier's fourth defensive player to become first-team All-America. Wide receiver Jack Jackson blossomed into an All-American after leading the '93-'94 team in receptions, but Doering would take over that spot with 1,045 yards in 1995 as he became Wuerffel's favorite target. Although Doering wound up with a school- and SEC-record 31 touchdown catches, the P. K. Young grad was never named to an All-America team, but he did make All-SEC first team in '95. Fittingly, Doering was inducted into the University of Florida Sports Hall of Fame in 2006 with Wuerffel—his quarterback, good friend, and former roommate.

In addition to his skills, Doering brought leadership and a good sense of humor to what he called "a team full of clowns" in 1995. James Bates was always playing a prank or pretending to argue with defensive back Lawrence Wright, who would refer to the popular white linebacker as "Cracker." It was a tossup between Judd Davis and Jason Dean as to who could do the better Spurrier imitation. Shea Showers and Jacquez Green could make their teammates laugh, too. Plus, the tough talk in the off-season from seniors like defensive end Mark Campbell—and the toughness of guard Donnie Young—seemed to define the team as well. Doering brought a "Rudy-like" inspirational quality for having earned the utmost respect as a player who took the long route to stardom.

Like some former P. K. Yonge athletes who felt gypped by the university for making them walk on to earn a scholarship—remember Bernie Parrish and his three Blue Wave teammates?—Doering used that to fuel his burning ambition. "The best thing that could have ever happened to me was to go through what I did—walking on and not being given a scholarship," Doering said, "So many times you see these blue chip prospects come in and never make it. I think that has made me a better person."

Going into the 1995 season, both the leadership and the sense of humor would be needed as Steve Spurrier was prepared to take his team to new heights.

Can Losing Ever be a Good Thing?

Though legend has it that Steve Spurrier has never found anything beneficial about losing, and that his dad taught him that winning was the only objective to playing sports, the truth is, the Ol' Ball Coach has often gained wisdom from defeat—and at least one tie.

From the 1966 loss to Georgia as a player, Spurrier learned that he and his teammates shouldn't have let their heads swell after beating Auburn the week before, 30-27. As a coach, Spurrier learned from the 1990 loss to FSU that the celebration of beating Kentucky for the mythical SEC title had disturbed his team's focus. From the loss to Syracuse in 1991, he learned a lesson about being true to his own coaching personality; and after losing to Tennessee and Mississippi State the following year—for his only regular-season back-to-back defeats as coach of the Gators—he learned that, at times, he needed a running game.

Although Spurrier would never admit to those lessons, the last game of the 1995—when an undefeated Florida team had a train wreck in Tempe, Arizona—would prove otherwise. From the ashes of Spurrier's most lopsided loss as a coach, a 62-24 whipping administered by Nebraska in the Fiesta Bowl, arose a national champion. First, however, came the thud of a team dropping from the high clouds of prosperity to a pit of despair. Florida's only unbeaten team, and one that many people feel was even better than the 1996 national champions, crashed and burned after spotless 12-0 regular-season record and the SEC title game victory. This 1995 squad was so good that some of the players admitted they walked on the field expecting the Cornhuskers to lie down.

"We were full of ourselves," said wide receiver Jacquez Green.

Earlier in the season, that Gator team had beaten eighth-ranked Tennessee, 62-37; seventh-ranked Auburn, 49-38; non-ranked Georgia, 52-17, in Athens; and sixth-ranked Florida State, 35-24. There was the satisfaction ahead of thumping Arkansas for a third straight SEC title, 34-3—highlighted by the interception of a lateral by Razorback quarterback Larry Lunney, which was returned 95 yards for a touchdown by linebacker Ben Hanks.

"We thought we were in for a dogfight," Nebraska defensive coordinator Charlie McBride would say a year later.

Had the Gators drawn anybody but the Cornhuskers' dynasty, we might be talking today about the best Florida team of all time. "I think that '95 team," Captain Donnie Young said, "was a lot better than the '96 team."

Quarterback Tommie Frazier of Bradenton inflicted pain on his home state with a brilliant 75-yard touchdown run—part of his 199 yards rushing that night. But that wasn't nearly as painful as the serious hip injury to wide receiver Jacquez Green, which stopped play for several minutes as he was carted off the field in intense pain. Green's fellow offensive teammates seemed to vacate the game emotionally, although Florida only trailed Nebraska by 10 points at the time.

Meanwhile, pain medication was administered to Green, who was hauled away to a medical facility, where he kept a watchful eye on a television. "I wasn't thinking about football right then, I was thinking about whether I'd ever walk again," Green said. Jaquez drifted in and out of consciousness due to the medication and soon became painfully aware of what was happening to his team. When he left the game, the score was still relatively close. "By the time I woke up in the hospital bed," Green said, "it was like 53-20, or something crazy like that. And I said, 'Good Lord! How did they score that many points that quick?' Every time I looked up at the TV, there was another Nebraska guy scoring a touchdown."

He wasn't hallucinating—the Huskers scored 29 unanswered points in the second period and took a commanding 35-10 halftime lead.

Dr. Pete Indelicato said Green's separated hip, caused by being pushed backwards when his leg was pinned behind him on a kickoff return, was one of the worst injuries he'd ever seen. "That's usually an injury you see in the emergency room after a head-on collision," Indelicato said.

Green did walk again, and ran again well enough to make All-America two seasons later.

Apparently, Wuerffel has exorcised that night from his mental scrapbook. "I'm not sure it's selective memory loss or what, but I don't remember much about that game," Wuerffel said. "They really did pummel us in every sense—offense, defense, special teams. They had a scheme [on defense] to come at me, and they were really getting after us. We weren't using the shotgun at that time, so the guys came clean off the ball. But their offense was so powerful that we could have maybe scored 50 points and lost."

Young couldn't erase the pain as did his good friend Wuerffel; and, in fact, he even bristles today when talking about the bitter taste. "It was in none of our blood to lose a game—to be at the pinnacle of college football and take a whippin' like that. It was pretty bad. I remember my quote from *Sports Illustrated*: 'I felt like my father had taken me out in the middle of the field and spanked my ass right in front of 85,000 people,'" said the senior guard from Venice.

The '95 Florida offense was a statistical buzz saw, averaging 44.5 points on four touchdowns passes and two rushing TDs per game. It also rang up 27 first downs per game on 7.4 yards per play. Wuerffel would snag the first of two straight All-America honors in '95, passing for an amazing 35 touchdowns, and the first of two SEC Player of the Year awards. Offensive tackle Jason Odom joined Wuerffel as a first-team All-American. Doering caught 70 passes—tying for the most in the nation—for 17 touchdowns, most in school history. He also led a parade of nine Gators to make first-team All-SEC.

What did they learn from this defeat? Young said it was painful, but educational. "They were on and had a perfect night," he said, "and we were off and had our worst night; not a very good cap to a great season. But we learned at lot about ourselves. ... It was a growing pain we needed to have—not just as athletes, but as coaches as well."

Spurrier wasn't going to give in on his philosophy. "I don't know what we learned," Spurrier said, reflecting back over 10 years later. "The '95 team had a good group of seniors—Chris Doering, Mark Campbell, Henry McMillan, Johnny Church—that weren't with us in '96. What we learned was, Nebraska was probably, some say, the best team in history. I talked to Tom Osborne later, and he said, while he wouldn't say one team was better than the other, that team was the only one he ever had that didn't have a close game all season. That team clobbered everybody he played, including us. So we learned that."

That's not all exactly. Spurrier learned his team needed to be bigger and stronger. "To get beat like a drum as we did—we knew we had to make some changes to get back the next year," said defensive end Cameron Davis. "We knew we had to get much tougher out there. I know Spurrier hired a strength coach named [Jerry] Schmidt. He really pounded us in the weight room in that off-season and that next summer. We were going to be dominant, not take any crap from anybody, and go out there and play. That's the kind of attitude we had throughout the year—we needed to be tougher out there."

Green said the Fiesta Bowl convinced the team that they had a ton of work to do in the off-season, and they were ready and willing to do so. "The main thing that summer was the leadership from our older guys—Anthone Lott, Lawrence Wright, and those guys. They made every workout. They were real good guys, and I looked up to them, so I wanted to do well in the conditioning part of it."

Florida was going to need a new defensive coordinator after Bob Pruett left, signing on to be the next head coach of his alma mater, Marshall. One day after the '95 season, Athletics Director Jeremy Foley brought Spurrier a stat sheet listing the leading defensive teams. Bobby Stoops, co-coordinator of Kansas State's nationally top-ranked defense, became of paramount interest.

No hire in Florida football—aside from Spurrier—would ever have a bigger impact.

That Championship Season

Spurrier soon found that former K-State coach Bill Snyder could be stingy when it came to helping his assistant coaches get ahead, evidenced by the several calls Spurrier made that were never returned. He sought permission to speak with Stoops, but such permission was mere formality anyway, so Spurrier phoned Stoops directly. Allegedly, the call was made by assistant coach Lawson Holland, a friend and former associate of the Kansas State co-coordinator.

A former Iowa player and coach, Stoops was a Big Ten guy who knew very little about Florida. He'd never met Spurrier, but greatly admired him. Stoops' K-State defense had held mighty Nebraska to 262 yards just two years earlier, but the stat Spurrier loved was that K-State defenders forced opponents to surrender possession after three downs 48 percent of the time.

"You know what that means," Spurrier said in semi-jest. "That means more ball plays for Stevie Boy."

Certainly Stoops wasn't expecting to be hired by Spurrier back in 1996, or even to receive a telephone call out of the blue. Stoops' secretary told him his friend and former coaching associate—Holland, then a Spurrier assistant—was on hold. "When I picked up the phone, Lawson wasn't on anymore," Stoops said, "but it was Coach Spurrier. He said, 'Bobby, this is Steve Spurrier calling from Florida.' And I didn't think it was, because I'd never talked to him before. So I didn't say anything for a long time. We got to talking, and I realized it was [Spurrier], so I said, 'Geez, I better start talking, because this really is Coach Spurrier.'"

Spurrier told him he was reviewing candidates for the job and asked if Stoops would be interested, which he said he was. They talked over the phone off and on for three days straight, and virtually Stoops was offered the job without a face-to-face interview.

"I remember when Coach called my home, after about the second day after we had talked," Stoops said. "My wife got the messages, and it was a Mary Kay [Cosmetics] recording, because I don't get messages at home; and my wife is a Mary Kay national director. His message said, 'This is Steve Spurrier, and I'm not looking to buy any cosmetics, but I wanted to talk to Bobby.' My wife was excited because she said, 'Hey! Steve Spurrier is calling for you!' I hadn't had time to talk to her yet, and I said, 'Yeah, we need to sit down and talk.' She remembered just after Thanksgiving I was watching the SEC Championship game, and I said how much I thought of Steve Spurrier and what a great job he had done. That team really had it going on right then and had one of the best programs out there. Then all of a sudden, there's Steve Spurrier on the phone."

Eventually they did meet when Stoops stopped in Florida on a trip home to Ohio, but before that, Holland was asked to go along and identify the guest from Manhattan, Kansas. The meeting sealed the deal, and it seemed like an ideal situation for Stoops to grow and for Florida to install a new, more aggressive defense. In retrospect, perhaps Spurrier should have bought some Mary Kay makeup—he and Stoops would be in the bright lights of college football fame right away.

That Spurrier often jousted with defensive coordinators was no big secret. Of course, each coach had to feel the other out, but they never really discussed the Xs and Os of Stoops' system before the hire. "Through the interview process, there was very little [discussion] on game plans," Stoops said. "He wanted to know a little bit about my style, but he trusted what I was doing." He brought his own defense to Florida with the understanding that the present staff would have to learn the Stoops way.

During the first practice scrimmage of 1996, Stoops received a baptism by fire—a proper introduction from Spurrier in which Stoops' first-string defense would have to contain Spurrier's first-string offensive onslaught.

"I looked out there, and there's the Heisman Trophy winner at quarterback," Stoops recalled, "with Fred Taylor at tailback. You got Reidel Anthony and Ike Hilliard split wide, and Jacquez Green was in the slot. They go about four plays, touchdown. Coach says, 'Okay, flip it around.' They go four or five plays, touchdown. 'All right, flip it around again.' Three more plays, touchdown. You talk about stretching out a defense! Coach looks over at me and says, 'Stoopsie! We gonna be able to force a punt this year?'"

Points were given, but that point was taken. Bobby Stoops was clearly the missing piece of the puzzle.

Cameron Davis said Stoops had a calming quality. "I don't know what it was," Davis said of his new coordinator, "but he made you comfortable, and he made you listen. That made it a whole lot easier to buy into his system. I always thought he was going to be successful once he left the University of Florida [for Oklahoma]—and that has obviously happened. He was a helluva players' coach, and his system wasn't difficult. It was just trusting everybody 'in the box' to do their job."

The 1996 coaches and players had the right man to run the defense, and, for the most part, Spurrier let him be. Together they had big plans. "At the beginning of every season, we set our goals for the year, and the '96 team was to win 'em all," Spurrier recalled. "They said, 'We want to win the Eastern Division; we want to win the SEC, want to be in a bowl game—and we also have goals in case we miss those.' But the '95 and '96 team started feeling like we were capable of doing that."

After two ho-hum preseason wins to start in '96, the No. 1-ranked Florida Gators took on the No. 2 Tennessee Vols in Knoxville, where Stoops' defense would face Vols quarterback Peyton Manning before college football's largest home crowd ever (107,608) in what would be a weird night.

"I've been in big games—played in the Rose Bowl as a player, played at Michigan as a player, and had many big games at Iowa and Kansas State," Stoops said. "But I guess I'd never been around the attention we were getting that year, coming into the season with Danny Wuerffel and a great team. Peyton Manning had emerged at Tennessee in that rebuilt stadium with 107,000 people, and the publicity and hype around that game created an amazing atmosphere that I'd never experienced ... just seeing the players and [Spurrier] and the way he rises with the great demeanor and leadership in those situations."

The rain fell hard in the first half, and everybody on the Florida coaching staff was immediately concerned about Wuerffel's inability to throw a wet football—a trait he had exemplified previously in several rainy games. Their fears were soon allayed. This was a night for defense, and Stoops' Troops were up to the occasion, allowing just three yards rushing in the first half. They intercepted Manning four times over the course of the game, deflected eight passes, recovered two fumbles, and tackled ball carriers for losses five times.

In his first big game with Spurrier, Stoops was awestruck by his boss' aggression. On fourth-and-11 at the Tennessee 35-yard line, Spurrier signaled his offense to stay on the field. "Coach doesn't even consider punting," said Stoops. "He probably did, but in his mind, he makes the decision so fast that he just called the play, sent it in, and, *boom*! ... We hit Reidel Anthony deep for a touchdown—and Reidel catches it, runs through the end zone, jumps up, and kisses a Tennessee girl—we go for it all, and there it is! I could tell he was doing his best to get that crowd sitting on its hands right off the bat and letting our guys know we are going to be aggressive. And I then look around—10 minutes to go in the second quarter, and we're up 35-0, with a defensive touchdown on the last one [Anthone Lott's fumble recovery]. And I remember thinking, 'Wow, it doesn't get much better than this.'"

At the half, Florida led, 35-7. Perhaps that was a big lead for some people, but Donnie Young's memory went back to a time when his Gator team was enjoying a 31-3 lead going into the fourth quarter when it blew apart like a love bug hitting a windshield. "I'd love to have slapped 100 on them, because we all remembered the game in Tallahassee," Young said, "but we certainly weren't comfortable."

Spurrier had a different perspective about his fourth straight win over the Vols. "We had them 35-0, and there were 10 minutes left in the second quarter," Spurrier said. "They [Tennessee] got the ball at the 20-yard line; and I looked up, and they threw a post route for 80 yards and a score. And I walked over to Bobby and said, 'What in the hell are we doing?' He said,

'I substituted the starting safety, and the other guy I put in there let Peyton Manning throw it over his head.'"

In his book (with Mike Bianchi), *Tales From The Swamp*, Wuerffel wrote that he'd had a near-epiphany during the timeout leading up to the touchdown to Anthony. That afternoon he had read a passage from a book called *My Utmost for His Highest* by Oswald Chambers, which said: "We find to our own amazement that we have the power to stay wonderfully poised even in the center of it all." He said he felt a sense of calm and peace on the sideline, giving him assurances that this football game was not his obsession.

Even though Florida won the game easily—Tennessee did score in the last 10 seconds to make it look good, 35-29, and Manning did pass for 492 yards—the Florida coaching staff wasn't happy. The team reflected that by showing humility in victory. Wuerffel had thrown four touchdown passes, but only managed 155 yards passing. And the defense let the Vols back in the game.

"We didn't play that well. We certainly weren't full of ourselves after winning in Knoxville," Spurrier said. "One of the Tennessee writers said, 'Big Crowd, Big Game, Big Stadium—No Big Deal To Gators.' [The article] said our locker room was subdued, nobody was yelling and screaming, that it was just another day at the ballpark. And it was, because we didn't like the way we played after having a big lead."

It must have been a good lesson. The Gators ripped through the next five SEC opponents by the whopping combined score of 261-37—Kentucky, 65-0; Arkansas, 42-7; LSU, 56-13; Auburn, 51-10; and Georgia, 47-7. They struggled at Vanderbilt, hanging on for a 28-21 victory, then wound up the conference schedule unbeaten with a 52-25 win at home against South Carolina. By the big game against FSU in Tallahassee, the Gators had rolled up a 10-0 record with an average score of 49.5 points, allowing fewer than 13 per game, averaging a 37-point average margin of victory.

The Florida staff had learned a valuable lesson about Wuerffel, too—what you saw on the practice field wasn't going to be what you'd get in the game. Wuerffel required intense pressure to summon his best game, which so many Gator fans witnessed during his remarkable run as their starting quarterback. During this stretch, Spurrier's brain and Wuerffel's body synergistically morphed in a new creation that some called "Spuerffel." This transformation, alongside Wuerffel's impregnable concentration, allowed Spurrier to change plays with the subtlest hand signals at the last possible moment—at near-*impossible* moments.

Wuerffel was asked to explain the difference. "Good question ... I think everything speeds up in the game," Wuerffel explains. "Kind of like when you're golfing sometimes—you're sitting there on the driving range, and you think about it so long that you figure out ways to mess up. Just go play, and you'll feel like you don't have to worry about it all the time. I just seemed to, in the flow of the game, get into a good rhythm and do well.

"I guess I have the incredible ability to focus on certain things and block everything else out. I'm blessed with that ability, which is a great advantage on the football field. In marriage, it drives my wife nuts because while I'm thinking about one thing, she can have an entire conversation with me; and I won't hear a word of it."

Wuerffel's idiosyncratic, somewhat-unorthodox throwing motion was never pretty in practice or warmups, either; but when the game was on, Wuerffel could throw lasers or lobs to his trio of All-Americans with amazing results. His three receivers—Reidel Anthony, Ike Hilliard, and Jacquez Green—were smart and played as a unit, reassuring him that if two of them were covered, one would be open.

With Wuerffel's hot hand, Spurrier's Gators swept through the SEC schedule in 1996 ready to complete their second straight undefeated regular season. "That team was in the habit of scoring a lot of points," Spurrier said. "Of course, we had Danny, Reidel Anthony, Ike Hilliard, Jacquez—we scored a lot of points, threw a lot of touchdown passes, and our defense got the ball back quickly, which we had never seemed to do. We were just playing at a high level. Going to Tallahassee, we felt like we had to win there to win them all."

More often than not, the Seminoles had gotten the better of Spurrier. He was 2-4-1 against FSU entering the game and had never won in Doak Campbell Stadium. If ever Spurrier needed to break his Tallahassee jinx, it was on November 30, 1996. Florida was No. 1, Florida State was No. 2—and the winner of that game most likely had a lock on the Nokia Sugar Bowl. It would be only the fourth time in history that two unbeaten college teams had met in the final game of the season. The loser would drop a notch in the poll and leave a backdoor for Arizona or Ohio State to jump over them.

And in the poll-sitting world of college football, every little nuance is critical. Even more critical now would be the decimation of Florida's offensive line, which had played so well all season—center Jeff Mitchell; guards Donnie Young and Ryan Kalich; and tackles Mo Collins and Zach Piller.

Echoing the "Echo of the Whistle"

In the root-hog world of Donnie Young, territorial imperative could be a matter of yards, if not feet or inches. His pugnacious attitude and ferocious competitive spirit exemplified the heart of the Gators' veteran offensive line.

Florida's right guard and captain could be as light-hearted and funny as anyone on the team, which he called "the perfect blend" of personalities. Going into the game against unbeaten, No. 2-ranked Florida State in Doak Campbell Stadium; however, he was in no mood for laughs—after lining up and looking at all the new faces on each side of him.

"I remember looking down the line," Young said of the greenhorns, "and going, 'Holy cow! I've got more experience that all these guys combined.'"

Piller had been injured against Vanderbilt and would not start against the Seminoles. Mitchell had been hurt against Georgia and was unavailable. Collins was suspended over a ticket issue. And here were the Gators about to play against the best pass rush they'd faced all year.

Young, however, felt confident the Gators could win. "We just knew if our tackles could hold up, the game was a non-issue," he said. "Obviously, history proved it didn't go too well."

When you're going up against two of the best defensive ends ever to play on one college football team, the absence of key offensive linemen like Mitchell, Piller, and Collins can be a recipe for disaster. Peter Boulware and Reinard Wilson of FSU—both NFL No. 1 draft choices waiting to happen—were licking their chops (Boulware would be the fourth player picked, Wilson the 14th). They were going to be a load for Florida's offensive line no matter who was playing.

Some people would call it good, hardnosed football; others call it dirty football; but Florida State defense's style of play under Mick Andrews was certainly aggressive. Meanwhile, the knock against Spurrier's offense was that he sometimes didn't protect the quarterback—odd, considering he won a Heisman Trophy playing that position. The combination was going to be lethal for Wuerffel, though, especially with the rumor afoot that a bounty was on his head. Wuerffel was in for the beating of his life, even worse than in the Fiesta Bowl against Nebraska.

"There were rumors—and I don't know if they were ever proven—that some people put up some money, that whoever could knock him [Wuerffel] out would get $300," Spurrier said over a decade later. "That was just a rumor, and I don't have verification of it; but we heard that rumor from several sources up around Tallahassee."

FSU's Boulware made no secret of what the Seminoles were trying to do. "Our plan was to hit him [Wuerffel] every time he raised his arm," said Boulware. "We'd hit him; he'd get up; we'd hit him again. You stop Danny Wuerffel, and you stop Florida."

A big-game feeling was in the air. "The anticipation before the game was incredible," said receiver Reidel Anthony. "Their crowd got there early. We were pumped, they were pumped—typical Florida-Florida State. Before the game is always the best part. Everybody out there jawing at each other makes for a great time and lots of excitement."

FSU's offense did its part to win the game. The contributions of pint-sized Seminole running back Warrick Dunn, who always seemed to be Florida's nemesis, could not be dismissed. Dunn rambled for 185 yards rushing. Quarterback Thad Busby made no mistakes and hit a key third-down pass in the fourth quarter to Peter Warrick that set up the "Pooh Bear" Williams' clinching touchdown run, his second score of the day.

"They competed hard," recalled Anthony, "but we had a bad eight minutes that turned the game in their favor."

Ike Hilliard had perhaps his worst game in several seasons. Field-goal kicker Bart Edmiston missed two attempts. Wuerffel was sacked six times and had three interceptions, but still managed to complete 23 of 48 passes for 362 yards. According to other "unofficial stats," Wuerffel was hit another 30 times, legal or otherwise. Yet, Wuerffel's nature was to keep quiet and keep competing, which turned out to be a big plus for Florida's title hopes. Hardly noticeable was a Wuerffel-generated drive during which his touchdown pass to Anthony in the final two minutes—a pass that not only made the score close, but would become a huge factor in the final balloting as well.

"Florida State actually blew us out that day," recalled receiver Jacquez Green. "Most people don't realize the score was 24-14 until the end. That's before we had the shotgun, and Danny didn't really have a chance. We were just throwing the ball, throwing the ball. I think we got away from our running game. Ike Hilliard had a bad sprained ankle, and I kept cramping up."

Despite that, Green said Florida's receivers were open all day. "Danny just didn't have time to get the ball to us," Green said.

Although Florida's last touchdown appeared meaningless, it was anything but. "We weren't very happy that we had lost one," Spurrier said. "But I'll tell you what Danny did. We did go down there and score to make it 24-21, which may have been very important in the final voting. When they're voting—and that's what we have in college football, voting for championships—to only lose by three was better than to lose by 10. But I didn't think we had any chance for a national championship."

Many members of that Gator team claim to have thought that they could still win it all back then. However, I was in the postgame interviews that day in Tallahassee and only heard one of them say it—although some may have been thinking it.

Cameron Davis and others said they all felt there was a piece of unfinished business. "I remember sitting next to [defensive back] Lawrence

Wright on that bus after the game, and we were saying, 'This is just *NOT* supposed to happen—it just doesn't feel right.' I don't know what it was, be there was just a weird feeling that we were somehow going to wind up in the national championship game."

Later, defensive lineman Ed Chester would tell the media: "When we lost that game to Florida State, you could see the look on everybody's face. We lost that game, and we knew we were better than they were. We knew that, if we got another shot at that game, we would kill them."

Still bearing the marks of his beating, Wuerffel stood on a folding chair in the postgame press conference, held in a makeshift interview room underneath Doak Campbell Stadium. At one point, he was asked if he thought the Gators were still in the national-championship picture, and he replied, "Yes."

Of course, there was still the SEC title game to be played the next week.

When Wuerffel took off his T-shirt, some of his teammates and coaches were horrified at the sight of the marks on his upper body. "He had bruises from his neck all the way down to his ankle," Davis recalled, "and yet he never complained about that one time. I've never seen anybody bruised like that in football. And that just took my respect level for that guy a lot higher—he was a tough cookie."

Hilliard, though, had seen this from his quarterback before. "He pretty much took a beating every other game. It's just amazing that he could twist and turn his body as he did. And he would get right back up. Danny is one of the toughest guys I've ever been around."

Once back home, Danny's father, Jon, watched the replay and called Spurrier. He'd counted 30 times that his son was hit, mostly after the whistle. After watching the tape, Spurrier was livid—he felt that brutality went beyond the rules of football.

Through it all, Danny Wuerffel said nothing.

"There's no question that they were very physical and aggressive," Wuerffel said. "And they were really coming after me—they made that known. I think what it comes down to is, there were several late hits that were called, and there were a few that they missed. But it really wasn't my place to bring that up during the game. I just have to get up and go play the next play. Coach Spurrier was the one who brought that to everybody's attention. They [the officials] did a great job of watching it closely in the Sugar Bowl, but it's one of those things that's not mine to worry about."

For each ounce of physical pain Wuerffel suffered, Hilliard matched him shot for shot with mental anguish. For reasons that even he still doesn't understand, Hilliard failed to show up with his game in Tallahassee. He dropped balls, ran sloppy routes, and missed blocks. Ike was held to three passes for 34 yards, not exactly All-America numbers in the biggest game of his life. Conversely, Anthony and Green did more than their part. Reidel had 11 catches for 193 yards and a touchdown; Jacquez caught four balls for 44 yards and two touchdowns. Reportedly, Ike and his friend Reidel didn't speak about it for several days.

"I let my team down that day," said Hilliard, now a Tampa Bay Bucs receiver. "I didn't play well at all. I was very fortunate—and I'm being selfish now—to get another shot at FSU in the Sugar Bowl. But I don't think it's a situation we should have been in, because of our poor play—and my poor play."

The loss to FSU was so devastating that Spurrier called off Monday's practice, telling his team to go home and regroup. "Get this crap out of your system, and let's get ready to win us another SEC championship," the Gator coach said. They came back on Tuesday with a changed attitude.

Meanwhile, as host of a Monday morning sports talk show on WMOP/Ocala and WGGG/Gainesville, I interviewed guest Paul Finebaum, a Birmingham talk-show host, who began an impromptu rant against what he perceived as the dirty-trick tactics of Mickey Andrews and Bobby Bowden. "What they did to Danny Wuerffel was 'criminal,'" said Finebaum, whom Spurrier numbers among his friends in the media. "I'm surprised Steve hasn't said something about it."

The next day, Spurrier joined the fray, lambasting Bowden and the FSU coaches for hitting after the whistle. "All I did was try to defend Danny Wuerffel," Spurrier said years later, denying that his outburst was in any way strategic, given that he didn't even know there would be a rematch. "I don't think, as coach, when your player takes a beating like, that you can sit back and say, 'That's just part of football—the referees have to control it.' To me, you have to speak out and defend your players in that situation. So I did. But it was only meant to support one of my players when he needed strong support from the coach."

Oddly, the victorious coaches wound up in a defensive position as Spurrier's charges rippled forthwith. When Andrews and Bowden were being forced to explain why FSU tacklers were taught to hit the quarterback up to the "echo of the whistle," were they using new football jargon that escaped readers of the rulebook? Spurrier jabbed back, telling the media, "I don't know what the ACC rule is on hitting the quarterback. They seem to say, 'If you're within a step or two, it's okay to clobber them.'"

Spurrier fielded heavy outside criticism about his complaints, but it set well with his players and diverted the focus from them. "Whether there were late hits or not," Green said, "we appreciated our coach standing up for his players like that. That's why you enjoy playing for him, because you know he will look after you if you look after him."

Even to this day, Spurrier is bitter about what he perceived as poor overall officiating.

"They [FSU] somehow won the game," Spurrier remembered. "We got a touchdown called back on a terrible call by an SEC referee. We were sort of used to terrible calls back in those days."

What also torqued Spurrier and Young, his captain, was that the touchdown was nullified by what they considered a "phantom" holding call. "Our guy had missed his block completely and was laying face first on the ground!" said Young. "He never even touched the guy."

Center Wyley Ritch says he can't remember for sure, but thinks the holding call was against him. "Coach Spurrier was a little upset with me about it, but the tape showed that I didn't hold the guy," Ritch said. "I cut the guy, because he had beaten me; so I didn't hold him."

Still, a sense of failure and denial permeated the team. Hilliard felt responsible for the loss. Young felt the offensive line hadn't performed up to their capability, but from those feelings came an awareness of responsibility and resolve. "Being a senior and captain of the team, I thought, 'What a chickens—t way to lose a football game,'" Young said. "It was an offensive-line problem. We needed to buckle our chinstraps and quit being a bunch of sissies—and that's exactly what we were in that football game."

Suddenly, the Florida-FSU series—one of the nation's most heated college-football rivalries—had become white-hot with contention. Yet, no one could've predicted the combustible result of their Nokia Sugar Bowl rematch.

Florida 52 - Florida State 20

The odds of Florida winning the national title were about as good as Steve Spurrier and Bobby Bowden exchanging Christmas cards that year. Meanwhile, a couple of other pieces of business had to be addressed before the Sugar Bowl matchup could be consummated. Florida had a crack at winning its fourth straight SEC championship and its fifth in seven years—sixth, if you counted Spurrier's way. As always, Spurrier would push aside the pain of the loss to FSU and say that the goal had been to win SEC all along.

Deviating from his past philosophy, Spurrier relented and installed the shotgun formation for the SEC championship game against Alabama—a move that would have monumental impact in the national championship, offering Wuerffel reprieve from the pressure of pass-rushers Boulware and

Wilson, more time, and better vision. Among others, Wuerffel's father was a staunch proponent of the formation and would later take part of the credit for convincing Spurrier to use it.

The shotgun was sprung on Alabama, so often on the wrong end of Florida's quest. Once again, the Tide would feel the wrath of the Gators, 45-30. Despite his previous FSU mauling, Wuerffel's brilliance was never more prevalent, as he passed for six touchdowns on 20 of 35 completions for 401 yards with one interception—much of it from the shotgun formation.

"We came out in the shotgun," said Wyley Ritch, "and I believe we ran it about 60 percent of the time. What I remember is, Alabama had only allowed six touchdowns passing all year, and Danny threw for six against them."

Although Hilliard caught one of the six, he had to come off the bench. "Just to let you know how bad I played [against FSU]," Hilliard said, almost shamefully, "I didn't even start."

If not before, Wuerffel seemed to punch his ticket for everlasting fame as the Heisman winner. The following week, he captured the honor.

Already, the football landscape was changing. After the SEC Championship victory, the top four spots in AP poll would look like this:

1. **Florida State (62 first-place votes)**
2. **Arizona St. (5)**
3. **Florida**
4. **Ohio State**

The SEC title and Nebraska's Big 12 Championship loss to Texas provided Florida the necessary credentials to land the Sugar Bowl bid. With that in his hip pocket, Spurrier continued to bash the Florida State defense. Some said it was a brilliant piece of coaching strategy. Most of the senior players had seen it from Spurrier before, purposely taking on all the pregame heat. "That was Coach's deal," Young said. "He was always outsmarting the other coach. He would turn the media on to them, let the other team deal with all the crap while we went ahead and studied our game plan."

Spurrier wouldn't acknowledge that. "Nah, I don't think that played a factor in the game later," Spurrier said upon reflection. "If we'd have gotten beat, then people would have said, 'If he'd have kept his mouth shut, he'd have probably won.' But since we won, the neutral people said, 'Well, maybe that helped the Gators.' I don't think any of it did. What happened is, we went to the shotgun offense against Alabama and against them. We were a lot healthier the second game. We had two offensive linemen, Zach Piller and Mo Collins, who didn't play in the regular-season game but were ready to play in the bowl game."

As for whether Spurrier psyched Bowden out, his players felt he did. "If he didn't mean to do it, then that's how it worked out," Young conceded. "Maybe it just comes naturally to him."

The most bizarre set of circumstances was about to unfold—almost if some higher power were parting the sea of Orange and Blue to allow these Gators their day in the sun.

From their remote outpost in a secluded Gonzalez, Louisiana, motel on the night before the Sugar Bowl game, nearly every television set in every Gator's room was tuned to the NBC's Rose Bowl telecast. Defensive lineman Reggie McGrew remembers that, upon arriving at the hotel around eight o'clock that night, everybody stayed in their room and watched the game. When backup quarterback Joe Germaine found receiver David Boston with 20 seconds for a 20-17 Buckeye victory over Arizona State, pandemonium ensued.

"I was rooming with Ed Chester," McGrew remembered. "We both jumped up and looked at each other like, 'We've got a chance!' We dropped the high-five, walked out of the room for the meeting, and guys were really hyper outside." Gator players bounced out of their rooms abuzz, but were careful not to celebrate too much, too soon.

"Everybody knew what it was," Green recalled. "We had been talking about the whole scenario for about a week and a half, although we really never thought it would happen."

Offensive guard Cheston Blackshear remembers the atmosphere in the meeting. "When we got in the room, nobody was saying anything," Blackshear said. "But we were looking around, and you could see it on everybody's face: 'Do you know what we're going to be playing for tomorrow night?'"

The next day, they would play their hated nemesis for the national championship. "I don't know if it was the thing that put us over the top or not," said Ritch. "But it seemed like it was meant to be—like it was in the stars. It felt like we were meant to win."

The Florida Gators got an opportunity to score some sweet Sugar Bowl redemption—

Redemption for the "Choke at Doak" …

Redemption for the Fiesta Bowl blowout by Nebraska …

Redemption for stumbling in Tallahassee and allowing the brutal beating of their Heisman-winning quarterback …

Sophomore running back Terry Jackson, a Gainesville resident from a long line of Gator-playing family members, had vowed, "If something happens, and we get one more chance to play these guys, they're going to be sorry."

Jackson, who would have a big role in the title game, felt like they owed Wuerffel a do-over. "You want to take it upon yourself and say, 'Can we do better to take the burden off Danny and give him the opportunity to show people what he can do?'" Jackson said. "Because he was a great player and didn't get a chance."

"We weren't about to lose another national championship," vowed Donnie Young.

Reggie McGrew, like others, had a bitter taste in his mouth. "Most of us knew that we didn't play a very good game that day in Tallahassee and that we were definitely going take full advantage of his opportunity."

Many Gators were totally confident that, if they got this chance, failure would not be an option. Said cornerback Fred Weary, "We knew we had it in the Sugar Bowl."

Nobody was nearly as overjoyed as Hilliard, who felt he owed his team and desperately wanted a chance to redeem himself. And there was no place better to earn that than at the Superdome, just a two-hour drive from where he grew up in Patterson, Louisiana.

For such a famous game—the biggest one in Florida football history—reports on the 1997 Nokia Sugar Bowl game played on January 3 are somewhat sketchy, lack depth, and are nearly nonexistent on the Internet. I was at the Superdome that night, but a decade has taken its toll on many of the game's finite details. A glance back at the official play-by-play sheet from the Florida Sports Information Department is a reminder of just how close the Florida-FSU game actually was through three quarters.

Gator fans remember three huge moments—the first of which insiders refer to "Ike's Stop & Go," Hilliard's brilliant plant-and-go touchdown reception on an inside-slant pattern. He hauled in Wuerffel's pass before he virtually "stiff-legged" an oncoming Seminole defender. Some people were surprised Hilliard didn't hurt his knee, the way he slammed his foot on the artificial surface so hard and so suddenly.

"James Colzie was covering me," Hilliard recalled. "Danny got the ball out to me rather quickly. I was trying to protect myself, because I thought Colzie'd hit me from behind. I happened to see a linebacker coming out from the hash—I don't remember who it was—and as I was coming down, I just kind of leaned back. We ran into each other, and I scored. I didn't spin out of it, but I did cut it back. I was going left, planted my left foot, and ended up going right."

Ike came to a complete stop on that left leg, shifted gears, cut back, got up a head of steam again, and sprinted to the end zone on the 31-yard scoring play that put Florida up 24-10 with just over five minutes to play in the half. This would be the first of three Hilliard touchdown receptions, tying a bowl record at Florida held by his receivers coach, Dwayne Dixon.

Hilliard had picked the right night to make up for his bad game in Tallahassee, but he took none of he credit. "I just happened to be in a good situation because I got a lot of *isos* [isolated, single coverage]," Hilliard said. "Reidel had a big game a couple of weeks before that, and they were really paying him a lot of attention. Danny followed me on the isos, and I was able to have some success."

"Ike's play was like a video game," said teammate Anthony. "I've never seen anything like it—the catch, stopping on a dime, reversing out, and going for the touchdown. It was one of the best plays I have ever seen. I've done stuff similar to it, but nothing like that."

Although the Seminole defense appeared to be tiring, FSU made it a close game in the third quarter, closing the difference to 24-20 on Warrick Dunn's run and Scott Bentley's field goal. That's when everything began to become unraveled for Bowden's bunch. Some of the Gator players say that, because Wuerffel kept the Gator offense rolling, FSU's defense was on the field so much that it began to fatigue. "You could see it in their eyes that they were getting tired," said Ritch.

Big Play No. 2 came with 23 seconds remaining in the third period on third-and-10 at FSU's 16. Wuerffel dropped back, saw no receivers, and scrambled to the end zone for the back-breaking score as the Gators went ahead, 38-20. Hilliard threw a key block on the play. The game was nearing blowout range for Florida, but it would be left to Terry Jackson—whose father, Willie Jackson, had been one of two players to break the color line at Florida just 26 years earlier—to add two exclamation points.

Big play No. 3, a 47-yard run, also is credited to Terry Jackson. This was a moment he had waited for since he was a small child, so he ran the ball like he was running for his life.

"They were such a fast team that they over-pursued at times," Jackson said, looking back over a decade ago. "But they were still playing hard. With a team like that, they put a lot of people in the box. But this was going to be a good play. I took the ball, ran right, cut back, and saw a big hole up field."

Young didn't see the hole, but knew he had cleared the path for Jackson. "We called '18 sweep' on one of my last plays of the game," Young said. "Jackson got the ball. I kicked my man out—just annihilated him—and I looked up to see Terry running down the field for a touchdown."

Once in the end zone, Jackson was overcome by feelings he'd never experienced.

"I'd never danced before," Jackson said, "because I was the kind of player who just handed the ball to the referee. It's a funny thing, because I dove into the end zone and jumped right up," Jackson recalled. "I wanted it to be sort of a [special] moment, because I have been a Gator all of my life. It was a jumping thing, with a little bit of 'The Squirrel.'"

No flag was thrown for the celebration.

Just over six minutes later, Jackson was standing in the end zone again, having scored from the 1-yard line to top off a 52-20 final. "I actually danced that time, too; but the game was over, and they didn't get the cameras on me," he said. "I really got down on the second one."

That touchdown came with 2:12 to play, crippling the Seminoles end assuring Gator fans there would be no FSU comeback, which surely would have been dubbed, "Chokia at the Nokia."

"It's great ... to be ... a Flor-i-*DA* Gator!" cheered the crowd, whose Gator chomps provided the percussion for their chorus.

Jackson's spectacular night included 118 yards on the ground, the third time a member of his family eclipsed the century mark in the Super Bowl. Terry's brother, Willie, did it twice, crossing the 100-yard threshold in the air against Notre Dame in 1992 and against West Virginia in 1994 (148 and 131 yards, respectively).

The shotgun and the return of offensive linemen Mo Collins and Zach Piller gave Wuerffel enough time and protection to hit on 18 of 34 passes for 306 yards and three touchdowns. Ironically, Wuerffel was sacked five times, but it didn't affect his composure, and the officials watched closely for any late hits by FSU.

The injury that benched starting center Jeff Mitchell had caused concern that backup Ritch might not be able to make all the reads and take all the snaps. It never fazed him, though, especially the snaps, for he'd done it at Santa Fe High School.

"Danny was getting hit, but not as often," said Ritch. "I think, if anything, it disrupted their cornerbacks and other defensive backs, because they were used to seeing the quarterback under center and trying to get the jump on him. I think it hurt them in their man-to-man coverage."

Downfield in the secondary, the receivers saw plenty of openings. "We had a great game plan, and we had guys wide open," said Green. "We also had guys wide open in the last game against FSU, but Danny didn't have time to throw it then."

Cameron Davis remembers many of the details because, after making a tackle of Warrick Dunn and then sacking Thad Busby, he came out with an injured knee in the final minutes of the first quarter and didn't return.

"That," said Davis, who was reduced to watching as a spectator after his injury, "was a good football game to watch."

When coaches, players, and fans know they are about to accomplish something that their school had waited 89 years to achieve, they don't always know how to react—except maybe dance a little and look for somebody to hug, and Spurrier, Wuerffel, and all the Gators did just that.

"After the game, the media was just hounding me," Wuerffel remembered on a spring day in 2006 from the new headquarters of Desire Street Ministries in Northwest Florida. "It was a really unusual situation, because I was just trying to run around and hug a teammate. There was a swarm of media, and I was looking for someone to hug—and it wasn't them."

Wuerffel's coach was searching, too, and found plenty of willing subjects. Spurrier even stooped so low that he hugged a couple of media members he considered semi-friends. (It was the only time in 12 seasons that I recall seeing Spurrier hug anybody after the game, including his players and assistant coaches—with the possible exception of his wife, Jerri.)

After the Sugar Bowl, the final Associated Press rankings were:

1. **Florida (65 first-place votes)**
2. **Ohio St. (1)**
3. **Florida St.**
4. **Arizona St.**

The next day, upon leaving the Hyatt Hotel in New Orleans, ardent, longtime fan Shirley Lovell Ritch turned and—as if speaking on behalf of "The Gator Nation"—said: "I can die now. I've finally seen the Florida Gators win it all!"

• • •

Wuerffel became the most decorated Florida Gator football star of its first century. He is the only player to win both the Heisman Trophy and Draddy Trophy. He also won two Davey O'Brien Quarterback awards.

Young cannot sing Wuerffel's praises loudly enough.

"You look back and think about Danny and what a good person he was, ut what a *helluva* player he was. People can take stabs at his arm, but there's never been a quarterback to walk through University of Florida and put that many points on the board—or one in all of college football. Danny was a helluva athlete who did a tremendous job for us. You could always count on him. I think that was our mentality: 'Don't worry about me—you can count on me.'"

Never one to praise his players effusively, Spurrier will defend Wuerffel's quarterbacking abilities to his grave, and believes that, given the chance, Danny could have won a Super Bowl. When he worked for the Redskins, Spurrier contended that Wuerffel should be brought back a second time—a move that was denied by his boss, Daniel Snyder.

"Danny is one of the biggest all-time winners in football," Spurrier said. "He won a state championship in high school for Fort Walton Beach. I watched him lead his team over St. Thomas Aquinas of Fort Lauderdale. St. Thomas had about eight or nine players that signed scholarships. I think Danny's team had two. I watched him win four SECs and a national championship at Florida. And also, he led his team to that NFL Europe World Bowl Championship [for the Düsseldorf Fire]. And I wouldn't doubt that with a really good NFL team that he might've lead them to a Super Bowl championship. That part didn't work out for him. He's the kind of young man who makes the play when it has to be made, and his game rises in the moment of competition—and all the players around him play better because Danny is on their team."

Rarely does a team have depth or talent like the '96 Gators, especially at the receiver position. In their last season, the two All-Americans, Hilliard and Anthony, posted strong numbers. Hilliard caught 10 touchdown passes and led the team with 19.2 yards per catch. Anthony set a school record with 18 touchdown catches and set an NCAA record by scoring in 11 straight games. All-America-to-be Green complemented the two of them beautifully. All three agree that being unselfish was the key to their success, along with Spurrier's preparation and productive, competitive practices.

"If you showed you could catch the ball in practice, Coach Spurrier was going to get the ball to you in the game—whether you were a freshman or whatever," Green said. "And so we all took pride in knowing the plays, knowing all the assignments of each receiver position."

Reidel Anthony agrees, but also emphasizes the role of his coach. "It's not hard to be successful when you are put in the right position. And Coach Spurrier did a great job in putting us in a position to succeed. Then you've got to get out there and execute. Coach Spurrier could come up with the game plan, Danny would get the ball off, and my job was pretty easy. It wasn't hard to get open with the plays he designed."

Anthony also said the surrounding cast of talent made everyone better, especially the receivers. "They can double two guys," Anthony said, "but not three. One of us was going to be doubled and taken out of the game, but that's when the other ones step up. We knew anytime could be our day, so that's why we prepared the way we did."

As he thinks back to head-to-head matchups with his defensive teammates, Anthony feels the quality of the defensive unit helped his game. "Going against guys like Elijah Williams, Fred Weary, Anthone Lott, Lawrence Wright, Shea Showers—the list of great talent around us just goes on and on."

Hilliard paid tribute to his teammates on defense, too. Ike looks back at some of the practice skirmishes as vital to keeping his edge—particularly his daily battles and trash-talking with teammate Lawrence Wright, whose competitive spirit he loved. "I got tired of Lawrence's mouth," Hilliard said in semi-jest, "just as I'm sure he got tired of mine. He always felt like he was a cornerback trapped in a safety's body, but he competed. That's why he was the best defensive back in the nation his senior year."

Hilliard still shakes his head at the great talent around him, the intelligence of his coaches, and the good fortune that befell his team. "We were just a blessed group," Hilliard said.

Florida would lead the nation in scoring average (46.6) and touchdowns (76). Wuerffel finished his career as the most efficient passer in college football history—with a rating of 163.56, passing for 114 touchdown tosses and just under 11,000 yards. He passed for 42 scores in 1996 alone. Wuerffel was named first-team All-America, along with teammates Anthony and Hilliard—all three also made first-team all conference. Tying the 1991 team for most spots, 10 players made first-team All-SEC, including Young, Mitchell, Chester, James Bates, Anthone Lott, Lawrence Wright, and Fred Weary.

The Florida defense, under Stoops, did get the ball back more and gave Spurrier more plays on offense. Stoops and Spurrier looked to be an almost unbeatable combination, and the future of Gator football had never been brighter.

"The way we put it together that year—with blood, sweat, and tears—really meant a lot," Anthony said, "One of the most special things for me were the guys who came in with me and played. And our class [1994] wasn't that heavily recruited. Over the three-year period, we had some great teams. And I feel like we could have had three national championship teams. ... To finally put it together with the same guys you've been around for three years and all the hard work we put in—that's what you play this game for. We play to win championships."

The memories are sweet for Ritch, a lifelong Alachua County resident and Gator fan. "I've got a picture of the football field during a night game that Coach Spurrier signed for me," Ritch said. "It's hanging in my living room. I don't wear my ring as much as I should. It's so big. I've got my jersey from the national championship game framed. I experienced something special that nobody else will ever live again because it was the first one. It means a lot to me that I was able to be a part of that, and it seems like the Gator fans still love that '96 team."

Members of the 1992 freshman and red-shirt freshman class walked away with five rings. Donnie Young loves the memories, but doesn't cling to the bling. He gave all of his rings to his father, Donnie Young Sr., of Venice. "It's not that I'm not proud of it," Young said. "It's the people who made it special."

Saying Goodbye to Gainsville

There were many more games to be played and coached by Spurrier, but never another national championship. Although his teams won 10 games in four of his last five seasons, there would be only one more SEC title, which Spurrier's team would capture by beating Auburn in 2000. Ten more of his players were named All-America: Weary, Green, Fred Taylor, Jevon Kearse, Mike Peterson, Alex Brown, Lito Sheppard, Jabar Gaffney, Rex Grossman, and Mike Pearson. Spurrier's teams would appear in five more bowl games, including the 2002 Orange Bowl, where Florida would smack No. 6 Maryland, 56-23, and wind up No. 3 in the nation. But there were no titles that year.

"We led the conference in scoring offense, scoring defense, total yards offense, total yards defense," Spurrier lamented, "and yet we didn't win anything. Third in the nation and we didn't win anything."

"Statistically, the 2001 team was the best we ever had at Florida," Spurrier said. Florida took a 10-1 record with only a three-point loss to Auburn into the game against Tennessee at Florida Field, which had been rescheduled due to the September 11 tragedy. Ironically, Spurrier would lose to the Vols, 34-32, in what would be his last appearance at "The Swamp."

"That whole season was fun," quarterback Rex Grossman said in 2001. "We had Reche Caldwell, Jabar Gaffney, and Taylor Jacobs, and all those guys were special athletes. Those three great receivers and Coach Spurrier just had a great relationship and feel for the offense—we could change the play at the line, get into the right play versus the right coverage. We got into a good rhythm, and it was a good process in the passing game that year."

Good process, indeed: Grossman threw for 34 touchdown passes and a school-record 3,986 yards.

"Tennessee kicked our butts," Spurrier said. "I thought we were ready to play, but obviously we were not. Their running back, Travis Stephens, ran for about 175 yards. They only punted once the entire game."

On several occasions in the mid-to-late 1960s, Spurrier reminded friends that anybody could wear out his welcome because "... people get tired of you." Spurrier didn't like having to attend 20 Gator Club meetings a year, where more and more autograph seekers dominated his time. He was unhappy about the fact that his own administration kicked blue-chip lineman Santonio Holmes out of summer school, although he was later made eligible to attend almost every other school and wound up signing with Miami. He was furious at what he considered another cheap shot by FSU— an injury to Gator running back Earnest Graham, whose leg was twisted by Seminole defender Darnell Dockett after a tackle, forcing him to the sideline. Spurrier said some of these things aggravated him, but that his main motivation to leave was the challenge of the NFL.

He doesn't dwell on it, but Spurrier celebrates 1996 when the occasion calls for it, which is why he agreed to return to Florida Field for the 2006 opener and 10-year anniversary of the championship team.

"Fortunately, I've still been coaching, albeit it not very much for a couple of years up in Washington, D.C.," Spurrier said in a self-deprecating poke at himself. "We look back occasionally at that season. Gosh, I look back on 2000, when we beat Auburn to win the SEC, which was the only one since '96. I've only got one championship in 10 years now. So for a team or a school that won, gosh, six in the first seven years there, we had a little dry spell over the next five years. But you don't sit around and look back a lot until your days are over."

Afterword

Danny Wuerffel's happy ending at Florida goes beyond what he could have imagined. It is probably not an accident that the "Mr. Nice Guy" of Florida football wound up with his Desire Street Ministries headquartered in Niceville, Florida. Although he is still the understated, somewhat-reluctant hero, it must be hard to be humble when your name is still all over the campus, including on the façade of the Florida Field south end zone. Sometime his celebrity even gets him through a barricade, which seems to astonish him.

"When I was a kid, I used to dream about the perfect four years and the perfect ending," Wuerffel said, "I don't even think my dreams had the capacity to match the reality that I faced at Florida. I even sometimes pinch myself to make sure I'm not dreaming when I think about it. It was a storybook career and a storybook ending—and I was blessed to be a part of it.

"It really is a special feeling when I go back to Gainesville and around the campus; people are so kind and helpful. I went back to a game last year [2005], and I was selling copies of my book. I had to get over to the north end zone, but all the roads were blocked. I couldn't get in. I was with Chris Doering and his wife. They said, 'Just go talk to the police officer.' And I said, 'I'm not going to go talk to the police officer!' And when I started walking over there, he saw me and said, 'Oh, Mr. Wuerffel, come on through.' It really is bizarre to be treated like that, but it really is great."

Wuerffel shares that honored spot on the façade with his coach, the other Heisman winner from Florida. Spurrier's legacy is a standard that probably will never be equaled at Florida. His 12-year coaching mark was 122-27-1, a winning percentage of .817 that ranks among the top three in conference history. He also enjoyed 12 seasons of making the Top 15 in final polls and nine consecutive January bowl games, both SEC highs.

Revisiting the issue of why Spurrier left Florida is pointless, but when asked in 2006 the motivation for leaving Florida he said: "In the back of my mind, I thought, 'Maybe I wanted to coach in the NFL four or five years before my days were over and hang it up.' I was wrong about wanting to hang it up, as I found out. Whether I went to the right NFL team or not—and obviously I didn't. We didn't have a general manager at the Redskins; I thought we were going to have one. It just didn't work out. I did a bad job, and that's all you ever have to say. But I like to have an off-season. Even if it's a bad day, I enjoy the challenge of golf … and working out … and having some time for family and children and grandchildren. So I found out that the NFL lifestyle is not as suited for me as the college."

All those other underlying reasons as to why he might have departed from his alma mater are irrelevant. He points out that it was his decision to quit, which put him in the category of the only modern Florida coach to have enjoyed that privilege.

"I left Florida on my own. I quit that job because I thought, at the time, I wanted another job," Spurrier said. "Basically, I had done that job long enough and needed a new challenge. And, of course, they knew that, and I knew that."

As for any bad feelings left behind, Spurrier says he has none, but admits that at times there have been some strained relationships. "I'm okay, but when Jeremy [Foley] gets mad, he can stay mad at people a little longer," Spurrier said. "But I talked to him, and we're fine when we see each other. We don't talk on the phone much. Every now and then I call and congratulate him, like when the [Gator] basketball team won the [2005-

2006] national championship. I lea
congratulations, I know how importan
But that's about all. We're fine when
everything's okay. He says everything is

Around the pool on the shores of th
of golf during a weekend to celebrate hi
Spurrier reflected on the blessings of l
afternoon in August 2006. There in Hi
his children and grandchildren, coachii
members, ex-teammates, old friends froi
media pals, Spurrier was flourishing in h

"See this?" he asked, unfolding a gre
made of rubber, he announced: "I got th
St. Patrick's Day parade. And I *am* one lu

Spurrier went on to say that his father,
$10,000, and "… yet we seemed to have e
story of visiting a friend's house whose fatl
being treated to a cold soft drink out of a
have such a privilege. "I couldn't believe yo
drink and not have to put down a dime,"

Later that next night, gathered in the M
people all dressed casually, Spurrier repeate
has a song out called, 'I'm The Lucky One.'
able to meet up with Jerri Starr and the Uni

Everyone knew the ending of the stor
testimonies and then an evening of dining, c
among a group of people who seemed bond

No matter who followed the Ol' Ball coa
result or perhaps good fortune, either. Ron Z
period of time.

9

The Ron Zook Era

2002 - 2004

Following the Legend was Impossible

Jeremy Foley was fighting an uphill battle from the day he landed in Gainesville, returning from a three-city road-trip search for Spurrier's successor. His choice was a reach, especially since he had no head-coaching experience. Yet, both Oklahoma's Bob Stoops and Mike Shanahan of the Denver Broncos had turned Foley down, and the best remaining candidate appeared to be the defensive coordinator of the New Orleans Saints, Ron Zook.

To many Gator Fans, Foley had taken the University of Florida jet to shop for coaches without any intention of coming home empty-handed. Some believed Foley acted in haste, as if he were looking for a fire sale. Time was indeed an issue—the futures of two outstanding Gators were at stake, and the program was scrambling to ensure that quarterback Rex Grossman and wide receiver Taylor Jacobs stuck at "The Swamp." Both had agreed to wait until Foley made a choice before they decided about the NFL.

Grossman—he threw for nearly 4,000 yards in his sophomore season—was perhaps the purest-passing quarterback in Florida's history. Many wondered, "If Grossman had another year under Spurrier, would he become the greatest Gator quarterback ever?" Grossman was planning to stay under Spurrier, but now he had to be convinced that Zook had his best interests at heart.

Spurrier was a Grossman fan, but when you asked the Ol' Ball Coach to rank his quarterbacks, it was like asking a proud papa to rate his kids. "I always tell everybody Rex was maybe the best passer of any of the quarterbacks, but certainly Danny Wuerffel, what he achieved, was the most," Spurrier said. "And Shane Matthews was probably right after Danny as the quarterback who achieved the most. As far as production, it was Danny and Shane. As far as [being] a beautiful passer, it was Rex."

Grossman and his father had dropped by the Florida campus following his junior year in high school to pay an unannounced visit and found Spurrier in his office. "We just happened to run into Coach Spurrier on one of those days when he wasn't playing golf," Rex said in the spring of 2006, during a break from a Chicago Bears mini-camp. "He took me through the highlight tape of the '96 season and explained how he got the receivers open, what the quarterback was thinking, and how he would bring me along. And I got asked to show him my highlight tape, and he liked it."

After leading his Bloomington (Indiana) South team to the state championship his senior season, Grossman would arrive in Gainesville for his degree at Quarterback U. with the ultimate headmaster as his head coach, quarterback coach, and offensive coordinator all wrapped into one. Rex craved the constant tutelage.

"Just having a guy like that constantly looking over your shoulder as you're developing from one level to another … a Heisman winner himself and a great coach like that," Grossman said. "The two reasons I went to Florida was: one, to play big-time college football and be a national championship contender every year; and two, to play for a quarterback-offensive coordinator-coach like Spurrier."

Much of Grossman's passing ability was natural, but Spurrier refined it. "He fine-tuned my release point," Grossman said. "He made it even quicker and helped with my footwork." More than just fundamentals, however, Spurrier taught Grossman some secrets: "He taught me how to beat coverage, look off defenders to create passing lanes—and once I got that, it was really, really fun."

Even though Grossman played a season under Zook and then departed with a remaining year of eligibility, he still has fond memories of Gator football and treasures the experience. "It's hard to explain, the feelings you get Saturdays, game day, running out on the field. Especially the starting quarterback, who's able to go under center, complete a nice pass, with 90,000 people screaming. You're playing for your fellow students, the alumni, and everybody else—it's just a fun atmosphere."

That passion worked in Zook's favor. Keep in mind that Grossman was All-America the previous year, SEC Player of the Year, and had finished second in the Heisman voting. In the season he has played for the Bears, even fellow pros have thought of Grossman as a Florida man. "And I'm proud of that," he said. "Sometimes when a defender tackles me, he'll say, 'I gotcha Gator.'"

Taylor Jacobs was taking the place of All-America wide receiver Jabar Gaffney and had already become one of Grossman's favorite targets. Retaining these two offensive stars would be a huge jumpstart for the new coach. Zook walked in the door with a No. 1 draft choice as a quarterback—which is what Grossman would be with the Bears—and a second-round wide receiver pick, which Jacobs was for Spurrier and the Redskins.

So, while Grossman and Jacobs were crucial to the team's success, their presence also elevated the expectations of Zook's offensive production. Gator fans would measure each of his moves by Spurrier's gold standard. Having worked under him as defensive coordinator and special teams coach, Zook was no stranger to the program and its love for Spurrier. The decision to hire him, however, seemed an abrupt departure from proven commodities—and when Foley's plane went from Norman, Oklahoma, to Denver, to New Orleans, one Florida staff member asked in semi-disbelief: "You don't suppose we're going to hire Ron Zook, do you?"

Almost as much doubt surrounded Zook's chances at Florida as a first-night candidate on *American Idol*. After all, who'd want to follow Elvis?

In Zook, Foley knew he was getting a man who was all business. "The first thing I thought about," Zook said in a cell-phone interview from his car as he drove back to Champaign, Illinois, following a speech he made in early March 2006, "was that I had to hire a staff and then start recruiting."

"You didn't even stop to shout?" Zook was asked.

"I guess maybe I should have," said Zook, "but there was too much to do."

Zook is the ultimate clock-watching freak whose life is built around his day-timer and cell phone; he's always trying to get to the next place punctually to tackle the next job.

His parents drilled organization into Ron when he was a young boy, along with a strict work ethic. "For me, to be able to go to practice or go play baseball, all my chores had to be done," he said. "And if you haven't got time to do it right, then you aren't going to have time to do it over."

Rarely does he take time to smell the roses. He is always on the clock, even when he goes on vacation. One of his proudest moments was touring Disney World in 2003 with his family in a single day.

"You can get a lot more done in a short period time if you're organized and you have a plan," Zook said. "But my family said, 'It's impossible.' And I said, 'No, it's not—we're going to hit it.' It went so fast they didn't even know they were there. In fact, my oldest daughter said, 'We want to go back down there this summer.' And I said, 'Okay, we'll go again.' And she said, 'No, Dad—we want to go without you.'"

Zook loves the challenge of the "impossible." To counteract the odds, he crams as much into a minute as possible. He talks fast, walks fast, coaches fast, and probably even sleeps fast. The man is nothing but a blur, always full speed ahead. While recruiting for Florida, he once visited players in six different cities on the same day without a hitch. He goes through cell phones as often as a shorthand secretary does ballpoint pens. "I wore out a cell phone," Zook once said, almost sheepishly.

For Zook, perhaps it's the future and never the present or past. Unlike his predecessor, who lined his office with memorabilia from his past coaching jobs at all levels, Zook didn't surround himself with the trappings of success in his early years as the Gators' coach. In his Ben Hill Griffin Stadium office, there was one photo—of him waterskiing at his property at Lake Weir, southeast of Ocala—plus about a half-dozen game balls from his past. Books about positive thinking adorn the shelves, along with Bear Bryant's Texas A&M lore, *Junction Boys*.

When asked about his minimalist décor, Zook replied: "Come back next year—you'll see more." Very little was added to pack up and take with him to Illinois when left to become the Illini coach before the 2005 season.

Opening Night: One to Remember

One could certainly say that Ron Zook's opening and closing acts were blockbusters.

Looking back at his first year, his inaugural game was special, because he beat University of Alabama-Birmingham, 51-3, with his dying father in the stands. Even up in Illinois, Zook often thinks about the night of August 31, 2002, and his first game.

"My whole family was there," Zook recalled. "We knew it would probably be the only game my father would get a chance to see. And so it was special. I've thought about it a lot more than I did at the time. It was just a blessing that my father was able to be there. It wasn't me—it was my whole family. So it was an honor, a privilege, and a blessing for him to be able to see it."

Devastating as it was, the peripatetic Zook moved on to the next thing—he always keeps moving. Even in woeful times, he won't look up. That's how he handles adversity. It's how he handled his father's terminal illness when he became Florida's head coach. So opening night 2002, when he ran on the field, he had a plan. Nobody but his family knew that Zook would come out of the tunnel and point up to his father in the stands.

He had tried to keep it private. "I didn't mean for anybody else to see it. It's something my older brother Bob and I had talked about. And it was to him, and he knew what it was for. It was kinda for the Zooks," he said.

Three weeks later, Pete Zook died of lung and liver cancer. Even then, Ron kept on churning.

"Losing my father was a very, very tough thing," Zook recalled. "You don't stop, though. You play the hand you were dealt."

With Grossman at the controls, Zook's 2002 team got off to a 4-1 start, and although the Gators stumbled against Miami, they went to Knoxville and beat Tennessee, 31-13. Grossman threw for 324 yards and three touchdowns. Trouble was ahead, however, with back-to-back losses to Ole Miss and LSU—teams from Mississippi seemed to be Zook's nemeses—as inconsistency plagued these Gators, and they dropped out of the rankings. No sooner were they in hot water than they pulled off four straight wins, including the 30-23 overtime victory over Auburn and a 20-13 upset of No. 5 Georgia. Winding up with losses to FSU (31-14) and Michigan (38-30), Zook's team finished 8-5, the poorest showing since the pre-Spurrier days.

Having lost Gaffney, Caldwell, and starting left tackle Mike Pearson to the NFL draft, Grossman didn't have the surrounding cast.

"We were still left with a pretty good team, but we just didn't have the experience and firepower that we had in 2001," Grossman said. "But that 2002 team was a lot of fun. We were real close to going to that championship game—and we were better than how we finished out. Still, it was a great year. I felt like I got better as a quarterback in having to go through a new system, and having to do that helped me to where I am now [with the Bears]. I wouldn't trade it for the world. We didn't win the SEC, but we still led the SEC in offense and passing, etc. At the end of the year, I felt like I would be drafted pretty high. It was a great four years at Florida, and it was time for me to go."

The coach's view came from a particularly different standpoint.

"It was a whirlwind," said Zook. "The ups and down, beating Tennessee, then you lose to Ole Miss. You beat Georgia. You lose to Florida State. You beat Auburn in overtime. ... We won a lot of games." But not enough games.

Grossman was gone in 2003, and after the first few weeks, the Chris Leak era opened. The wolves came out when Florida dropped three of its first six games, including a home loss to unranked Ole Miss, 20-17. The Zook era had its milestones, though, including the 2003 run of four straight road wins (at LSU, at Arkansas, over Georgia in Jacksonville, and at South Carolina) after the Ole Miss defeat. Once again, though, the season closed with losses to FSU and in a postseason game—this time to Iowa in the Outback Bowl, 37-17.

Blowouts were rare, and in his final 2004 season, Zook's Gators lost four conference games by seven points or fewer: Tennessee (30-28), LSU (24-21), Mississippi State (38-31), and Georgia (31-24). Zook's future was in jeopardy halfway through his third season following an embarrassing loss to hapless Mississippi State—coming in 1-5, the Bulldogs would finish 3-8— who had dealt the Gators their third defeat in seven starts. The next week, Zook was terminated, but the university allowed him to finish out the regular season.

However, Zook will always have one night in Tallahassee. He became the answer to a trivia question on November 20, 2004, in what turned out to be his last game as Florida coach.

Q: Who was the first coach to win at the newly christened Bobby Bowden Field?

A: Rodney Dangerfield Zook, by Jove, who went out wearing his coaching boots.

Florida beat No. 8-ranked Florida State, 20-13, to finish 7-4 on the season. The Gators bettered their bowl future and, at the same time, dashed the hopes of the Seminoles in their bid to win the Atlantic Coast Conference title on a tiebreaker. Gator fans will always remember him for doing something no coach has done in 18 years, not even Gator icon Steve Spurrier: defeating Florida State in Doak Campbell Stadium. And Zook did it on the night that happened to be the 10th anniversary of what they call "The Choke at Doak."

"I'm so happy," Zook said that night. "And I'm so proud of them. It was an honor and a privilege to coach them [his players]. I love these players. Nobody gave them much of a chance. They deserve this. They've been through a lot. But they listened to us."

It was no fluke. Zook was almost Spurrieresque as he elected to go for it with a one-touchdown lead on fourth-and-inches at his own 26 with just 2:38 to play. Chris Leak sneaked it for the first down to keep the drive alive and eat up valuable time.

How rare was this loss at The Doak? Well, only one Atlantic Coast Conference team had beaten the 'Noles on their home turf in 52 tries—and only 21 teams total had defeated Bowden in 168 tries.

The Gators had not won in Doak Campbell Stadium since 1986. Of the victory in 2004 over FSU, only Florida's fifth against the Seminoles since 1994, Zook said: "It's something I will always remember. I was happy for 'The Gator Nation.' I was happy for our players—that they would have an opportunity to go out [like that]. And I was just glad that I was fortunate enough to be a part of it."

In the 37 games he lasted as Florida's head coach, the FSU win was unarguably the biggest, and it had to feel good—right down to that last pay stub.

Florida's strong November 2004 finish gave credence to those critics who say Zook wasn't given a fair chance to finish his work. After getting his pink slip, he won three of his last four games, which was as good as it would ever get for the frenetic coach with the platinum-collar work ethic. None of it was good enough to save his hide, though, despite winning 23 games and taking his Gators team to three bowl games.

So the tenure of Florida's 19th full-time coach would last just shy of three seasons—despite his sixth win on the road against a ranked opponent in three years. The victory over FSU proved the final chapter to his theme, "Ride Out," the slogan featured on T-shirts he gave his players.

Zook rode out—on their shoulders.

Zooker Gets the Bad News

The axe had come swiftly on Monday morning, October 25, 2004, as Ron Zook was doing his usual stroll through the weight room at seven o'clock to talk to players. He was a little surprised to see Foley approaching at this hour.

"President Machen would like you to meet with him at eight o'clock at his house," Foley said.

As if to shake the chill running up his neck, Zook stopped, looked directly at Foley, and asked: "You're not going to pull the plug on this thing, are you?"

Stoically, Foley repeated: "The president wants to talk with you."

And Zook responded: "Okay, I'll be there."

Zook knew something was amiss—"I assumed…"

He also knew he wasn't being invited to the president's house for high tea. At Machen's home, they broke the news that "… we're going to go in a different direction." They told him they wanted him to coach the remainder of the year. He had even hoped to coach the team through the postseason, a wish that was later denied.

Perhaps the firing shouldn't have been a total shock. Some had already seen it coming. The website FireRonZook.com was under assault. Patience is not one of the virtues of "The Gator Nation," yet Zook said he had "… absolutely no indication."

The series of events leading up to the Tennessee game that season didn't bode in Zook's favor either. According to police reports, several Pi Kappa Phi fraternity members got into a fight with three players, breaking offensive lineman Steve Rissler's nose. The Wednesday night before the game, a sworn complaint was issued against the fraternity members, alleging that they jumped the three football players. The following evening, several team members gathered at the fraternity house, perhaps seeking revenge. A rumble seemed imminent, and someone called the police. Word quickly spread to the athletic department, and Foley called Zook, urging him to collect his players in order to avoid an incident. An unconfirmed report arose that Zook swore at some of the fraternity members in a threatening manner.

"Coach Zook went there for the right reasons," Foley was quoted as saying in the newspaper. "He went there to get his players out of there and prevent an altercation. And he accomplished that." Foley, however, admitted that Zook's methods were "unacceptable" and said he dealt with the issue "internally." Zook confirmed that "Foley asked me to go over there …" in an interview. He said "absolutely nothing" happened involving him at the Pi Kappa Phi fraternity house.

And if that had any bearing on his eventual firing at Florida?

"I was never told anything about it."

Calling on Carlos Again

A period of dark confusion loomed over "The Gator Nation." An alumnus reached out to a former superstar to right the ship—a star who had faced this kind of travail. Thirty-five years removed from one of the biggest, game-changing, history-writing touchdown catches of all-time, former All-America receiver Carlos Alvarez came back in the fall of 2004 to provide a substantial impact. Yet, instead of a catch, he was there to make a pitch—for everyone to hang together in the midst of stormy weather.

At the suggestion of Lee McGriff, the former all-SEC wide receiver and ex-assistant coach and current member of the Gator Radio Football Network, Zook invited Alvarez to speak to the team just before the FSU game in 2004. McGriff remembers his introduction of Carlos and the disinterested group they encountered at first. "It was after practice, they were tired; they wanted to shower; and they're looking over at this gray-haired gentleman wondering, 'Who is this guy?'"

Quickly, McGriff jarred them to attention, as he introduced his own personal Gator football hero.

"This man has nothing to do with the athletic administration," McGriff said. "He has nothing to do with the coaches. He has nothing to do with the university. He is here for *you!*"

And then he laid down the challenge:

"None of you has done—or is currently doing—what this guy did. I repeat, none of you has done—or is currently doing—what this guy did."

It seemed to both pique their interest and rankle them a bit.

Zook was coaching his final four regular-season games. His last game would be in Tallahassee on the newly named Bobby Bowden Field. A successor was yet to be named. "The Gator Nation" was divided over whether Zook was treated unfairly, if Spurrier should be brought back to replace him, and if this new guy, Urban Meyer, was going to be the choice of his former boss at Utah, UF President Bernie Machen.

"After the Georgia game, I went down there and spoke to the team," Alvarez said. "I wrote a letter to Pat Dooley of the *Gainesville Sun*, basically, telling people in 'The Gator Nation,' 'Back off!' People were implying bad motives about many people there, including Foley.

"I think things were done right. We all ought to have been pushing in the same direction. It did seem to me there were some people who had an over-inflated ego about the way things should be. I won't go into details what I talked about, but one thing I did talk to them about—and this is sort of how I feel about the '69 team—that we are all part of Gator football. When it was our time to be the player, we all helped put a brick in that stadium. We all contributed to building what Gator football is all about.

"What we did was take a step forward—and every team that comes along needs to take that one step forward, in whatever fashion it comes to them. We're all basically part of a family. I told them, 'Any player who has ever played can call me up if they're in town, and he has a place to stay.' And a lot of Gator players feel that way. Don't feel isolated. Feel like you're part of—and it's overused—'The Gator Nation' and the Gator players. They are building for the future. No matter what, there is always the next game.

"And I said to them, 'No matter what happened this year, if you go up to FSU, and you beat FSU, and it's the first game at the Bobby Bowden Field, I will flat out guarantee you that, 20 years from now, people will remember that game. They'll forget all the other stuff, but they'll remember that this was the team that went up there and beat 'em. There's all kind of bricks you can still put in the stadium.'"

It was more like taking a brick out of Doak Campbell. The Gators went to Tallahassee and beat the Seminoles behind Ciatrick Fason's 103 yards on 24 carries, and Florida's defense held the 'Noles to a mere 34 yards rushing. His players hoisted Zook onto their shoulders and carried him off the field. Even in all his great seasons, Spurrier had never even won there.

In retrospect, critics may have been hasty and we rightly could be accused of a borderline lynch-mob mentality. Hysteria seems to be a precondition of the Florida football program. "The Gator Nation," once at the top of the mountain, didn't care for the view from halfway down. Suddenly, winning eight games the first two seasons—with a shot of equaling that in his third—wasn't enough for a pardon. Removing emotion from the situation, Foley and Machen upon further review may have "pulled the plug" (Zook's words) prematurely—and certain columnists did their part to stir it up.

Had Meyer not been a red-hot candidate, in the crosshairs of other schools like Notre Dame, though, would Zook have been granted a grace period? The numbers show that Zook's first three seasons, excluding Spurrier's 12-year reign, were better than four coaches prior to him, equal that of Galen Hall's. Zook won 23 games over three seasons, the same as Hall, and better than Ray Graves' 20, Bob Woodruff's 18, Doug Dickey's 16, and Charley Pell's 15. Under Zook, Florida played in two New Year's Day bowl games his first two seasons.

Zook's worst sin was that he wasn't Spurrier. His second was that he wasn't Urban Meyer, or that he had never worked for Machen. The fact that Meyer would be available and was being courted by other schools may have pushed the decision forward. Besides, Zook was already battling public sentiment against him. Truthfully, though many people felt he shouldn't have been fired, an equal number probably thought he shouldn't have been hired in the first place. If the hiring of Zook was curious, then his firing was even more so.

Zook is the ultimate soldier-coach. Even though his close friends will tell you that Zook was badly hurt by the manner in which Florida parted ways, they also know he would never roll over on any of his former associates or bosses. Zook has declined to talk to the media about it. Only after the intervention of a close friend did Zook consent to doing a book interview. Even then he was cautious, refusing to make any negative comments, saying over and over: "I was fortunate to have such a great head-coaching job in a program like Florida. My family and I loved Gainesville, and I will always be thankful for the opportunity." After a while, it sounded like a repeat on a Memorex loop. There was one caveat, though:

"I look back on the thing—and I really don't want to talk a lot about it—but I look back on the thing, as I told our players and our coaches after it was over: 'Fellas we didn't fail. We *DID NOT FAIL*! We were successful. We did a great job.' I felt like the program was in great shape when we left, and I'm not going to feel bad about it."

So was Zook a victim of circumstances? He stopped short of saying that, referencing the tough schedule he inherited—one at which even Spurrier certainly winced before choosing to leave.

"Obviously, that 12th game," Zook said. "In my first two years, we played the national champions and runner-up national champions [Miami 2001-2002] with the Southeastern Conference schedule, along with Florida State. It was a tough schedule, but it was what it was. The only thing I have to say is this: I loved it there. My family loved it there. I love where I'm at now. It was a great opportunity.

"My brother [Bob] asked me, right after I was let go, if I had it to do over again, would I do it again. And I said, 'Absolutely!' Everything happens for a reason. If I wouldn't have had the opportunity there, I probably wouldn't have the opportunity where I'm at now—and I'm excited about this opportunity."

His interviewer prodded Zook to "… tell us what we don't know about Ron Zook and other things that we may not know about what happened to you at Florida—without placing blame or criticism." The urging resulted in another neutral-but-polite response.

"You're not going to get me to say a word. No matter what I say—hey, it happened, it was a great opportunity for me. I can look in the mirror. I said it many times: I was not going to become held hostage to the job. I'm the same person I was when I took the job. I didn't change. I'm honored and privileged that I had the chance to be the head coach there."

History will have to judge whether Zook failed or not, and if a won-loss record is the only true measure. Fairness has never been an issue when it comes to firing football coaches at Florida. Just ask Hall, who posted those three nine-win seasons. But at least Hall, in his 59 games and five-plus seasons, was allowed to play a full hand. Zook was kicked out of the game while he still had money in the pot: more than two years of strong recruiting. He wasn't allowed to coach a class to its fruition.

Critics might say that Zook was doomed to fail because his performance would forever be judged against the paradigm of greatness. What, then, would make Zook think he could succeed; and why would he take the job in the first place, given the record of most coaches who try to follow in the footsteps of a legend?

"What was I going to do," Zook asked rhetorically, "turn down the job?"

Charlie Strong's Portraits of Coaches

For unexplained reasons, Zook was asked to leave before the Peach Bowl game against Miami. Those duties were left unexpectedly to defensive coach Charlie Strong, who has worked for the last five head coaches—and under Lou Holtz at Notre Dame and South Carolina. Perhaps it was fitting for the man who assisted so many Gator head coaches to have his shot for one game. But the fact that he was given the reins as an afterthought made it a tough assignment. Miami belted an uninspired Gator team, 27-10.

"I'm very grateful to the University of Florida for allowing me to be the coach," Strong said, "but it was so different, because none of those guys on the staff were going to be here. So how much are they going to put into that one game? People say, 'Charlie should be a head coach,' but you get your one shot, and you get those results."

Officially, Strong went down as Gator coach No. 21, but one game does not a career make. When you want to know something about the recent past of Gator football, however, few coaches know more than Strong, who has been on the staffs of Charley Pell, Galen Hall, Steve Spurrier, Ron Zook, and now Urban Meyer, for whom he serves as assistant head coach and co-defensive coordinator.

Here's Strong's portrait of those five former Florida head coaches:

Pell: "Coach Pell was very well organized, kind of like Coach [Lou] Holtz. You had to dot your I's and cross your T's. He was really concerned about the players and wanted them to be happy. Your job as a coach was to coach. He was an outstanding motivator, a great communicator, and very, very disciplined."

Hall: "He did a great job of keeping the team focused. That was right there during the probation time, and he was able to take this program and withstand that probation when Charley Pell was fired and he took over. The players really liked and respected him. He let his assistant coaches work. We had some really good players—Neal Anderson, John L. Williams, and Lomas Brown—and continued to play well. At one time, we were ranked No. 1 in the country under Coach Hall."

Spurrier: "Coach Spurrier was very competitive. People sometimes talk about him playing golf, but they don't understand: he was very competitive, and we worked hard. It was not a country club. You look aat what he did for this program—six SEC titles, a national championship—where everyone thought it couldn't be done. When we were winning in the 1990s, it brought attention to this program, and people wanted to come to the University of Florida. He motivated by winning. He wasn't a tough-talk kind of guy. He just let it happen on the field. He had an air about him. Some guys have a certain persona, how they carry themselves. He was one of those guys."

Zook: "He worked hard. A great recruiter, his coming back to this program was good, because he had been here. We didn't waste time under Coach Zook. We were organized when we hit the field, and the players enjoyed playing for him."

And his new boss, Urban Meyer: "Urban is, in a way, a young Charley Pell. Just the way he wants them to work—whether it is in the classroom or on the football field. If he doesn't know something about the history of this program, he's going to find out about it, no stone unturned. Look how he handled the pressure in his first year: he was able to keep his team focused and play well down the stretch, even though we had a couple of stumbles along the way. He was able to stay focused and not give in. Every time I look at him, I think of Charley Pell. He has a system in place, and the players understand it—just like Coach Spurrier had a system. The players know there are going to be consequences if they don't do the right thing."

Afterword

The Ron Zook era produced two All-Americans from the 2003 team, offensive guard Shannon Snell and cornerback Keiwan Ratliff, but none in 2002 and 2004. It broke a string of 10 straight seasons with at least one Gator All-American. The most first-team All-SEC performers Zook's squads produced were three in a season. Ciatrick Fason, the team's star offensive performer, rushed for 1,267 yards in 2004 and became a fourth-round pick of the Minnesota Vikings. Only three players were drafted, the fewest since 1993. Oddly enough, Zook was known for his great recruiting, but few of his recruits became stars in college or in the pros.

Charlie Strong watched Meyer learn the tough lessons about the Florida job in his first season, not the least of which was the pressure to win on the road in the SEC. "Many coaches have to learn about how tough that is," Strong said. "I just heard one of our assistant coaches say the other day, 'You never realize it if you're not in this conference—you heard about it, but after being here, I believe it now.'"

Urban Meyer is a believer, too. It only took trips to Tuscaloosa, Baton Rouge, and Columbia, South Carolina, for the new coach of the Gators to realize he wasn't in Utah anymore.

10

The Urban Meyer Era

2005 - ?

Urban and the 500-pound Gorilla

If history repeats itself, Urban Meyer will be dismissed in 2013, after his eighth season, and he will have won fewer than 52 times. Aside from Spurrier, Gator coaches from 1950 to Meyer's tenure lasted just over seven years each and won just under six games per season. The Ol' Ball Coach averaged 10 wins a year, which elevated the wins-per-season figure, and, more importantly, he was the only modern coach to leave of his own accord. The law of averages was set against the 22nd Florida coach succeeding.

"Average" is not a word anybody uses to describe anything about Urban Meyer, however. In fact, when the Utah man arrived to replace Ron Zook, expectations for the Gator football program were higher than the Century Tower on the Florida campus. The level of enthusiasm was off the charts, supercharged by the new Head Gator, who whipped his devotees into a feeding frenzy long before coaching his first game. Traveling around Florida like a rock star to speak before record crowds at 22 Gator Clubs, Meyer baptized Florida football fans with a fresh new spirit and, at the same time, healed some old wounds. If nothing else, this guy knew how to create mystique.

They came in droves, 58,000 strong, for the Orange and Blue Spring game. They thought they saw a little bit of Pell discipline and a little bit of Spurrier dazzle in their new man. He fed them fish-and-loaves football dreams, and they were ready to follow him into the desert—okay, maybe to the beach. Some of the swagger was back; however, it wasn't as though they believed other SEC teams were going to FedEx the white flag-swathed conference trophy directly to "The Swamp".

Urban's neighbor, Billy Donovan, showed him one piece of smart public-relations business by bringing the game back to the students. After the spring game, Meyer and the UF Athletic Association staged a contest to name the student section. The winning entry was "The Swamp Things," submitted by Tyler Boehling of Naples. All the hype was in motion—now came the time to stand and deliver.

When reality set in, Meyer realized his first Gator team wasn't going to be nearly as good as advertised—and he knew it back in August before the first game. That's why he spent so many restless preseason nights staring at the ceiling and worrying that his opponents would see through the façade. The pieces weren't fitting together. Some people were concerned about whether the spread offense would work in the land of blazing cornerbacks and sick 'em linebackers. Meyer was more worried that he and his coaches might not have their players on the same page, maybe not even in the same book—the Book of Urban. Florida had some excellent athletes, but it didn't have a great team—maybe not even a good team. Suddenly, a coach's dream was a coach's nightmare.

"We were hoping we could work through it," Meyer said a year after his first season as coach at Florida. "We were developing the team every day. In August [2005], when I was lying awake, staring at the ceiling, it wasn't about the spread offense. It was: 'This is *not* a good team. It is far from being a good team.' But there are some really good kids here, as good as I've ever been around. ... That's where the late nights came in. It wasn't so much designing plays. It was, 'How can we get these kids together?'"

And so began the wrestling match between Meyer and the 500-pound gorilla that is Florida football—that behemoth that had pinned six of the last seven Gator coaches. The gorilla that never leaves your door, whether it's the swarm of the media; the heartbreak of players being injured, giving up, or giving in to the temptations of college life; the pressure of a rock-hard schedule with a road through SEC hell; or just the endless demands of being band leader of "The Gator Nation."

Bare-knuckle brawlers such as Urban Meyer want to face all the gorillas in the same ring simultaneously—may best man or monkey get up and walk away. In his first 18 months on the job, they had him on the canvas a few times, but he eventually fought them to a draw, learning a life lesson about the difference in football cultures. Bowling Green, Utah, Notre Dame, and Ohio State all had their gorillas, but Florida's seemed a bit bigger, nastier, and more persistent.

And thus begun the fascinating struggle between King Kong and the Urban way.

Sitting Down with Urban

After chasing him around the state for an interview—a moment here, a moment there—we finally caught up for the first of several one-on-one sit-downs that would take place over the next 10 months. It was like chasing smoke. With the intensity of recruiting, the squeeze on time began to cast doubt as to whether the first of these interviews would ever materialize. Once Meyer began his whirlwind 10-state tour in May, during which he flew 14,615 air miles, drove 33 rental cars, performed 10 speaking engagements over three time zones and visited 99 high schools, time was scant. He was home three days that month, so we first connected in June 2005, in a second-floor room at the Ocala Gator Club. We talked about the 500-pound gorilla as he and his six-year-old son, Nathan, grabbed a dinner on the run. His focus alternated between answering questions and negotiating his knife and fork over a barbecued chicken thigh.

Q: What's the most important thing you have learned so far?

A: I've coached big-time football before at Notre Dame and Ohio State. And I think the level of this is a "wow", because it's so centralized. Obviously, Gator football in Seattle is not real powerful. But there can't be anything more powerful than this in the southeastern part of the country. There can't be. I mean 60,000 people at the [spring] game. People say, "Wow!" These Gator Clubs … and I'm sure there are 20 more just like it … that's a "wow," because it's not like that elsewhere.

Q: That "wow" is a 500-pound gorilla, with which every Florida coach has had to deal. You're coaching everything that moves—fans, students, players—can you do all this? And how long can you keep on doing it?

A: Dennis Franchione [Texas A&M head coach] is a great friend of mine, and I called him when I first became a head coach at Bowling Green. And I visited with Bill Snyder of Kansas State—had long talks. I think if you look at what I try to do, if it helps recruiting, if it helps our players, if it helps our staff, and most importantly, if it helps my family, then you probably do it. If it doesn't, you don't have to do it. And so the hardest thing for me—and I actually let my secretary do it—is I can't say no. I'm too appreciative of everything. She's been the "bad cop," and she does a good job of it. If I get my focus on my family, my players, and recruiting, I don't have to worry about that "gorilla." And I talk about it with the people I care about—the Lou Holtzes, Earl Bruces, Shelly Meyers—people who know me. I don't worry about it. I haven't had much [bad press].

These kind of getting-to-know-you sessions with Meyer were rare, because most of his time was spent answering questions from fans and media about Chris Leak's development, how his offense worked, whether he could win an SEC title, how this new Champions Club thing worked, and if he could beat FSU and Georgia. On this particular day, still more than three months out from the first official snap, we talked about some of that, but also what was in his CD player (Jimmy Buffett), and whom he thought was the best coach in football (Bill Belichick).

First impressions are valuable tools for assessment, and, after watching Meyer interact with the large crowd of more than 500 people at the Ocala Gator Club, he evidently had both a sense of purpose and a sense of humor. Meyer chided Bull Gator John Alvarez for asking him to sign something for Alvarez' grandson, Isaac, but when the coach asked how to spell "Isaac," he was told by granddad, "I don't know, I was hoping you knew!" Everybody laughed as Urban repeated that story, Alvarez included. And then he proceeded with a sermon from the Gospel of Meyer, bragging on the numbers of merit scholars at the University of Florida and stressing the importance of his players getting an education and living right. "If their mothers want them to go to church, then it's our job to see that they go to church," Meyer promised. Had he asked for it, Meyer could have elicited a few "amens" from the back row. This was the kind of living-room message that could—and would—close the deal for some of the best blue-chip prospects in the country.

In his ability to evoke preseason passion, Meyer ranked right up there with Charley Pell and Steve Spurrier. Although the new coach knew that he wouldn't have a championship team right away, he realized that responding to Gator fans' expectations by instilling hope in the immediate future was crucial to the program's success as September approached. Once the excitement of opening day had passed—and Florida had its first win, 32-14 over Wyoming—he could breathe easier. The following weekend the Gators polished off Louisiana Tech, 41-3; but the following Saturday, if was time for Big Boy Football.

Tennessee Comes to Town

In what has become one of college football's grandest rivalries, Florida was trying to reclaim "The Swamp," having lost to Tennessee at home the last two times and three over the last four. It was hot, it was loud, and nasty licks were being delivered on the grassy floor of Florida Field, where Tennessee was about the muscle and Florida was about the finesse—as usual. The endurance battle would test Meyer's plan to condition his athletes in the off-season for "finishing games."

Minutes before the kickoff, Meyer reflected the tension as he paced a trail to nowhere at the 45-yard line, stepping first one way and then the other, always tethered to the headset in self-imposed isolation. Wiping the sweat from his brow, he then slapped hands with passer-by Markus Manson.

Perhaps he had reason to be nervous. After all, at stake was the validation of his spread offense, plus his aggressive hands-on coaching style, his Champions Club rewards program, and how he would meet the challenge of SEC football. And that's leaving out his 18-game winning streak.

The congregation of 90,716 in The First Church of Gator Football witnessed the manifestation of what Meyer had been teaching and preaching. Before the largest crowd ever to attend a football game of any kind in Florida—college or pro—Florida beat Tennessee, 16-7.

Chris Leak was sacked three times, but wound up hitting 17 passes for 179 yards—several on key third downs to keep a drive alive—and for the third straight game he did not throw an interception. The offensive performance was less than the coach desired—"We're still a million miles away ...."—and he definitely wasn't pleased with the blocking of his veteran offensive line. "We're just not blocking people," Meyer said.

But it was a victory over Tennessee, always considered a harbinger of the season.

"What a great day for Florida football," the 41-year-old Meyer said after his first Southeastern Conference win—42nd overall, 19th in a row, and third at Florida. "I have great respect for SEC football. That was like two sledgehammers going at each other."

It wasn't picture perfect. Instead of opening to rave reviews, the spread offense sputtered a bit with just 247 yards, most of it passing. In the end, an unheralded defense, special teams, and three field goals by a non-scholarship player, kicker Chris Hetland, came through for Meyer.

The victory didn't come without a price. Defensive end Ray McDonald, one of the team's best linemen, suffered a serious injury and was lost for most of the season. And wide receiver Andre "Bubba" Caldwell, who scored Florida's only touchdown on a fake option-reverse, suffered a broken leg and would miss the year.

So while Florida was off to a 3-0 start—and the opponents had not yet discovered the Achilles heel that Meyer was attempting to disguise—danger lurked ahead. An easy 49-28 win at Kentucky set up Meyer's first road venture: a trip to Tuscaloosa.

The Ghost of the Bear

Alabama football reeks with tradition, thanks primarily to the Reign of The Bear. Yet the Gators-Crimson Tide matchup didn't really have enough legs to be considered a heated rivalry. Although the two teams dominated the early years of the SEC Championship playoff game, they'd only met 31 times previously, and the Tide had won 19.

The ghost of The Bear looms eternally over Tuscaloosa like the Goodyear blimp hovers over Monday night football games. Perhaps Alabama's clarion call for a return to glory invoked the spirit of this legendary, but very dead football coach, Paul W. "Bear" Bryant, who won 323 games at Maryland, Kentucky, Texas A&M, and Alabama. Bryant had pretty much owned the Gators with seven wins in eight tries. Six times Alabama won national championships under his guidance, and he was a three-time national coach of the year.

I'll never forget the first time I laid eyes on Bear in the early 1960s, when he suddenly appeared in a doorway of an SEC hospitality suite, filling it like John Wayne, speaking in a gravelly voice cultivated by too many unfiltered Chesterfield cigarettes and glasses of bourbon. I was in Silver Springs, Florida, sitting at the poker table with several coaches and writers, plus Bear's wife, Mary Harmon Bryant. She could call a bluff and drink a glass or two of whiskey herself and was always welcome. Her husband, while friendly and genial, was an imposing figure. Bryant's commanding presence could always be felt on the sideline or in a room when he was alive, and even then, after he'd been dead for 22 years, he was very much alive in spirit on that October 1, 2005 Saturday in Tuscaloosa.

Things began badly for the Florida Gators as they got caught in a traffic jam from Birmingham and arrived 45 minutes behind schedule. They just kept stalling out the rest of the day—and then they got run over by a Red Machine. In fact, some might say Urban Meyer's team never showed at all. Certainly the nation's No. 5-ranked team didn't, because those guys in the white jerseys and orange pants were impostors.

"The team in the red was more prepared than the team in the orange," Meyer admitted.

Final score: Alabama 31, Florida 3. Humpty Dumpty took a great fall from No. 5. Even if the Gators were thrown behind by the traffic jam, it didn't matter—once they arrived they were in for an old-fashioned butt whipping. They would have been better off missing the bus altogether.

In the postgame press conference, the first thing Meyer did was take a white piece of paper on which game statistics were printed and stare at it for a good 15 seconds before uttering a word. "The best thing for me to do is just eat it for a day rather than to name names," Meyer said. "There were far too many mistakes, and if we were going to start pointing fingers, it would be at the coaching staff."

Weaknesses popped up everywhere, especially in Florida's man-to-man defensive coverage, which concerned the Gators immediately because they knew then that they couldn't compete with the Alabamas without superb effort and preparation. Atop their fall from the rankings, Urban Meyer's 20-game winning streak was halted in his most lopsided loss as a head coach. Asked how it felt to lose, Meyer responded, "Awful!" Equally as ominous was that this was the first time since early in 1992 that the Gators failed to score a touchdown. Chris Leak, who had an awful day, ended his streak without an interception after just four passes at 117.

What kept Meyer up August nights had come to pass: the defense wasn't solid, the running game was suspect, the special teams were playing uninspired, and now that Caldwell was injured, the lack of a deep threat would put even greater pressure on his struggling quarterback.

All that with a road trip to LSU in two weeks and Georgia just around the corner …

Yes, There is Crying in Football

In a rare piece of fortuitous SEC scheduling, Mississippi State popped up at a perfect time. The Gators cruised past the Bulldogs 35-9, as they approached the next SEC road trip—destination "Death Valley," where the LSU Tigers awaited.

Baton Rouge is usually a vibrant football town, but not after Hurricane Katrina's devastation of the Gulf Coast. The Tigers had become one of the few bright lights in the lives of distressed Louisianans. With their new coach, Les Miles via Oklahoma State, still an unknown quantity—he came from Oklahoma State—LSU was a difficult team to assess. At any rate, Meyer knew Baton Rouge was no place for the faint of heart.

It began like a Tuscaloosa Redux. The Gators fell behind 14-0 in the first quarter, and this had all the making of tent-folding time. Instead of mailing it in as they did when they fell behind 17-0 to the Crimson Tide two weeks earlier, though, the Gators fought back to take the lead 17-14 before losing, 21-17. At least they showed a little fight. This time Meyer saw something different in the faces of his players: pride and passion, touching him to the point of tears as he spoke about their effort.

"I tell you what I liked: I liked the passion," Meyer said. "The way our guys played today. You'll never hear me say I'm proud of a team if I'm not. I see guys I've never seen actually act like they like putting on a Gator helmet—act like they wanted to play today."

There was the matter of the paltry 99 yards rushing and 107 yards passing with four sacks. With only half an offense and without the talent to run Meyer's spread, it wasn't likely to get better. There didn't appear to be much conviction in the offense, which was becoming more predictable by the week.

Then, of course, a shot too easy for the media to pass up: the teary-eyed coach who had been demanding more toughness from his players. "There's no crying in football," wrote more than one of the wise-guy columnists.

With an off week to get healthier before the Jacksonville showdown with SEC East leader Georgia, Meyer had a ton of work to do in haste.

Georgia: Time for a Change

Good coaches know how to adapt—and that means more than making changes at halftime. They know that personnel dictates strategy. At the core of these decisions is an underlying philosophy about how games are won. Good coaches never change who they are, but they also remain unafraid to make major tweaks. In the case of the spread-'em-out, run-first, pass-second Urban Meyer offense, too many holes showed in the Florida pass protection. The opposition no longer feared the running game or deep threat.

Since Leak was not a runner, he was unable to escape the swift linebackers and ends—or evade corner or safety blitzes. Meyer scrapped his ego and the high-tech portion of the spread offense, dumbing it down to a few effective plays.

Instead of the four- and five-wideout setup, he opted for the better protection, utilizing a fullback and tight end to fend off Bulldogs rushers. The result was two precision-like drives in the first quarter that put Georgia to sleep early in the afternoon. Leak took his offense 80 yards for a touchdown on the opening drive, sticking the ball across the goal line with a half-gainer. That was the first of two efficient scoring drives, and when the Bulldogs awoke, like Rip Van Winkle, too much had already happened.

Then the Gators held on for dear life.

Fortunately for Florida, starting Georgia quarterback D.J. Shockley was on the sideline with an injury, replaced by the not-nearly-as-quick Joe Tereshinski III. As the big quarterback was falling to the ground, he managed to hand off to Thomas Brown, who threw back across the field to Tereshinski for a touchdown. Despite the Bulldogs' rally, Meyer was up to some tricks of his own. Against Georgia, the biggest of the Gators' SEC rivals, Meyer saved his fourth-down fake punt for the fourth quarter, and it paid off when punter Eric Wilbur rambled 20 yards to keep a drive alive. Even if it didn't result in points, it ate up more clock.

After the 14-10 victory over previously unbeaten Georgia, you could see clear eyes and the look of a relieved man. He had the big monkey off his back—for now at least—and over a two-week period of hard work, he'd found some kind of elixir for his ailing offense, which produced a 109-yard rushing day for tailback DeShawn Wynn.

Later, he would say that the offensive changes were necessary because of the injuries, because of the speed of the opponents' defense, and because Leak wasn't comfortable trying to see over some of the taller linemen. "We had a six-foot quarterback. It was because of his comfort level, not my comfort level," Meyer said. "And that's why we adapted. The quarterback position was probably the No. 1 reason."

In addition to being a season-saving, SEC-rejuvenating victory, it gave Meyer some badly needed coaching cred. The Gators couldn't stand anymore major hiccups, but they nearly experienced one the next Saturday.

The unthinkable nearly happened. Vandy took an early 7-0 lead and counterpunched every time Florida scored before falling in double overtime, 49-42. Leak's 16-yard touchdown pass to Jemalle Cornelius in the second overtime, which had to be reviewed, proved the difference. It was his third TD pass of the night. In one of his best performances as Gator quarterback, Leak led his team in rushing with 67 yards and three touchdowns, while completing 32 of 41 passes for 257 yards.

Yet, Vanderbilt's brilliant Jay Cutler, who passed for 361 yards and four touchdowns, equaled and surpassed Leak. The difference was, Cutler's last pass was intercepted to end the game; Leak's created the winning score. The game may have never gone to overtime but for a celebration penalty called on Vandy after the touchdown at the end of regulation. Cutler was under center, ready to quick-snap what may have been the winning two-point conversion when the flag was thrown on receiver Earl Bennett, forcing the Commodores to kick for the tie and subsequent overtimes.

"We're still battling for the SEC championship," said Meyer, with an eye toward the next week's game against Spurrier. Little did he know then that Spurrier's team, not the Gators, would be in that position the following Saturday.

New Ball Coach vs. Ol' Ball Coach

When I found Steve Spurrier in his office overlooking Williams-Brice Stadium the day before Florida's visit to Columbia, he wasn't exactly full of angst. He greeted an old friend with a warm hello, we sat down, and he began chatting about a new condominium he'd just bought within a few blocks of his stadium office. He was in a good mood—realistic, but optimistic about his chances against his old team.

"We've got a chance. We're going to pitch it around and see what happens," he said, as he almost always did. "I'm just trying to get some ball plays drawn up right now. When you're the offensive coordinator, you've got to work on some ball plays. It takes time." But by now, he had kicked back.

This was vintage-1990 Spurrier, full of zest after dragging a quarterback out of the mothballs and finding a wide receiver stuck off in the corner, pushing their buttons, then saying, "Let's go play." Once he landed in the Low Country, he weeded out about a dozen of the problem players, found himself a promising quarterback in Blake Mitchell, and coached up a basketball player named Sidney Rice to be a wide receiver. The Ol' Ball Coach was off and running.

The Gamecocks had beaten Arkansas for their sixth win of the season the previous week to become bowl eligible. Frankly, you could tell he'd had just about enough of all this Godzilla vs. the Gators talk with so many visiting press from Florida in town. Of course, he was telling the media everything was just dandy; had worked out for the best; and by the way, thanks to his old boss, Jeremy Foley, and UF President Bernie Machen for their wisdom in not offering him his old job back right away, or he would have missed out on this South Carolina deal.

(Editor's note: Not that he would have taken it, of course.)

One reason the media always enjoys Spurrier is that he so often willingly fills up their notebooks and tape decks with pithy quotes and entertaining sound bites. In fact, he was so downright happy about his Gamecocks upsetting Florida, 30-22, that he even suggested a headline for our sports pages the next day—keeping in mind that, if Georgia got beat that night by Auburn, his Gamecocks could accomplish an outright football miracle.

"Guess who's pulling for Auburn now?"

Which some of us indeed used as our column headlines.

The headline above was suggested in his press conference after the first South Carolina victory over the Florida Gators since 1939. For South Carolina, it was a record fifth straight Southeastern Conference victory, assuring them no worse than second in the eastern division and the most points South Carolina had ever scored against the Gators.

Not a bad headline, either—after all, it was Carolina, and not Florida, which needed Georgia to lose Saturday night. That, coupled with another defeat of the Bulldogs the next week by Kentucky, would send the Gamecocks to the SEC title game. A little far out? Perhaps, but Spurrier has been living in the land of the Far Out. Though he claimed he hardly ever mentioned "Florida" to his players all week, his Gator roots run deep. He may have been wearing garnet and black, but his heart was still pumping orange and blue. "I still love the Gators, and I always will," he said. "But this is my team now."

It was still a bit rowdy at midfield as his players doused him with ice, and several of the Gamecock players tried to lift him to their shoulders. "They don't know yet that you aren't supposed to do that," Spurrier said, "except when you win conference championships. We've got to coach 'em up on that."

This was the way he won at Duke, with the Tampa Bay Bandits of the USFL—guile and guts. It had been a charmed life for Spurrier the previous five weeks. The ball bounced his way again Saturday, and he admitted it. "We got some extremely good breaks," he said. "That's the way it's been. Every long pass by the other team seems to go just off their fingertips. ... We [got] Chris Tucker's interception."

A tipped pass that Tucker returned to the Gator 5-yard line was the first break. With just over a minute left, the officials called Florida for illegal substitution for having 12 players in the huddle, thus giving Carolina a first down and a chance to kill the clock.

Spurrier was most grateful for the last call, because "... Chris Leak may have taken them downfield, and they might have scored and gone for two and made it.

"I tell our players that we are defying football logic because we're last in the SEC in rushing, and we're next to last in rushing defense," Spurrier admitted.

Steve Spurrier had made a career out of defying logic. Meyer had the better football team that day and knew it, but Spurrier came away with the win. As far as Jarvis Herring was concerned, the Gators got ambushed. "I knew that was going to be a tough game," said the free safety, who was recruited out of Live Oak and signed by Spurrier. "That was like walking into a door and getting jumped by 10 guys. He's just a mastermind. It doesn't matter what team he's got around him. He brings confidence to the guys, just by being on the sidelines. It wasn't that they were better than us. We warned them [the younger players] about him. I guarantee you they won't overlook him next year. "

A few months later I asked Spurrier if he felt, now that the Gamecocks had beaten the Gators, that South Carolina and Florida would become a real rivalry.

"It may change things, I'm not sure," said Spurrier, who was making plans for two trips to Gainesville—one for the anniversary celebration of the '96 national championship and another time to coach his Gamecocks against the

Gators. "One win in 66 years, I don't know how much that changes it. We were very, very fortunate in that game. Every good break went our way. Florida didn't play very well, and we won the game. Somebody asked me the other day, 'I bet you can't wait to coach against the Gators in 'The Swamp.' And I said, 'I am not looking forward to that game *at all*! If we had a lot better team than they have, I'd have been looking forward to it; but talent-wise, they are superior to us right now. If they don't play their best, and we get all the breaks, I'll be looking forward then."

Naturally, a little rumbling murmured in the "Gator Nation" after the loss to Spurrier, and the New Ball Coach needed to finish the season strong in order to quiet his critics.

A Sweet Victory Over FSU

The Gators picked a good time to play their best game of the year and beat the *bejabbers* out of the team that would represent one side of the ACC against Virginia Tech. So Florida got the Sunshine State bragging rights and a trip to the Outback Bowl—but no ring and no cigar. And FSU, despite a 34-7 drubbing, got to go play for its league championship.

Florida's game plan was nifty—and the execution was first rate, particularly on special teams and defense, which produced 27 points on four turnovers and a blocked field goal.

"That was one of my best games as a Gator. Being a captain, seeing our crowd, as loud as it was—it was a great experience," said Leak, who had a big night, throwing for two touchdowns on a 19-for-28 passing showing for 211 yards, including completions to nine different receivers. One of his touchdowns was an impressive corner-route connection with Dallas Baker, delivered where only he could catch it. That night, Leak became the first quarterback since Kerwin Bell (1985-86) to defeat Florida State in consecutive seasons.

"We had total focus that night offensively," Leak recalled of the win over FSU. "You could see it in the way the guys were playing. We were definitely ready and prepared for that game."

So I asked Meyer after the game why his Gators responded so impressively. Was it better preparation, better mental approach, more time to scheme with an open date? What? He couldn't really answer it, except to suggest it was the home-field advantage at "The Swamp," where the environment was "electric" and that the players were "committed to and believe in." Meyer might have pointed out that some of the injured wide receivers who had missed games during the middle of the season—especially Jemalle Cornelius and Baker—were back for the game. Losing them, along with the Caldwell's season-ending broken leg, had proved devastating to Meyer's spread offense.

The road in the Southeastern Conference being highway of hard knocks, Meyer found that in Baton Rouge, Tuscaloosa, and Columbia, you don't expect any love.

"We obviously have an issue on the road," Meyer responded, "which will be addressed. I will evaluate everything from Point A to Point C on what we do, what we eat, how much butter is on the table, and everything else. And [I will] figure out why we are struggling. We're going to change our routine and everything. Because if it's not working, you've got to change."

Though they won no championships, the 2005 Gators did earn a measure of success. They wound up 6-0 and unbeaten at home, with wins over Tennessee, Georgia, and FSU.

"We're a new program, and we hit a few speed bumps," explained Meyer.

The lingering sweetness that comes with beating your intrastate rival cannot be duplicated in any victory. So this would be a night of celebration for the Gators as they drank from the cup of golden nectar, the spoils of beating FSU. As the 41-year-old head coach ventured to the north end zone to join the players and the fans in singing the school song, he did a jog-by of the student section—with a special shout out to "The Swamp Things"—and pumped his fist multiple times. He knew now that speed bumps could be negotiated, and the future was already beginning to look better.

As for the Gators and championships in Meyer's first year, the only title they wound up playing for was a mythical one—but at least they could call themselves state champions.

If they had been members of the Atlantic Coast Conference, they probably could have won the Atlantic Division and gone to Jacksonville the next weekend, instead of the team they just thumped, 34-7. They just couldn't qualify for the Southeastern Conference title game.

Florida wound up with a 31-24 victory over Iowa in the Outback Bowl to go 9-3 on the season—the Gators' first nine-win season since Spurrier left. Leak passed for two touchdowns, completing 25 of 40 for 279 yards with no interceptions. Thus, the Gators had won a bowl game and had beaten three rivals—Tennessee, Georgia, and FSU—not a bad way for a coach to start off his career in a new job.

Meyer knew he needed to address the matter of finding a way to win on the road. He promised, at the end of his first season, that he'd evaluate everything right down to "the butter" in seeking answers. He never underestimated playing on the road in the SEC, he said, and the quality of competition had far more to do with Florida's struggle than "the butter."

"We played some really good teams," Meyer said, "but I'm not convinced the better team won those games. I don't think that was the case with the last one we lost [South Carolina]. I don't think we were a good team at all. We had good players. But good teams beat good players every time."

Not knowing the heart and soul of his team right away, Meyer wasn't sure how far to push his players. In retrospect, he might have been tougher. "I was a little disappointed, to be honest with you," Meyer would say almost a year later. "But we had some great moments. One of those moments was probably the way the season ended [wins over FSU, Iowa in Outback Bowl]. It took a little longer than I thought it would take to get to know these players. There was the respect issue for all of them. But I felt like at the end of the year we accomplished that."

Looking Back at the 99th Year

Nearly four months after the 2005 season ended, I spoke with Meyer a final time about the events of his first year and the expectations of 2006. As a supporter of all University of Florida sports programs, Meyer experienced a vicarious thrill through his neighbor and friend, Billy Donovan. Given Urban's quest for the secret to team chemistry, he watched with admiration and joy as the Gator basketball coach molded a young team into national champions. In fact, Donovan invited Meyer, who rescheduled his spring practice, to the title game to see Florida's 73-57 hammering of UCLA.

"I was fortunate to be invited into the locker room after the game and experience it firsthand," Meyer said. "Our conversations are not done. I'm a big fan of great teams, and that was one of the best teams, regardless of the sport, that I've ever been around. I talked to him at length and will continue to do so."

As highly as Meyer praised Donovan, he pointed out that leadership was the biggest reason those players jelled. "I've been part of a great team before where coaches get the credit," Meyer said. "That was a lot of fun to watch, and I think the words that epitomize a great team—certainly our national championship team—is 'a bunch of unselfish people who care about each other.'"

If he sounded a little envious, it's because Meyer is on a mission to bring about that kind of attitude for his football team and knows that without it, greatness is not possible. He was quick to point out that great teams are scarce. "There's a bunch of great players, but how many great teams are there?" Meyer asked. The talent is there, he says, but lacking are leadership and discipline.

The Champions Club, which offers players a chance to be rewarded with newer workout gear and special steak dinners, helped some. To earn membership, the players were required to perform in the classroom, remain good citizens, and attend regular workouts. Meyer was mostly pleased with the result.

"The whole program is based on treating secretaries, all the way to SIDs [Sports Information Directors]—whoever is associated with the program— treat them however they deserve to be treated," Meyer explained. "Not all the same. When I was in high school, I never understood why, if I worked out and the other guy didn't, we got the same kind of equipment. So I always promised myself that, if I ever got in this position, I was going to treat the good guys good and the not-so-good guys not quite as good as the good guys. That's the politically correct way of answering it. It's reward-based. If I'm a guy who doesn't have a lot of self-respect and discipline, then why am I going to work hard? Well, you get better stuff and you're treated a little better. Now to the guys with self-discipline and self-respect, it's not that big a deal, because they're going to do it the right way anyway. But what I'm finding out as I get older is that you don't have that many people with that self-respect, that self-discipline. It's just a way of motivation."

He was a little impatient about the progress in some areas. "I actually wish we were further along, but from the middle of the season to the end of the season, there was a really good situation," Meyer said of his 2005 experience. "I think the way the season ended up was very positive. Middle of the season, I was not pleased at all. The chemistry is coming around, but we are certainly not a great team. And that's all I'm worried about [in 2006]. Yeah, we have some issues at linebacker, and we have some issues at corner, but we're still dealing with issues that great teams don't deal with. And I'm anxious to move along and either make personnel changes, or we have got to change some of the behavior issues I'm dealing with."

The message was loud and clear: Meyer was going to be less tolerant about off-the-field incidents. He was clearly troubled about the players involved in the firearms incident that occurred at the apartment of Dee Webb, who had left the team early to play in the NFL.

Several present members of the Gator team were involved in handling some of the guns in Webb's collection—albeit legal guns—while visiting his apartment. One of them went off while receiver Kenneth Tookes was handling it. According to reports from the Alachua County Police Department, the bullet embedded in a wall of an apartment occupied by two women next door. After discovering an AK-47 rifle and an AR-15 in Webb's apartment, police found a .38-caliber revolver and a 12-gauge shotgun belonging to Webb in an SUV that receiver Andre Caldwell was driving. Cornerback Reggie Lewis was also involved in the incident.

Even though no charges were filed, the police said all were guilty of "bad judgment," a fact that didn't go unnoticed by their football coach.

"I was extremely disappointed," Meyer said of the incident. "Some people say that perception isn't important. Perception is very important for our program—for all the Gators and alums and 'The Gator Nation' and recruiting. We came down on them very hard. You'll never hear me bring out in public what the punishment was, because that's in-house. Some coaches come out in public because they want to say, 'That's what we did.' But I'm not going to do that—never have. I heard someone say, 'Well, there's no punishment.' If someone does their homework and finds out—they're not going to find out from me—but if they find out, there were some serious consequences."

For Meyer, the issue is repeat offenders. He's willing to accept the fact that young men will make mistakes as long as they're not grievous errors he calls "poor values" choices. He will forgive them, dish out the punishment, keep it in house, and move on. If you make the same mistake again, however, or one classified as a "poor value" issue, you're probably gone. "Last year [2005], we had several issues that we took care of internally, and we've got to maintain so that they're not repeat offenses," Meyer said.

For the most part, Meyer escaped the media unscathed. If you're scoring at home, give Meyer an A- for his dealings with the press in his first 18 months. The Florida media pretty much gave Meyer a pass. They were curious about his "Champions Club" idea, that inner circle of privileged players who earned better workout gear and tastier food through disciplined workouts and classroom excellence. They poked a little fun at him for shedding tears in his LSU postgame press conference. One columnist called him a "liar" for not revealing an injury to a player.

Long ago when he was an assistant coach at Notre Dame and his wife got angry at some of the things written, Urban told Shelley: "You understand, they have one job: to sell newspapers, to sell magazines, to sell books." He believes in First Amendment rights, "Everybody is allowed to have their own opinions, with little or no consequence and without any knowledge of what's going on," Meyer said. "I have no problem with that, which is why I am so open with the media, why I have fun with them. ... The way I look at it is, everybody has a job to do, and God bless him—do it to the best of your ability."

He has respect for the media at Florida, but does get a little piqued at some of the others who don't really do their homework: "I think the people here who do it on a daily basis do a good job. I have a hard time dealing with the media who have never been to your practice and never talked to your players, and yet they are overcritical. Example: ESPN. And I have great respect for Lee Corso and Kirk Herbstreit, because they come to my practices, they talk to players, they've done our games, but there are the ones that don't."

What annoys Meyer are the pundits who take shots at his players without any firsthand knowledge of them. "I'm not going to give names," he said, "but if you meet Alex Smith [his Utah quarterback], and you see him practice and don't think he's good enough, then you've never coached football—but that's a guy's opinion. But if you've never really seen him play, then I've got a problem with that. The people here—they do their work. And I didn't know that. But after every practice, there's a bunch of folks out there. And that's not the case in most places, including Notre Dame."

Some feel-good news arrived when Meyer was able to parade the prized recruit of his first class before the thousands at Florida Field for the spring game, once again setting off outrageous expectations for the future. Fans were still abuzz about Tim Tebow. Based on his performance in the spring game, the true freshman was going to be an exciting addition. Even Meyer was enthused. "The intangibles are the best part, and the fans haven't even seen it yet," Meyer said of his incoming freshman. "That's his leadership, his ability to run and his toughness. He's got a long way to go throwing the ball. He looked pretty good [in the spring game] throwing the ball against a vanilla defense, but there's a lot to Tebow."

It didn't matter that one guy was a senior with three years of experience and really had done nothing to lose his job as starting quarterback for the Gators, or that the other guy was a true freshman. After all, that's the nature of this beast called football—the backup quarterback, if at all talented, is almost always a fan favorite.

A quarterback "controversy" awaited Florida fans to chew on in 2006, at least for a season. "Controversy" may have been a little too strong, but "competition at the position" certainly wasn't.

Gator fans needed just two seconds to realize that Tebow, the nation's top-ranked high school quarterback, was going to be something special. After the Orange and Blue Game in the spring, they were starting to pencil in Tebow's name as "The Future Face of Florida Football." As the countdown to the '06 season began, however, the job belonged to senior incumbent Chris Leak, who had done nothing to lose it. Most comforting to Gator fans was the idea that, if Leak faltered or was injured, Meyer had a Plan B at quarterback.

Indeed, Tebow was impressive in his spring debut. Perhaps it was an omen that Tebow's very first pass as a Gator was complete, if only for six yards to wide receiver Kenneth Tookes. From there, Tebow completed 14 more of the next 20 passes for 197 yards and one touchdown. The fact that Tebow's Orange team beat Leak's Blue team, 24-6, had no bearing and wasn't really a good tool of comparison because the squads were not balanced. Leak was 17 out of 33 for 135 yards, with one interception and no TDs. So was there a quarterback controversy?

Meyer addressed that question early in the post-spring game press conference: "The good thing is, there's not a quarterback controversy in-house," said Meyer. "I think, as Gator fans and as college football fans, that's a great water-cooler story, that's a great discussion around the coffee thing in the morning. It's also great discussion upstairs [in the press box], but Chris Leak's our quarterback, and Tim Tebow is going to be the guy that's gonna play. His playing time is all dictated by Tim Tebow. We're going to let him grow as a quarterback. The complete negative is that you wish there was somebody behind him, but there's not. But these are two great men we are going to build an offense around and be successful."

It didn't take the rest of the media long to pounce on the "quarterback controversy." For the next few days, that theme was pounded home in the printed press, as well as on talk radio and television sportscasts.

Going on his very first appearance, Tebow looked like football's version of "The Natural" with his great football instincts. He was decisive with the ball, whether passing it or pitching it out. He stood in the pocket with poise, looking very much in command, dispatching the ball with such authority that it seemed to arrive ahead of schedule. His touch and accuracy were excellent as he hit several receivers on the dead run. Tebow's deep passing threat was immediately evident as he connected with redshirt freshman David Nelson on passes of 29 and 55 yards—although granted, he didn't get a lot of heat because there was no blitzing, and the quarterback couldn't get hit.

Most importantly, at 6 feet, 3 inches, 229 pounds, Tebow was a big, strong guy with quickness who could likely operate Meyer's spread offense the way Urban would like to see it run. It was a fit. And the new kid from Nease High in nearby St. John's County was clearly going to be exciting to watch. Meyer himself even got caught up as a spectator in watching his prized recruit. "He was nervous in the first half," said Meyer. "His huddle was a mess. The tackle could hear what he was saying. But in the second half, he got better, and he played pretty good."

Playing before 45,000 in "The Swamp" had a little to do with that. "You dream about it all your life," said Tebow.

Standing at the main lectern in the interview area, the strapping quarterback with the movie-star looks "yessired" and "nosirred" reporters to death. Wearing a T-shirt bearing the words "Gator Strength," which seemed to fit the occasion, Tebow said all the right things: "Chris Leak is a great quarterback to learn from … I have a lot to learn" … *yada, yada, yada*.

The words didn't matter. The actions spoke. You could swear Tim Tebow was born to play quarterback for the Florida Gators.

What Urban Meyer had wished for after his first season was better backups. He often spoke with concern about the lack of depth after his first unit and the lack of competition. He got what he wished for at the quarterback position, plus a bit more.

That doesn't mean there will be a change at quarterback. "Chris Leak is our quarterback, and Chris Leak has made great progress. He's won a lot of games here, and he is our best option to win games," Meyer said. "Certainly the way he played at the end of the season and the people around him—that gives us our best chance to win. If we were going to make a change at quarterback—I don't see that happening—and Chris and him are tied, Chris is our quarterback. Tim will play. You have to have your quarterback have some reps. So hopefully, he will play and improve."

He was asked to explain his offense. "It's an offense based on run first, but you want to be balanced," Meyer said. "It's an offense based on creating numbers, which means you don't want to run the ball with unblock defenders. If they're putting unblocked defenders, you've got to be able to throw the ball. We want to spread everybody about and make them defend the field; and if they're not defending the field, we want to be able to get the ball there—fast."

Meyer prefers to call it his "system" and not his "offense," because it defines the intent better. "I believe in our system, which is to get the ball into the playmakers' hands and force the defense to play honest," Meyer said. "I would not say there is a set offense."

In addition to some of those aforementioned "bumps" for the Meyer regime, possible contention sprang up in the summer of 2006 in a clash over offensive philosophies: the Meyer Spread versus the Spurrier Fun 'N' Gun. At least one member of Meyer's staff has experienced minor conflict with ex-Gator stars over the proper way to teach young quarterbacks.

In 2006, the BMW Quarterback Camp ruin by Shane Matthews, Kerwin Bell, and Danny Wuerffel was moved from Ocala to Gainesville, where Florida offensive coordinator Dan Mullen became involved. The problem was that Matthews, Bell, and Wuerffel were teaching kids the way they knew—The Spurrier Way—and Mullen preferred The Meyer Way. A heated discussion ensued about passing routes—they were running 12-yard curl routes—and Mullen commented: "You can't run that stuff in the SEC today."

Mullen was informed that "that stuff" had gotten these three former Gator quarterbacks six SEC titles and a national championship—not to mention five SEC Player of the Year awards. Some felt Mullen had not yet gotten the best out of his own quarterback.

One should take into account that Leak has been asked to run different offenses under three different coordinators—first Ed Zaunbrecher, next Larry Fedora, and then Dan Mullen. Since taking over the starting job early in his freshman year, Leak had 33 straight starts, with a 15-8 record in SEC games. In 2005, Leak was 235-for-375 for 2,639 passing yards and 20 touchdowns with just six interceptions. In his first three seasons, Leak passed for 45 touchdowns.

It fell upon Leak during the 2004 Zook firing to help keep his team together. "My main thing was to stay focused on trying to win games," Leak said of his experience during the 2004 coaching-change carrousel. "We had to keep our minds on Georgia, which is one of the biggest rivalries in college football."

As for having to switch to the spread offense just before his junior season, Leak played down the difficulty. "It was just a case of getting some reps. I think our guys did a great job of making the adjustments," Leak said, "and the coaches did a great job of getting us the reps during spring."

Meyer was feeling good about his senior quarterback, but what he wanted from Leak in his final season was stronger leadership. "There's a common denominator about national champions in college football," Meyer said. "The more I study it and talk to the coaches … the guy on the championship team is that great leader who gets everything going. When people are struggling, they don't look to the center or the wide receiver. They look to the quarterback. He's got to have an ability to rally people. And we are not there yet at that position."

Of that personal challenge, Leak said: "That's what you want to do, find a way to improve, become a better player, become a better leader. That's what you want out of a coach. You want a chance to compete. Coach Meyer came in and said he was going to build the whole thing around me, and that gave me a great deal of confidence, as well as the coaches and players around us."

Leak arrived at Florida in 2003 with a big reputation that incited great expectations. In his first three seasons he played reasonably well, but in comparison to those before him, he hadn't measured up to the likes of Danny Wuerffel and Rex Grossman. He does not shirk the pressure, though.

"It comes with the territory," Leak said. "It comes with being a Gator."

Clearly, the injuries to his wide receivers hampered Leak's performance in '05. "It's always hard when you train with the guys all spring and in the off-season, and then they go down," Leak said. "It can be tough sometimes when you've got younger guys, especially in mid-season when you need to get that timing down. But that's just college football. Sometimes you've got to play through things."

Then there was the shoulder injury Leak suffered against Alabama that he pretty much kept secret throughout the year—but he said he was injured the rest of the season. He estimates he was at "… about 75 to 80 percent the rest of the season."

For the most part, the players learned to accept the changes Meyer brought about, but it took a while. Senior Jarvis Herring realized how important it was to start off right. One of Meyer's favorite projects was restoring the safety, who had fallen out of grace for some off-the-field problems earlier in his career. The graduating senior remembered what it was like to arrive on campus as a small-town boy from Live Oak. "A shock," Herring said of his first time running out of the tunnel at Florida Field. "I was like a deer in the headlights. I couldn't even see the faces of the crowd. Everything is a blur at first."

Since Herring actually got into a game for one play when Steve Spurrier was the coach, he played for three different coaches. "It was more of a nonchalant environment," Herring said of Spurrier's team. "They were expecting to win. It didn't matter who they were going up against. They had a swagger and an attitude that nobody could touch them—nobody deserved to be on the same field with them."

Dealing with the loss of Spurrier as his coach was tough for Herring, and it took several days for him to come to grips with it. In his redshirt freshman year, Herring began to hear older players whispering questions about the hiring of Zook. "'He never had any head coaching experience?' they asked. 'How was he going to walk into the SEC and measure up?'" Herring recalled.

To this day, Jarvis thinks that those negative thoughts impacted Zook's team from the start and that they became a self-fulfilling prophecy. "I never blamed Coach Zook for those losses," said Herring. "But that was the biggest part of the battle, because nobody ever expected anything."

Herring blamed himself for being one of the negative thinkers and decided that, when Meyer signed on at Florida, he wasn't going to be one of those nay-saying older players setting a bad example. "I regret not doing that in the past," Herring said, "and wanted to make sure the younger guys had the right attitude."

Herring knew the doubters would raise questions about Meyer's spread offense, asserting that, although it had worked in the Mountain West Conference, it wouldn't in the SEC. "There's speed around here on these defenses," said Herring, "so we could have easily made it a negative vibe when he first came in, but instead of doing that, we embraced it. It wasn't easy. There were a lot of changes that it were hard. Some of the older guys kept things together."

Herring said one of the biggest missing pieces was the specials teams. "Guys didn't seem to realize how important it was," said Herring, "but that was the piece that was missing to become a team. It came in at the end of the year, in the Florida State game, when we started dominating. And we were starting to become a team. I guess we started to develop what Coach Meyer needed around here."

Meyer had correctly identified the problem back in August when he was staring at the ceiling: shaping the team up would be a challenge. Team chemistry remains high on Meyer's list. He wants to recruit high-character players who are talented, teach them discipline, and hope that they will unify. The challenge falls equally on the shoulders of coaches and players to lead. Thirteen members of the squad were named to the leadership committee in the spring of 2006. One was linebacker Brandon Siler, who was asked how the Champions Club impacted his teammates. "You could definitely tell the difference because people have a goal to work toward in the off-season—and they had stuff they could get," said Siler. "Me, I've always set my standards high, whether you put a goal up there or not."

Some of the team's early struggles under Meyer, Siler said, had to do with so much change. "Changes are hard for a lot of people," Siler said, "and when he came in, he made a lot of changes—different living arrangements, different styles, all kind of different things. It took a while to get used to, and I think that's what happened."

There was also the issue of keeping players from having delusions about their pro careers. "Coach [Steve] Spurrier would say this to Jeremy [Foley], and we've actually had a brief conversation about it," Meyer said. "I think it's very similar to the Notre Dame athlete—and especially in this era, with the Internet and the media buildup of players. I read things about our players that are mind-boggling. Who's leaving early for the draft? I often ask myself, 'What draft are they talking about?'"

Two other valuable lessons learned were about dealing with the heat:

1. The heat of the day that drains players when long practices are necessary in preseason to get it right.
2. The heat brought to players by members of their families whose expectations include everything from tickets for themselves to instant stardom for the player. There was one absurd claim by at least one parent that Meyer was hurting the chances of their son winning the Heisman Trophy. "Their son has about as much chance of winning the Heisman as I do," Meyer said. "Where does a comment like that come from? That's just illogical."

The pressure brought by expectations from his family and community drove five-star recruit Cornelius Ingram to the brink of quitting and transferring to another school. Two of Meyer's favorite players, Herring and graduating senior cornerback Vernell Brown, convinced Ingram to stay, and as a result, Ingram worked his way up to the No. 1 tight end and H-back spot.

"You talk about an education," Meyer said. "Cornelius Ingram was going to transfer. Charlie Strong and I drove to Hawthorne and got very upset with him. And I don't understand how a kid could think this. I probably wasn't going about it the right way and neither was Coach Strong. We think he's gone. So I happened to run into Jarvis Herring the next day, and he suggests we get with Vernell Brown. We had a meeting with Vernell, Jarvis, Coach Strong, Cornelius, and me. And it had nothing to do with him wanting to play quarterback. It was all the pressure on him from his family and friends."

Brown, from Gainesville, explained to Ingram that it had been that way for three years. He couldn't go get a hamburger. He couldn't get a haircut. He couldn't get the newspaper in the morning without somebody saying, "Vernell, what's the problem?" And eventually, he wanted to run from that.

"C.I. was trying to run from that problem," Meyer said. "Vernell Brown handled it, and it eventually worked out for him. That kid [Ingram] wouldn't be here today if it wasn't for Vernell Brown and Jarvis in my office that day."

As for dealing with the other kind of heat problem, Meyer planned to put more of a premium on running the plays correctly the first time and not re-running them to extend the practice into the hottest part of the day.

He thinks he'll be able to handle the rest of the heat, along with that 500-pound gorilla.

Afterword

Meyer has a strong appreciation for those who've come before him to lead Florida football. He makes it a point to learn as much as he can about the past, good and bad. Although he had been around just over 18 months, he was aware of whom some of these men were when he was asked:

Bob Woodruff: "I know his name, I don't know much about him."

Ray Graves: "I'm a big admirer of Ray Graves. He's been tremendous to me. I called him when I took the job. I'm just a big fan. He stands for all the right things."

Doug Dickey: "Met Coach Dickey—he was here. I used to admire him as a coach."

Charley Pell: "I think Charley Pell made a couple of bad decisions, but other than that, Charley Pell had as much to do with Gator football separating itself from everywhere else. He was ahead of his time, going out and speaking to people. … It's all the stuff I had to do at Bowling Green and Utah. He was doing it years ago. The other thing that stands out to me about Charley is that Ward Pell and Charley were a great team. I've researched that. She was involved in all the stuff as well."

Galen Hall: "Don't know Coach Hall, but I spent some time with Joe Paterno talking about him. Galen Hall loves Florida; and Florida loves Galen Hall."

Steve Spurrier: "Steve Spurrier was the master of Florida football in the 1990s. He had it going. He kind of brought a new style of football to the SEC, and I think his personality is very good for college football. It creates interest. A lot of people like him, dislike him, whatever."

Ron Zook: "Great recruiter. I know Ron—I won't say very well, but fairly well. I knew him when he was an assistant coach. An extremely hard worker, he was involved in many great games in Florida football."

On its 100th anniversary, Florida football is in the hands of a man who respects its history and its impact. Meyer grasped the meaning of "The Gator Nation" early on, and every time he makes a trip around the state, he is reminded of the pride shared by its citizens.

"'The Gator Nation' is extremely powerful and it goes beyond the fans," Meyer said. "I'm finding that out because of the quality of the education here. Every school I went to, the principal was a Gator. Most of the time, when I deal with people who work for a company, the company is run by a Gator.'

"And I tell our players, 'You're not just a Gator—you're part of 'The Gator Nation.'"